Advertising, The Uneasy Persuasion

ADVERTISING, THE UNEASY PERSUASION

Its Dubious Impact on American Society

MICHAEL SCHUDSON

BasicBooks
A Division of HarperCollins*Publishers*

Library of Congress in Publication Data

Schudson, Michael.
Advertising, the uneasy persuasion.

Includes index.
1. Advertising—United States—History. I. Title.
HF5813.U6S38 1984 659.1'042'0973 84-45076
ISBN 0-465-00078-9 (cloth)
ISBN 0-465-00080-0 (paper)

Printed in the United States of America
Designed by Vincent Torre
95 MPC 10 9 8

To Charlie

and in memory of Hod

CONTENTS

ACKNOWLEDGMENTS

I WOULD never have written a book about advertising had it not been for the keen interest that students took in the topic in my course on "Mass Media and Society" at the University of Chicago. When I told them of social science research that indicates there are limits to the power of the communications media to mold thought and action, they were skeptical. When I suggested that people attend to messages they already agree with, perceive primarily those parts of complex or ambiguous messages that fit their preconceived ideas, and rely on trusted friends and relatives to develop opinions about the world, my students quickly responded: "But look at advertising!" So I looked. And I found that advertising, too, is as capable of dramatic failures as of remarkable successes. My students heard me out but insisted, "Businesses wouldn't pour so much money into advertising if it didn't work." To that, I did not have an adequate response. Coming up with an answer became an extended research project and this book is the result.

Well-launched on my study of advertising with the help of a Rockefeller Foundation Humanities Fellowship in 1979–80, I moved from Chicago to the University of California, San Diego, and began teaching a course on "Advertising and Society" in 1981. In that course, students all chose a product that interested them and wrote term papers on the manufacturer's marketing strategy and the social context of the product's use. The students' papers broadened my knowledge of the subject enormously and I would not make the claims I do in this book with as much confidence were it not for them.

My Rockefeller grant allowed me to spend time in Washington and New York where my research included interviews with officials at the Federal Trade Commission and advertising executives. A quarter's sabbatical in 1983 enabled me to return to New York for additional interviews, including second interviews with some of the people I talked with on my first trip. I also interviewed advertising executives in Chicago and San Diego. I am grateful to all of them for sharing their time and thoughts with me. A few of the people I interviewed were generous enough to read and criticize drafts of my chapter on "What Advertising Agencies Know." I also benefited from the use of several specialized libraries, the library of the Advertising Research Foundation and the reading room of the Direct Mail/Marketing Association, both in New York.

Many colleagues in the Department of Communication and the Department of Sociology at the University of California, San Diego, have been of great assistance in providing encouragement and critical reading of parts of the manuscript. Don McQuade, of Queens College, was a colleague at San Diego in 1983 and was of great help with a close reading of several chapters.

Early in my research, at the University of Chicago, I received advice and encouragement from Paul Hirsch and Morris Janowitz. I benefited from sitting in on Harry Davis's class on marketing at the Graduate School of Business. My colleague in the Social Sciences Collegiate Division, John MacAloon, was a great source of support.

Other friends and colleagues have been generous, too. Hillel Schwartz read chapter 6 with a rapier red pen and prodded me to ask myself hard questions. Todd Gitlin and Herb Gans plowed through the entire manuscript at a stage when that was a more daunting task than, I hope, it is now, and their criticism was most helpful. Robert Manoff had the patience and care to read through three full versions of the manuscript, and I am grateful beyond words for his efforts to hold me to my own best ideals of honesty, clarity, and concern. In addition to all else, he is the best editor I know. The late Cathy Covert provided me my first forum to try out the ideas in chapter 6 and made available her Cape Cod cottage to my wife and me for my writing sabbatical in 1983. I feel lucky to have known Cathy and I hope this finished book is one she would have admired.

Other students of advertising have graciously shared their own published and unpublished work and have responded with interest and criticism to mine—I mention especially Leo Bogart, Robert Goldman, Albert Gollin, Morris Holbrook, Daniel Horowitz, T. J. Jackson Lears, William Leiss, Roland Marchand, Richard Ohmann, and Richard Pollay. My teachers from graduate school days, Daniel Bell and David Riesman, whose own works on aspects of consumer culture have been a powerful influence on many besides myself, provided new leads and continued encouragement. Martin Kessler at Basic Books was able to see the forest through the trees in earlier versions of this book and to insist that I see it, too.

I have benefited from the work of several student research assistants—at the University of Chicago, Abbe Fletman; at UC–San Diego, Randy Coplin, Ken Cornwell, and Haida Massoud. Jillaine Smith did some of the manuscript typing. The cooperation of Jane Geddes and the entire office staff in the Department of Communication at San Diego, especially during my term as department chair, was invaluable. The Committee on Research provided small research grants that made a big difference.

This project has taken a long time from its conception in 1978 as a research proposal to study "The Problem of Credibility in Modern Society" to its final form. Begun several years before I met my wife, it would have moved to completion without Suzie, but her love has made this a better book than it otherwise would have been—and a work much more truly my own.

My first book was dedicated to my parents. This one owes much to them, too. My father began his business career as a copywriter for Sears, Roebuck & Co. and I got my own measure of participation in advertising working summers for him. I learned a lot those summers, putting out a catalog for Personalized Inc., his bowling and billiards supplies business, and acting as an emissary to the Rumack-Abert Advertising Agency and the B&C Letter Service in Milwaukee. While I did not develop a taste for a business career myself, I am glad to have acquired an inability to share the academy's contempt for business enterprise.

I dedicate this book to my brothers: to the memory of Hod and the music he gave us; and in honor of Charlie, for his ideals, his courage, and his love.

PREFACE TO THE PAPERBACK EDITION

ADVERTISING is much less powerful than advertisers and critics of advertising claim, and advertising agencies are stabbing in the dark much more than they are practicing precision microsurgery on the public consciousness. These points—made in chapters 2 and 3—have only been reinforced in the past two years. One of the more striking examples concerns television advertising for the 1984 Olympics and the 1985 Superbowl. The naïve observer must assume that businesses reap extraordinary rewards for their elaborate and expensive sponsorship of these events. But, it turns out, *no one really knows* if they do. Video Storyboard Tests, Inc., a market-research firm, found that Olympics advertising was not cost effective. Leading Olympics advertisers paid $62 for every 1,000 "retained impressions" (consumers who report that they remember an ad or have "retained impressions" of the ad) compared to the $27 they normally spend for the same result. As for the Superbowl, some firms were pleased to advertise. Soloflex, a mail-order exercise firm, advertised because, as the firm's president put it, "Look, it's the Superbowl! Advertising [on the game] gives the company more credibility; it's a statement that we have arrived." On the other hand, some leading companies, like General Motors, decided in 1985 that the growing cost of Superbowl air time ($525,000 for 30 seconds) was simply not worth the cost.[1]

Advertising, the Uneasy Persuasion argues against the most commonly held view of advertising—that advertising affects sales by leading consumers to change their minds or to think a certain way about a product. In the common view, advertising associates a given brand or product with a prestigious person or a romanticized lifestyle, and suggests that the use of the product will transform the consumer into a more beautiful, more desirable, or more energetic human being. The consumer, believing or half-believing this, and consciously or subconsciously coaxed by the ad's suggestion, buys the product. With most Americans most of the time, as I argue in chapter 4, this notion that advertising directly affects consumer choice explains scarcely anything about why consumers buy what they do. Nevertheless, there may be ways, not touched on in my book, that advertisements *indirectly* affect consumer buying decisions. Advertisements may affect the *goods available to consumers* even if they do not persuade consumers which goods to buy.

This can happen if business people *think* ads affect consumers directly (even if, in fact, they do not). A marketing executive at a major food company told me he thinks most of the money spent by his own company on advertising does little good in convincing consumers of anything. However, he has failed in efforts to limit the advertising budget. Why? His explanation is that when the company executives make presentations before meetings of their stockholders or others in the investment community, the first thing investors want to see is a reel of the company's television advertisements. Expensive, well-executed, and familiar ads convince the investors, as nothing in the black and white tables of assets and debits can, that the company is important and prosperous.

This, naturally, can have major consequences for the firm. If investment in advertising keeps the firm's investors happy, the company can count on a flow of capital for its operations. In this way, the investors' *belief* that advertising is an index of a prosperous company helps make the company prosperous.

This "self-fulfilling prophecy" also works with a company's own sales force. It is much easier for a salesperson to walk into a retailer's store and say "I represent Procter & Gamble" than to say "I'm selling Product X, you probably haven't heard of it, but. . . ." Visible consumer advertising gives salespeople confidence in the public presence of their company and its products. An announcement of an advertising budget is also an indicator to the sales force of how seriously the company believes in a given product. In publishing, for instance, it is common lore that advertising has little impact on consumers. Still, the announcement at a sales meeting that a book will be backed with a sizeable ad budget signals to the sales staff that the company expects a big hit. The salespeople communicate this to retailers, the book gets widely distributed, and its general availability leads to sales. (Perhaps an experimentally minded publisher might some day announce a big ad budget to the sales force, not buy any ads, and see what happens.)

The belief that advertising works may affect the behavior of retailers as well as investors and salespeople. Retailers generally prefer to stock well-advertised goods than nonadvertised or poorly advertised goods because they think that advertising directly influences consumers and that consumers will ask for or look for widely advertised brands. The result, of course, is that widely advertised brands become the brands most widely available; consumers pick up what they find on the shelves whether ads influenced them or not, and the retailers are thus "confirmed" in their conviction that advertised products sell.

It is entirely plausible, then, that advertising helps sell goods even if it never persuades a *consumer* of anything. So long as investors, salespeople, and retailers believe advertising affects consumers, advertising will influence product availability and this, by itself, shapes consumer choice. Availability, as marketers sometimes say, equals sales. Advertising may be an important signal system within the business world.

I want to add one more point about the direct and indirect impact of advertising on product sales. The argument I make in chapter 4 does not stand out with the emphasis I intended. Chapter 4 does not argue that consumers are too smart or too well informed to be affected by advertisements. It starts with the premise that with current evidence, we cannot calculate the independent effect of advertising on sales. It then argues that we should not ask whether advertising works or not but *under what conditions* it is most likely to work. This changes the question from a "yes/no" question to a "more/less" question and opens up new angles on the advertising controversy. Chapter 4 then shows that consumers normally have access to many information sources besides advertising when they make a decision to buy something. *Some* consumers, however, and *all* consumers under some circumstances, are deprived of alternative information sources and are more dependent on and vulnerable to advertising. This is the case with children, with people in transitional states in their lives, and with Third World peoples, who are relatively new to the world of mass marketed consumer goods, and whose governments have few agencies and laws of consumer protection. T. J. Jackson Lears has rightly observed that these "exceptions" account for most of the people on the planet—and, I would add, *all* of the people on the planet at some point in their lives.[2] I acknowledge this. I wish I had made two points stand out more sharply: *different groups are differentially vulnerable to advertising;* and *their vulnerability varies not so much with the character or quantity of advertisements as with the informational resources they can claim by age, education, station in life, and government guarantees of consumer protection.*

The notion of people's differential vulnerability to advertising should provide guidance for efforts at the regulation of advertising. Take the controversy over alcohol advertising that made its way to the Congress and to state legislatures in 1985. There is no impressive evidence that advertising has a significant impact on total consumption of alcohol. When the alcoholic beverage industry pleads before congressional committees that companies advertise to influence market share (distributing consumers among brands), rather than to increase the total number of consumers, they are stating a generally valid rule of marketing. (This is discussed in chapter 2.) It is not a rule that perfectly fits the alcohol business of late. Major firms in the alcohol industry target nondrinkers (young people) and nontraditional drinkers (women) in their advertising. As competition becomes intense, as aggressive marketers like Philip Morris enter the alcohol field and break the norms of market behavior, and as marketing efforts for some alcoholic beverages, like whiskeys, repeatedly fail, alcohol companies have desperately searched for new customers.

But there is not much evidence that they have succeeded. Hard liquor sales have ranged from flat to faltering, wine sales did not skyrocket as most marketing wizards forecasted but have bumped along slowly since the peak of the late 1970s, and the rapid increase in per capita beer sales from 1970–80 (about 22 percent) can be largely accounted for by the spectacular increase in the size of the population of the primary beer-drinking group, fifteen to thirty-four-year-old males (25 percent) in the same period. (Indeed, it would have been astonishing if beer sales had *not* boomed in the seventies.)[3]

The evidence, then, for powerful advertising effects in alcoholic beverage sales is pretty slim, even when the marketers have energetically sought new consumers. But, unhappily for the beverage companies, the argument does not end here. Suppose that social critics recognize not only the hypocrisy but also the element of truth in the business community's claim that its advertising does not create new drinkers. Suppose critics argue not that there is a measurable direct impact of advertising on sales but that there is a *differential* impact on different populations and that some groups, young people for instance, may be especially at risk. There is good common sense to support this as well as some suggestive (but not overwhelming) empirical evidence. If society has some special interest in protecting the affected group (minors in this case), legislative action might well be contemplated. It is clear that government holds a special obligation to the young and has long recognized that minors' liberties (to hold office, to vote, to make private contracts, to drive automobiles, to have access to sexually explicit literature) may be restricted in their own interest. There is more constitutional room to restrict advertising directed to young people than to limit the same ads shown to an adult population. The burden of proof to show that advertising affects behavior should be correspondingly lighter for young people than for adults.[4]

Still, the alcohol industry might reasonably respond that young people's drinking behavior is affected by much more than advertising. Alcohol advertisements are but one of many symbolic representations of drinking in our culture. Movies, television, fiction, and news also shape the mental world in which people develop attitudes toward drinking. Of course, the representation of drinking in all cultural forms besides advertising shows liquor in both a positive and negative light while ads picture drinking uniformly as positive. Ads tilt the symbolic environment in a direction affected neither by real world events (the way news is affected), nor by the intentions of artistic communities (the way television, film, and fiction are to some degree affected), but almost solely by the profit motives of large corporations.

But the industry could well reply that young people are influenced most of all by the drinking behavior they see in adults in their own homes and that advertising will do little but reinforce existing patterns and attitudes about drinking (while coaxing the teenager toward a particular brand loyalty). What answer is there to this claim?

I tried to address this argument in chapter 7 when I characterized advertising as a peculiar symbolic system I call capitalist realism. I stand by that argument, but it is important to see, also, that what is fundamentally at issue is not just how advertising works but how *culture* works. To ask if a beer ad leads a teenager to drink beer is not essentially different from asking if television violence leads people to commit crime, or if a crucifix has the power to keep a person a practicing and believing Christian, or if Wagner's music contributed to the rise of Hitler, or if Harriet Beecher Stowe helped start the Civil War.

What difference does culture make? What influence do cultural products have? Does American television programming cultivate a certain set of attitudes in regular television-viewers? Do cockfights in Bali enable Balinese to rehearse the emotions and attitudes that distinguish them as a people? Does the theater weaken democracy by demoralizing its citizens, as Rousseau argued two centuries ago? How can we, or can we, specify the meaning of terms like "cultivate," "rehearse," and "demoralize"?

That in some sense culture *works,* that our symbolic environments affect the way we see the world and act in the world, no one would deny. But how does this cultural work get done and how important is it? Surely a steady diet of "The Untouchables," "Kojak," "Starsky and Hutch," "Cagney and Lacey," and "Miami Vice" (pick your favorite television era) does make people more fearful of their worlds; and cockfights in Bali, like baseball in America, helps the natives know more who they are; and theater of various kinds distracts people from participatory democracy. At the same time, people would be fearful of city streets even without television crime shows; Balinese can learn to be Balinese, or Americans American even if they are not keen on cockfighting or baseball; and most democracies have many impediments to citizen participation more worrisome than the theater.

Yes, cultural products matter. But how? And how much? A full appreciation of this issue awaits a more adequate theory of culture than the human sciences have yet provided. But *Advertising, the Uneasy Persuasion,* and especially chapter 7, inches toward a theory of culture that I plan to write about at greater length one day but can now state in brief and, I hope, suggestive terms.

Advertising is one of the institutions Joseph Tussman has called "awareness institutions."[5] It is not the most important of them. The schools, government, and news media are all more powerful in shaping people's basic concepts of how the world operates and what kinds of lives are worth living. Still, advertising is a powerful cultural institution in this country (less so in other capitalist countries, though its presence is growing). Part of its power comes from the fact that it has only one message. As I argue in chapter 7, it glorifies the pleasures and freedom of consumer choice. It defends the virtues of private life and material ambition. It idealizes the consumer and consuming. It holds implicitly or explicitly that freedom, fulfillment, and personal transformation lie in the world of goods. As John Berger has written, advertising "proposes to each of us that we transform ourselves, or our lives, by buying something more."[6]

The simplicity of this message, its ubiquity, and its repetition help impress it on the public. This makes advertising a different sort of communication from, say, works of serious fiction that tend not to be simple, not to say the same thing over and over, and not to reach very many people. On the other hand, if we continue the comparison to fiction, an individual's involvement with a given ad is very slight, usually close to zero, while his or her investment and involvement in a novel may be very high. The credibility of the two genres differs, too: people often disbelieve ads that claim truth while they often take as truth a novel that claims only to be fiction. The ad lasts for 30 or 60 seconds, the novel for many hours, often over a period of weeks or even months. The ad comes and goes and the individual cannot return to it at will (unless it is a print ad in a monthly magazine or annual), while the novel has greater permanence. In these respects, the power of an advertisement appears to be modest.

But the ad has a unique grip on the public nonetheless. This has to do not with the substance of the message but its location in social context. First, the ad provides the viewer a clear-cut impetus to action. The individual who sees an ad knows exactly what response is wanted: go out and buy the product. Not only is the desired action clear but it is an *individual* action—it does not require difficult intermediate steps of forming coalitions, joining a party, developing new skills, or undertaking new resolves. (What, in contrast, is the "response" a novel or painting asks for? What should a person go out and do after reading *The Grapes of Wrath* or seeing "Guernica"?)

Second, the advertisement is just one small piece, even if the most visible piece, of a major economic enterprise directed at getting consumers to buy (and getting people to think of themselves as consumers).[7] An individual's connection with a novel is usually isolated from other aspects of his or her life. It is a rare novel that gains a larger cultural installation by becoming part of the canon of school instruction. In this unusual case, an individual may read the novel several times over and may read it along with other readers. Important consequences (grades in a course, for instance) may depend on the reader's attentiveness to the work; the individual's ability to comprehend references in popular speech and literature may also depend on knowledge of the text. Here, then, there is great cultural support for the novel's influence—but this is the rare exception.

The advertising message is more like the canonical novel than the typical novel because it is *normally* supported by other institutions. The most important of these is the retail store. The consumer not only sees a product ad but also views the product. If the product comes from a large company with good channels of distribution, it is probably visible close to home in a store that the consumer passes by or shops in regularly. The product can be seen in the homes, yards, or garages of friends or neighbors, in restaurants, bars, and ball parks, or in someone else's picnic basket at the park or beach.

Only the direct mail advertiser leaves the ad by itself in the cold world of indifferent consumers. In most advertising, the ad is but one part of a larger marketing design that includes attention to retailers, "point-of-purchase" display, attractive packaging, proper placement on retailers' shelves, the training of a sales force, and the use of coupons and price incentives to promote consumer "trial." If the product is expensive and of some degree of permanence, service and repair institutions grow up around it. The advertisement merely names, marks, and reminds consumers of something that is almost inescapable in other parts of their lives.

An understanding of the impact of culture concerns the term "merely." I used it as a kind of entrapment: it is exactly the *wrong* word. Little is more important than naming, marking, and reminding. Reminding is not something that only advertising does—it defines the work of culture in general. Culture is the set of socially available names, markers, and reminders that guide human action and establish the meaning of human experience. Attention is a scarce resource that culture organizes and directs. Culture is an attention-focusing institution. A "dominant" culture includes the most available, credible, and legitimated reminders, those most fully backed by social authority.

Names and markers may sometimes strike an individual as novel. They may be "news." No one knows everything about his or her culture and all human beings begin by knowing nothing of it. We learn culture constantly. But most of the names an adult encounters in a normal day are familiar. *This does not make them unimportant.* Culture works by taking things we already know and *making them actionable.* Culture works by reminding people of what they already know; dominant culture reminds people of what they already know, backed with the authority of the whole society. When the judge charges the jury in a trial, he or she repeats things the jury has already heard. Yet the judge gives these things a special emphasis and social authority, and so focuses and shapes the jury's deliberations. To take a more humble example, when a man ties a string around his finger to remember to water the lawn, he adds no new information to what he already knows, but he gives himself a way to remember, a way to focus attention. This, on a private and individual level, is precisely what cultural symbols do socially. Does it matter? Yes, it does. It gets the lawn watered.[8]

This is a fairly primitive understanding of culture but it is an important beginning because it strongly suggests that symbols do not "merely" remind us. They re-*mind* us. They make us mind, make us focus—and on some things rather than on others. Ads do not "merely" reinforce existing social trends: they re-*enforce* social trends, and some trends and not others.

This is not enough of a theory to serve all purposes. An executive with a big marketing budget wants to know *how much* reminding a given ad will produce and how many sales the reminding will generate. Unfortunately for the executive, there is no satisfactory answer. Nor can solutions that work for a given brand of a given product at a given time in a given market condition be generalized as rules for advertising effectiveness, for reasons this book examines.

If a scholar wants a social theory of culture, the question of "how much" may not figure importantly; the problem will be to understand the ways that culture affects human action, what different forms of culture exist and what different kinds of influence they have, and the circumstances under which culture will be more or less powerful. This may be a very personal question for a scholar: How do I put my own ideas into words, how do I give my words energy, and how do I put them before people who might be influenced in the way most likely to influence them? (The scholar, unlike the advertiser, also asks: How can I communicate with people who can influence *me,* lead me to change my view, and reorganize my understanding of the world?)

If a society's civic leaders and the people who elect them want a public policy to help make commercial activity serve human values and democratic institutions, then it will have to reconcile the absence of clear answers to how and by how much symbols "work" with the need to act in the world. Political choices in this realm, as in others, depend on values and priorities that social science can usefully inform but will not now, or ever, be able to decide.

NOTES

1. Jube Shiver Jr., "Firms Split on Value of Bowl Ads," *Los Angeles Times,* Jan. 18, 1985, sec. IV, p. 1; and Ronald Alsop, "Study of Olympics Ads Casts Doubts on Value of Campaigns," *Wall Street Journal,* Dec. 6, 1984, p. 33.

2. T. J. Jackson Lears, review of *Advertising, the Uneasy Persuasion, Wilson Quarterly* 9 (Spring 1985):42–43.

3. See Michael Jacobson, George Hacker, and Robert Atkins, *The Booze Merchants: The Inebriating of America* (Washington, D.C.: Center for Science in the Public Interest, 1983) for documentation of the industry's efforts to target new drinkers. Data on population and sales trends comes from U. S. Bureau of the Census, *Statistical Abstract of the United States 1985,* 105th ed., (Washington, D.C.: U. S. Government Printing Office, 1984).

4. The empirical evidence that exposure to advertising influences drinking behavior among teenagers comes from the studies of Charles Atkin and his colleagues. See, for instance, Charles Atkin, John Hocking, and Martin Block, "Teenage Drinking: Does Advertising Make a Difference?" *Journal of Communication* 34 (Spring 1984): 157–167. Atkin, et. al. find that high exposure to advertising (as self-reported by high school students in a survey) is significantly related to high alcohol consumption (also self-reported) for beer and liquor but not for wine. Advertising exposure appears more closely associated with liquor drinking than is peer influence, but peer influence is more strongly associated with beer drinking than advertising exposure. These differences are interesting and suggest, again, how hard it is to come to across-the-board conclusions about the influence of advertising on consumption. Atkin and his colleagues make a good argument that the causal relationship in their correlations runs from advertising to consumption—that advertising encourages consumption rather than frequent drinking behavior leading to greater exposure to advertising. I suspect, however, that frequent drinkers *remember* alcohol ads they see more readily than non-drinkers or occasional drinkers—if I am right, this could confound the Atkin findings.

The legal argument that children or youths should be treated as a special group is summarized in *FTC Staff Report on Television Advertising to Children*

(Washington, D.C.: Federal Trade Commission, 1978), pp. 239–288. For an important Supreme Court case supporting a state ban on the sale of sexually explicit literature to minors with implications for other First Amendment situations involving youths, see *Ginsberg v. New York,* 390 U.S. 629 (1968).

5. Joseph Tussman, *Government and the Mind* (New York: Oxford University Press, 1977), p. 20.

6. John Berger, *Ways of Seeing* (Harmondsworth: Penguin Books, 1972), p. 131.

7. George Hacker emphasized this point to me in a personal communication.

8. Mary Douglas uses a very similar example of the Dinka herdsman stopping by the roadside to tie a knot in the grass before hurrying on home to dinner. See *Purity and Danger* (London: Routledge and Kegan Paul, 1966; Harmondsworth: Pelican Books, 1970), p. 79.

Advertising, The Uneasy Persuasion

Introduction

I FIND it hard to pay close attention to ads, especially on television. In this regard, it seems I am like most Americans. About 60 percent of adults remain in the room with the television on during an ordinary commercial break and most of them read, talk, eat, or do household chores. It is little wonder that, on average, less than 25 percent of a television audience can remember an ad they saw on television the day before, even when prodded with various clues. Unprodded, about 9 percent of viewers can name the brand or product category they saw advertised on television immediately before answering the phone call from the market researcher.[1]

Advertisements ordinarily work their wonders, to the extent that they work at all, on an inattentive public. If we think of popular culture as a variety of forms ranging from those that are avidly followed to those that are barely acknowledged, then popular movies like *E.T.* or *Star Wars* or celebrations like the 4th of July fireworks would be at the high-involvement pole. They are cultural forms that people go out of their way to see, they become "events" in the foreground of people's lives, and they may provide grounds for talk and even for critical reflection. At the low-involvement pole are forms of culture that surround us without our taking notice. Design, typically, touches people without their focusing on it—the design of buildings, of products, of packages. Television and radio are somewhere in the middle, with soap operas and sports near the fireworks end of the spectrum and most other programming far closer to the unattended end, existing for most people as a kind of background noise. Television commercials, though often noticed as a phenomenon—they are interruptions, after all—are less attended to than television programs. They are, as Shakespeare said of the cuckoo in June, "heard but not regarded." Loud and brassy as they may be, and technically as sophisticated as they are, they rarely stop viewers in their tracks. Unlike radio disc jockey programs, television sitcoms, professional football games, or feature films, they do not command rapt attention or allegiance, at least, not until they are old enough to be remembered nostalgically. The most avid watchers of commercials are the men and women who create them, the preschool children who do not readily distinguish them from regular programming, the important but inevitably small segment of the audience actively in the market for the advertised product and uncertain about which brand to buy, and students of popular culture looking for deeper meanings.

This does not mean that the ads are ineffective. In fact, as I shall discuss later, television ads may be powerful precisely because people pay them so little heed that they do not call critical defenses into play. But why do most people most of the time tune out advertisements? Because, to put it simply, advertising is propaganda and everyone knows it.

To put it another way, commercials regularly miscommunicate by addressing an audience different from the actual audience. Fred Posner, research director at N. W. Ayer, Inc., writes that to attract his interest the best ad would be one that begins, "This message is for all those people named Fred Posner." Any other message sacrifices personal relevance for marketing reach.[2] If I have just bought a Toyota Tercel (which I have) and if it seems to me a substantial investment (which it does), then all the other automobile ads do not speak to me. I am not a car buff and I am not in the car-buying market. I cannot be moved. I might be amused but few car ads try to amuse me. Most car ads bore me. I have not tried a Ford lately and will not, even though I am bright enough to remember the slogan after I have heard it a few dozen times. Most of the time most consumers are not in the market for most of the products most often advertised.

Perhaps more important, ads address an audience different from what the actual audience *wants* to be. Commercials have an "implied viewer" who is someone, I find, I do not wish to be.[3] Take soft drink ads, for example. They are evocative of "freshness"—scenes of people jumping into a swimming hole and splashing in crystal-blue water give me the impression of freshness and I like that. But I take some pride in living my own life, growing older and doing it as well as I can, and I do not worship youth nor do I care to imagine myself as a sixteen-year-old. Even more, I do not want to be thought of as someone who worships sixteen-year-olds. It is not so much that I do not respond to the fun-loving blondes on the screen (although I tend not to identify with blondes) but that I do not want to be equated with the implied viewer, twenty-nine or forty-five or sixty and fat, bored, and dull, sitting in his living room wishing he were sixteen. Nor do I much like the idea that some advertiser *presumes* I am such a person and walks uninvited into my living room to talk to me on that basis.

The primary messages in most ads are simple. The power of ads rests more in the repetition of obvious exhortations than in the subtle transmission of values. Advertisements in themselves will receive modest attention in this book until the final chapters. I will perform no high-wire acts of semiotic analysis, no magic tricks to draw out of a hat of commercials a rainbow of cultural messages. My subject is not advertisements but advertis*ing:* advertising as an institution that plays a role in the marketing of consumer goods, advertising as an industry that manufactures the cultural products called advertisements and commercials, and advertising as an omnipresent system of symbols, a pervasive and bald propaganda for consumer culture. In considering advertising as propaganda, my question is not what the ads say. This seems reasonably clear, though I hope to make their general message more clear in chapter 7 on advertising as "capitalist realist" art. The ads say, typically, "buy me and you will overcome the anxieties I have just reminded you about" or "buy me and you will enjoy life" or "buy me and be recognized as a successful person" or "buy me and everything will be easier for you" or "come spend a few dollars and share in this society of freedom, choice, novelty, and abundance." My question is: What does the repetition of these messages over and over again *do* to the minds and characters of people?

People *think* ads help create a consumer culture. Many people believe, with Christopher Lasch, that advertising "manufactures a product of its own: the consumer, perpetually unsatisfied, restless, anxious, and bored. Advertising serves not so much to advertise products as to promote consumption as a way of life."[4] That is the chief offense social critics charge to advertising, and it is the central concern of this book. While an occasional apologist for capitalism takes it to be a virtue of advertising that it promotes "consumption as a way of life," I think we know enough of the "externalities" of goods-intensive economic growth in acid rain, black lung disease, oil spills, endangered species, and in general the poisoning of the earth we hand over to our children to dismiss uncritical praise of consuming. Many observers, from various positions on the political spectrum, have taken advertising to be a cause for alarm. Criticism includes the neo-conservative view that advertising undermines character and "strengthens not only individualism but attention to one's own interests and needs at the cost of attention to anyone else's."[5] It includes the neo-Marxist position that advertising is a " . . . cultural apparatus aimed at defusing and neutralizing potential unrest."[6] There is also the liberal concern that advertising inverts the democratic principle by which the market, in theory, operates; it makes producers rather than consumers sovereign in deciding what goods shall be produced and forces people to "buy things they do not need."[7] And there are feminist views that rightly see women as the main target of most advertising and object to advertising's role in encouraging them to take shopping as their work and way of life.[8] Whatever form the criticism takes, it sees the emergence of a consumer culture as a devolution of manners, morals, and even manhood, from a work-oriented production ethic of the past to the consumption, "lifestyle"-obsessed, ethic-less pursuits of the present. The image of a consumer society loosely couples images of the grabbing, status-climbing nouveau riche obsessed with material possessions with the laid-back, poolside affluence that takes the shopping mall as the normal and expected center of life activity.

At the simplest level, a consumer culture is a society with a lot of consumer goods. This, in itself, is rarely the object of criticism though by itself it may give rise to many of the habits and values that do come under attack. More often, a consumer culture is taken to be a society in which human values have been grotesquely distorted so that commodities become more important than people or, in an alternative formulation, commodities become not ends in themselves but overvalued means for acquiring acceptable ends like love and friendship. The criticism is either that people sacrifice people to accumulate wealth or that they sacrifice themselves to the pursuit of goods in order to accumulate people. In the former case, the participants in consumer culture are seen as philistines; acquisitive and upwardly mobile, with sturdy character, perhaps, but bad values, working long hours and saving money to satisfy obsessive longings for whatever the next prestigious consumer good may be—the stereo, the home computer, the food processor, the videotape recorder. In the latter case, character has degenerated and values have, in a sense, disappeared. There is no longer an obsessive striving after things but a mindless indulgence in them, and the problem is not so much the quest for the stereo or home computer but the assumption that all values inhere in or grow out of these objects. In this image of consumer culture, narcissism runs wild, the unguilty desire for objects and experiences to "pleasure" oneself runs free.

All of this is especially abhorrent in a puritan culture suspicious of pleasure in any form and certain that waste is sinful. It is especially dangerous in a society that depends on a healthy civic culture; attacks on consumer culture are often linked with a critical concern for the growing privatization of life and a decline in concern for public good. The profusion of private luxury and indulgent triviality is compared to the poverty of the public sector with its understaffed schools, deteriorating city services, and hospitals unable to care for the poor. The consequences of the present lack of public regard are on-going, extending into the future as well; current plundering of natural resources for the sake of air-conditioned cars and backyard swimming pools is measured against the difficulties that a shortage of energy and resources will very likely present to our children and our children's children. It seems to many critics that the American materialism that, 150 years ago, Alexis de Tocqueville found "decent" and "virtuous" in its restraint seems to have become unhinged.[9]

Very often the criticism of consumer culture is not that people of such a culture value goods unduly but that they value the wrong characteristics of goods—not workmanship but convenience, not character but cheapness and portability, not aesthetic design but glitzy showiness, not *substance* that goods once supposedly had but *image* which, in a world of mass marketing, goods must have to be successful. They consume and discard rather than use and maintain; they take a care-free or care-less attitude toward possessions rather than a responsible one; they do not love things too well but use them mindlessly instead of caring for them. Their attitude toward things of the world is profane rather than sacred. They value appearance over substance and easy disposal over maintenance.

Criticism of this sort links critics of the left who oppose consumerism with critics of the right, who oppose the debasement of culture by democracy. It also confronts the role of advertising in consumer culture which is under attack not just because it contributes to consumer culture but because it is that culture's emblem, its embodiment, its caricature. When Daniel Bell writes that "a consumption economy . . . finds its reality in appearances," it is clear that advertising is the foremost example.[10] It is all show, no substance, all illusion and no reality, the perfection of the fraudulence of modern society. Critics of capitalism who attack the economic system through assaults on advertising have not gone after a scapegoat; they have identified a sitting duck that voices the messages of contemporary materialism in its most vulgar and most accessible form.

Still, I have grave doubts about the conviction shared by both the critics of advertising and its most enthusiastic promoters that advertising is highly effective in manipulating the minds of consumers and so in promoting a consumer culture. Critics of advertising contend, in one form or another, that advertising powerfully shapes consumer values and choices. While some critics point simply to a global consumer mentality as advertising's creation, most blame advertising for the sale of specific consumer goods, notably luxury goods (designer jeans), frivolous goods (pet rocks), dangerous goods (cigarettes), shoddy goods (some toys for children), expensive goods that do not differ at all from cheap goods (nongeneric over-the-counter drugs), marginally differentiated products that do not differ *significantly* from one another (laundry soaps), and wasteful goods (various unecological throw-away convenience goods). Advertising, it is often claimed, persuades people to buy these things that they do not need or should not have. Advertising shapes consumers' desires and makes them feel a yearning for things they do not really need.

The response of advertisers and marketers to this criticism would be comical were it not so serious. Advertising, they say, cannot do any of these dastardly things because advertising is ineffective or only modestly effective in changing people's habits of consumption. The reason advertisers advertise is not to change people's product choices but to change their *brand* choices. Advertising is not a war on consumers' minds but a competitive war against commercial rivals for a share of a market whose size is either constant or, if changing, changing for reasons far beyond the power of advertising to affect. The marketer with any sense tries not to persuade people to gamble on a new product but to find consumers who already use a product or are already predisposed to a product by their situation in life and to *remind* them that a certain brand of the product is available and attractive.

This argument may at first sound very dubious. Certainly it is self-serving. It is the kind of argument that marketers regularly take before federal agencies that seek to regulate advertising.[11] But the marketers have a point—so crucial a point that I will devote much of the next chapter to discussing it. The role advertising actually plays in marketing and sales is quite circumscribed. I will show that, despite the saturation of print and air waves with advertisements, few businesses invest great percentages of their budgets in advertising and most businesses organize their advertising so as to rely as little as possible on its persuasive powers.

Nevertheless, the marketing ideology that advertising does not have great power (and so can do society little harm) is disingenuous. There are conditions under which advertising has a significant impact on sales. Beyond this, advertising may influence cultural life in the large even when it is not doing much to sell goods piece by piece. Whatever advertising's direct effect in stimulating sales and making people buy more goods, it fully merits its reputation as the emblem of fraudulence. I do not mean fraudulence in a sense the Federal Trade Commission would recognize. The vast majority of ads are not "unfair" or "deceptive." A great many are positively informational. But there is a persistent, underlying bad faith in nonprice advertising. I take as emblematic the old McDonald's slogan, "We do it all for you." That, of course, is a lie. McDonald's does it all for McDonald's. It may be that what's good for General Motors is good for the country, but that is not why General Motors takes the actions it does. Even if, as is generally the case, everything that the ad says about the product is scrupulously honest, or at any rate scrupulously avoids outright dishonesty, the implication of the direct address of most commercials—that the announcer speaks with the viewer's welfare at heart—is fraudulent. The advertisement seeks to promote sales, it does not seek to improve the lives of consumers except as a means to the end of sales.

What does it do to human experience to live in a society where people are incessantly exposed to messages ostensibly addressed to them that they cannot take as truthful communications? A 1976 survey found that 46 percent of the public holds all or most television advertising to be "seriously misleading" with 83 percent responding that at least "some" television advertising is seriously misleading. A 1981 *Newsweek* poll asking people to rate the honesty and ethical standards of people in different fields found advertising executives with the lowest score (just slightly below Congressmen).[12] And yet advertising is said to be a kind of new religion that, as Christopher Lasch put it, "addresses itself to the spiritual desolation of modern life and proposes consumption as the cure."[13] But if advertising is part of a religion of consumption, it is one whose priests are invariably on the defense; if consumption is a road to salvation, many seem to take it without believing it will lead anywhere. National consumer product advertising is the art form of bad faith: it features messages that both its creators and its audience know to be false and it honors values they know to be empty.

This, it seems to me, is the primary fact to understand about advertising. The question, What work does advertising do in the culture? quickly becomes the question, How can it do any work if people are so inattentive to it? and when attentive, so critical, so able at recognizing its propagandistic intent and techniques? Apologists are wrong that advertising is simply information that makes the market work more efficiently—but so too are the critics of advertising who believe in its overwhelming power to deceive and to deflect human minds to its ends. Its power is not so determinative nor its influence so clear. Evaluating its impact is more difficult than these simplicities of apology and critique will acknowledge.

This book, then, is about the role of advertising in shaping American values and patterns of life. I will consider what influence advertising may have in promoting materialist values and a consumer culture (acknowledging, however, that the very notion of "consumer culture" is vague, and promising to ask some of the questions that will help to know it better).

This is not a comprehensive account of all types of advertising. I will say little of what is widely acknowledged as the most effective form of advertising—price advertising—because critics do not object to it. Nor will I discuss classified ads or industrial product advertising, and for the same reason—these are not subjects of controversy. I will not discuss corporate image advertising because, controversial as it is, it still is a small element in overall advertising volume. Nor, regretfully, will I say much about political advertising, which deserves book-length treatment itself. But political advertising is only peripherally related to the concern about advertising that is my subject here: the impact of advertising on American attitudes toward goods, money, and the good life. I will focus, then, on national consumer goods advertising—the advertising people see most often on television and in national magazines, recall most vividly, and think of most readily when the topic of advertising comes up.

I see this book as an essay in the sociology of culture. I have learned from advances in this field in the past decade that it is insufficient to examine the symbolic content in culture, be it ads or television programs or paintings or science or literature, without attending both to the social situation of the symbol makers and to the responses of the audiences or clients for the symbols. Studies that examine the symbols alone can make vital contributions but take the risk of sociological irrelevance if they do not consider the intentions of the symbol makers or the meanings that the audiences actually take from the cultural products in question. Studies of the symbol makers that assume that the meanings the symbol makers intend *are* the meanings, and the only ones, communicated to audiences also risk error, for communication is rarely so simple, even with a cultural form as industrialized and as stylized as advertising. As for studies of audiences, these are still very rare, and more are needed. One of the advantages of studying advertising is that market research makes available valuable information about how audiences perceive advertising and respond to it. The complexity and variety of audience response is probably better documented here than in any other field of cultural studies. But there is danger in audience studies, too. It lies in the seductiveness of pluralism: when one discovers that different kinds of people assimilate very different meanings from the same mass culture, it is too easy to conclude that the symbols of mass culture have little authority in the face of human diversity. That tempting conclusion, I think, lights on the variety of immediate audience responses and ignores the channeling of human experience, however difficult to identify or measure, in which mass culture participates.

In chapters 1 through 3 of this book, then, I look at the use of advertising by businesses, the creation of advertising by agencies, and the place of advertising in the consumer's decision making about buying products. That is, I examine in turn the symbol makers, their clients, and their audience. In the next three chapters (4 through 6) I examine the historical context in which advertising arose and discuss the emergence of a modern infrastructure of consumption—patterns of life that, quite apart from advertising as such, have helped produce a consumer culture. No one has been so crude as to imagine that advertising created "consumer culture" single-handedly, but few critics of advertising have thought very hard about *what else,* besides advertising, has brought us to the kind of consumer culture we have today. These chapters address that problem. In the final two chapters (7 and 8) of this book, I look at advertising as a system of symbols and stand as an analyst, outside, interpreting the cultural form of the advertisement in its social context.

What is the work that advertising does? Where does it fit in the culture? Indeed, what kind of a culture has been historically required to nurture it? These are the questions I shall explore, trying to comprehend not so much whether we have a consumer culture or not, a rhetorical issue, I think, but what place consumption holds in the culture, what *kind* of consumption we have, and what can be said of the role of advertising in it.

We live and shall live, barring nuclear or other disaster, in what has been called a "promotional culture."[14] America has long been a nation of salesmen and the "shoeshine and a smile" that were Willy Loman's stock-in-trade are now the tools of politicians and religious evangelists and hospital administrators as much as of advertising agents and public-relations directors. The promotional culture has worked its way into what we read, what we care about, the ways we raise our children, our ideas of right and wrong conduct, our attribution of significance to "image" in both public and private life. The promotional culture has been celebrated and indulged in. It has been ridiculed and reviled. It still needs to be understood.

1

The Advertiser's Perspective

"THE BASIC FACT to remember about advertising," Jeremy Tunstall wrote in his study of British advertising agencies, "is that little is known about what effect it has; even to talk of advertising having an effect is misleading."[1] This is not exact. More precisely, *much* is known about the effects of advertising, but the results do not, and by the very character of business practice, cannot add up to a simple or consistent conclusion.

Manufacturers and retailers who want to use their advertising dollars efficiently worry about the effectiveness of advertising. So do advertising media that live off advertising revenue and seek to encourage businesses to advertise. So do advertising workers themselves. One of the fathers of American advertising, George Rowell, reminisced in 1905 about advertising in the 1860s, and observed:

> Then as now the idea that "advertising always pays" was promulgated and the assertion was made then as frequently as now, and is now made as frequently as then that advertising does not amount to anything and is a waste of money.[2]

In the 1980s, as at the turn of the century, the same thing can be said. Indeed, the view that advertising works and that it doesn't work may be expressed by the same person. A copywriter at one of the ten largest ad agencies wondered out loud, when I spoke to him, if advertising really sells products:

> Ads don't sell products, do they? Take Charlie the Tuna. Do you really go into the store and buy Starkist because Charlie the Tuna said they're picky about what they put in the can? The kind of ad that sells, that has to sell, is retail advertising, the one that says, Starkist Tuna, fifteen cents off.[3]

Then the same man, in the same interview, noted that Procter and Gamble spends enormous sums on advertising and that "they have research up the ass to show it works. They know their ads work." Well, does she or doesn't she?

The few economists who have studied advertising closely conclude that it has modest effects, at best, on general consumer demand for advertised goods. Julian Simon, for instance, concludes his overview of the economics of advertising in this astonishing manner:

> Those branches of advertising which are most in dispute—advertising for such products as beer, autos, soap, and aspirin—do not seem to have much effect upon the economy in any way, direct or indirect, and hence from an economic point of view it is immaterial whether they are present or absent. . . . All this implies that the economic study of advertising is not deserving of great attention . . . (As the reader may realize, this is not a congenial point at which to arrive after spending several years working on the subject.)[4]

Not everyone takes so dubious a view. While economists tend to be skeptical about the power of advertising, many television and radio stations, magazines and newspapers, market research firms, and the trade associations representing these various groups, generate data to suggest to potential advertisers the power of advertising. The advertising agencies and the media can argue the point either way. If they are trying to convince an advertiser to increase its media budget, they can cite examples of devastatingly successful advertising campaigns. But if they are defending themselves before the Federal Trade Commission (FTC) or a civic organization decrying television advertising to children, they trot out the data that demonstrate that advertising has slight or no effect on product sales. Advertising research, advertising trade journals, and conferences of advertising practitioners repeatedly assert that advertising is an effective business tool, but one wonders if they do not protest too much and reveal an underlying uneasiness about their trade.

Does advertising help sell products? That is the question I will address in this chapter.[5] Again, I focus on the national consumer goods advertising that makes up most of what people see on network television and national magazines and some of what they see in newspapers and other media. This is the advertising that plays a role in shaping the values of a consumer culture and is the advertising most often a subject of controversy and cultural and political criticism. This is the advertising most often said to deceive or mislead people or to persuade them by a variety of emotional means to buy things that they would not, rationally and independently, choose to buy on their own.

Does this advertising move goods? In particular, does it move goods in a *socially significant* way, not just shifting consumers from one brand to another, but leading consumers to try and to be loyal to categories of goods they would not otherwise have wanted? Strange as it may seem to the citizen bombarded with hundreds of advertisements every day, this is not an easy question to answer.[6] Even when advertising works, it works *in concert with* other tools of marketing and it attracts the attention of consumers who are simultaneously influenced by product information from a wide variety of other sources. As I shall now detail, the realities of marketing lead businesses to use advertising while limiting the weight they place on its power to persuade. Advertisers' goals for advertising and their strategies of deployment reduce the risks they take on advertising and, at the same time, limit their ability to evaluate the direct impact of ads in selling goods.

The Realities of Business Marketing Practice

THE ADVERTISING/SALES RATIO AS ARTIFACT

How does a firm decide how much money to spend advertising its products? From the point of view of a marketing professor, the rational approach to determining an advertising budget would be for a firm to arrive at a decision model based on "marginal analysis" so that it would keep increasing the budget as long as the increase is outstripped by the marginal revenue it brings in.[7] In practice, there is rarely adequate data to make marginal calculation possible. Most firms resort to rules of thumb. A. J. San Augustine and W. F. Foley found that large American advertisers rely on "essentially illogical" approaches to determine their advertising budgets. Colin Gilligan replicated their survey in Britain and found that the British are also "irrational." More than three-fourths of the ninety-two British companies surveyed calculated their ad budgets as a fixed percentage of either the previous year's sales or profits or the next year's expected sales or profits.[8] In most cases, the percentage taken had remained unchanged for at least four years and was applied regardless of market conditions. Marketing scholars David Aaker and John Myers find this procedure "disturbing," and well they might.[9] Instead of acting as if advertising causes sales, businesses create a situation in which sales are quite literally the single determinant of advertising expenses. This practice makes it "almost always impossible to estimate the impact of advertising on sales volume."[10]

In one of the most thorough econometric studies of the effects of advertising, Richard Schmalensee found that there was a closer correlation between consumption in a given quarter and advertising in the *next* quarter than between consumption in the given quarter and advertising in the *previous* quarter. Schmalensee concludes:

We find . . . that total national advertising does not affect total consumer spending or consumer spending for goods. We find that changes in total national advertising can be well explained by a model which postulates gradual adjustment to changes in the sales of consumer goods.[11]

More recent studies have replicated this finding. This aggregated data may simply not be appropriate to the questions at issue. But to the extent that there is an answer to the problem of whether, in the aggregate, advertising causes sales, the answer seems to be no, sales cause advertising. And business practice ensures that this will be so. Field experiments varying the amount of advertising and measuring the results on sales have been relatively rare. Especially rare are experiments that dare to *lower* advertising expenditures below current rates. In a number of these cases, including a celebrated set of experiments at Anheuser-Busch for Budweiser beer, reducing advertising expenses actually led to *increases* in sales. It is very likely that many firms spend more on advertising than, for their own best interests, they should.[12]

CONFOUNDED VARIABLES: QUALITY OF PRODUCT, ADVERTISING, AND SALES

Not only do ad dollars tend to follow high sales; ad dollars also tend to follow good products, or at least, pretty good products. That is, within a product area, firms will tend to put advertising power behind products that they genuinely believe (and that independent studies actually find) to be products of high quality. This point is made by an FTC study of prescription drugs. In the oral-diuretic drug market, brands offering "important therapeutic gains" were promoted on the average $1.25 million more annually than brands offering no therapeutic gain. There was, however, an even greater promotional expense for brands offering "modest therapeutic gains"—$1.44 million per year more than brands offering no therapeutic gain. Similarly, with antianginal drugs, brands offering modest or important therapeutic gains were promoted with more dollars than those offering no therapeutic gains. Firms tend to put advertising dollars behind products whose high quality—or pretty high quality—is likely to be a stimulus to sales itself.[13]

Indeed, it can be argued that advertising promotes or encourages quality products. The more advertising for a product, the more incentive a manufacturer has to keep quality high, since with advertising the consumer has a resource for identifying the product and can stop buying an unsatisfactory product. For repeat-purchase products, the argument goes, advertising can at best lead a consumer to make an initial purchase. From then on, the consumer is greatly influenced by experience with the product itself. For the many household items on which so much advertising is lavished, manufacturers count on repeat purchasing. And repeat purchasing depends on consumer satisfaction. Product quality, then, may have more effect on brand loyalty than advertising does.[14] This is a preponderant view among advertising workers themselves. In the advertising industry, one of the most frequently repeated slogans is, "Good advertising kills a bad product." Good advertising, that is, can lead a consumer to try a product once. If it is a bad product, the consumer will shun it thereafter and let others know, too, that it is a bad product.

Advertising ideology of this sort should not be taken at face value. The idea that good advertising kills a bad product, first of all, actually refers to bad *brands* in a product category. It does not mean that consumers will shun dangerous products like cigarettes. Nor does the aphorism accurately account for the sale of products whose quality or cost-effectiveness the consumer cannot easily judge. Life insurance and medicines are notorious instances where consumers continue to buy advertised "bad" products because they are not able to make sound judgments about quality.[15]

Not all advertised goods, clearly, are quality products; advertising can be used to give the sheen of status and quality to inferior goods. Nevertheless, in product categories where consumers can judge quality for themselves, there are strong business reasons that advertising will follow quality. If so, it can be argued that quality of product leads to sales (or repeat sales) and that advertising acts only as a mediating factor.[16] Generally, this is well accepted. No one doubts that product quality combined with moderate prices brought on the Japanese challenge to the American automobile industry. Datsun, Honda, and Toyota advertising is certainly attractive but none of the hand-wringing about the decline of Detroit has suggested that marketing practices have won the American consumer to the imported car. Quality and price have made the difference.

THE "MARKETING MIX"

Advertising is but one part of the "marketing mix" of a firm. The advertising most visible to the consumer is a very small part of the marketing efforts of most businesses. Personal selling—human sales representatives—are still vital to businesses. Firms that sell industrial products rather than consumer goods tend to rely heavily on sales representatives. So do some consumer goods firms. Drug companies employ more than twenty-five thousand "detail men" earning \$25,000 to \$50,000 each to call on the two hundred thousand private physicians and seven thousand hospitals in the country.[17] Even when a firm uses consumer advertising, it may work not only by moving consumers to buy but by motivating the sales force to sell. Coca-Cola advertising, a McCann-Erickson advertising executive has said, "tells the salesmen how to sell a product. It gets them excited about it. It creates an elite product for them. It energizes them."[18]

Only part of a firm's promotional budget goes to advertising. What is called "sales promotion" is generally distinguished from advertising. Advertising is an announcement, a kind of informational or persuasive message about the product for sale. Sales promotion is the provision of some material benefit to the consumer who buys the product (cents-off coupons, premiums, games, sweepstakes) or to the sales people who push the product (travel awards, electronic equipment, cars, and trucks for outstanding sales records). And sales promotion is a major marketing tool in many industries. The food industry, for instance, spends more money on coupons than on television advertising. In a 1979 survey of fifty major package good companies, less than half of marketing dollars were found to go to advertising: 40.5 percent to ads, 34.7 percent to promotion to the trade, and 24.8 percent to non-advertising modes of consumer promotion.[19]

Sales promotion often emphasizes a reduced price as enticement to the consumer—as in coupons. This kind of promotion is not only an alternative to advertising but an antagonist of it as well. National advertising is designed to attract consumers to a product at a given price and to keep consumers loyal to the product. It seeks to promote "brand image" and to achieve a "consumer franchise"—a following of consumers who feel psychologically attached, loyal, to the brand. Its task, then, is to make salient product characteristics *besides* price in order to, as one executive crudely put it to me, "own a piece of your head." To the extent that marketers rely on price-related sales promotion (or, for that matter, price advertising) they surrender to the very criterion that most of their advertising seeks to play down in the consumer's mind.

Overall, media advertising represents about 20 percent of all selling costs—the rest going to sales promotion and personal sales. This varies dramatically from one industry to another, with an industry like proprietary drugs spending 57 percent of its selling expenses on advertising, breads and cakes just 7 percent.[20] (See table 1.1.) Given the importance of sales promotion and personal sales, it should not be a great surprise that in a study of marketing executives in fifty of Britain's largest corporations, only 10 percent felt advertising to be vital to their marketing efforts. Less than half rated advertising as either "vital" or "very important."[21] American marketing managers, in a country with many more channels of commercial television and with nearly twice the percentage of the gross national product (GNP) devoted to advertising, are not so hard on advertising. In a survey of managers of two hundred American industrial and consumer goods companies that asked which marketing elements matter most, product research and development, sales research and planning, and management of the sales staff all were mentioned more often than the combined category of advertising and sales promotion. However, if one looks only at the responses of executives from firms producing non-durable consumer goods, advertising and sales promotion is mentioned more often than the other factors.[22]

One key factor connected with the sales force is distribution. An advertising executive familiar with the soft drink industry

TABLE 1.1

Media Advertising Expenses as a Percentage of Sales and Total Selling Expenses as a Percentage of Sales (for the Ten Industry Categories with the Highest Advertising/Sales Ratios)

Description	*Advertising Expenses/Sales*	*Total Selling Expenses/Sales*
Drugs, proprietary	19.1%	33.7%
Perfumes, cosmetics, and other toilet preparations	14.3	29.5
Cutlery	12.5	25.6
Periodicals	12.1	20.7
Distilled liquor	11.3	24.2
Hosiery	10.9	25.6
Cereal breakfast foods	10.8	20.3
Dog, cat, and other pet food	10.7	22.4
Flavoring extracts and syrups	9.3	26.9
Cigarettes	8.1	15.0

NOTE: Of the ten industry categories with the highest total selling expenses/sales ratio, six are listed above but the other four have relatively low advertising/sales ratios: bread, cake, and related products, for instance, has an advertising/sales ratio of 2.3 percent (and sales expenses/sales of 30.9 percent) and soft drinks an advertising/sales ratio of 3.4 percent (and sales expenses/sales of 24.1 percent).
SOURCE: Federal Trade Commission, *Statistical Report: Annual Line of Business Report 1976* (Washington, D.C., U.S. Government Printing Office, May, 1982), pp. 11, 12.

explained to me that the success of Pepsi-Cola in recent years has had as much to do with an understanding of distribution as with its advertising policies. In soft drink merchandising, there are three avenues of distribution: vending machines, restaurants and fountains, and supermarkets. Pepsi recognized that Coca-Cola had an unbeatable edge in the first two categories, thanks to long-standing arrangements and ties of loyalty with these outlets. In supermarket sales, however, Coke was more vulnerable. Pepsi went after the supermarkets, pioneering the two-liter plastic bottle, returnable bottles, and the plasti-shield package, then giving local bottlers advice and incentives on how to display Pepsi for better sales. Pepsi also provided supermarkets with the first end-of-aisle display racks for soft drinks and promoted cold product displays, too. Finally, Pepsi worked to improve relations between local bottlers and retailers and so made marketwide promotions possible for the first time in markets with more than one bottler. What Pepsi received in return was good will, more and better shelf space, and more end-of-aisle displays. The result: Pepsi outsells Coke in supermarkets.[23]

Distribution is not unrelated to advertising. Sometimes advertising can lead the way for a product into new channels of distribution. Maker's Mark bourbon, for instance, a successful Kentucky bourbon with a sales area that included only Kentucky and bordering states and sales that grew primarily by word-of-mouth, began advertising in the *Wall Street Journal* in 1980. Its unusual ad campaign "pulled" the product into markets in New York, San Francisco, and elsewhere even without a national sales organization.[24] Some decisions regarding shelf display are responsive to advertising. Heavily advertised sugar cereals tend to be placed at a child's eye level. Since most shoppers are right-handed, the supermarket house brand, where profit margins are generally higher for the retailer than on the more expensive private-label brands, will be placed directly to the right of the leading national brand—usually a heavily advertised product.[25]

Good distribution is a matter of organizational quality, business management, and the maintenance of good relations with regional and local distributors and retailers. The consequences of poor distribution are serious for a firm. A 1962 A. C. Nielsen Company study of shoppers leaving supermarkets found that 24 percent did not find a brand they had intended to buy. Of these, 42 percent did not buy at all but 58 percent bought a substitute brand—which thereby gained a chance to wean the consumer away from the previously favored product.[26]

What gets on the shelf makes a big difference in consumer choice; how it looks on the shelf matters, too. Packaging is a part of product promotion that is distinct from advertising and strongly affects consumer choice. A 1981 Nielsen study found that 46 percent of consumers interviewed said they returned or discarded a product in the previous year because of defective packaging. About a fifth of these unhappy consumers said they would not buy the same product again and many others expressed more modest degrees of caution.[27]

MARKET SHARE VERSUS AGGREGATE CONSUMPTION

It is possible that advertising may increase the sales of the brand advertised without increasing the aggregate consumption of the product category. Thus, a clever ad campaign for Coca-Cola might increase sales of Coke while total soft drink sales remain constant. What the campaign succeeds in doing is to increase the market share of Coke by taking market share away from competitors. In cases of this sort, advertising works for the advertiser *without* having a significant social effect. Indeed, this is the ordinary situation. Advertisers rarely set as a goal an increase in aggregate consumption of the product they promote; much more often, their aim is to increase their share of the market by taking a share away from a rival. The market share necessary for success differs according to the market. In a highly competitive area with many brands and large sales, the requisite market share may be very small indeed. In cigarettes, for instance, the rule of thumb is that .5 percent share is a commercial success for a brand. A new brand, then, will be a winner if it attracts no new smokers and just convinces one current smoker in two hundred to change brands.[28]

A celebrated case in marketing is Hershey Foods Corp. Hershey became very successful without any media advertising. From its beginnings at the turn of the century until 1970, Hershey refused to advertise, founder Milton Hershey claiming that a good product, well distributed, sells itself. In Hershey's experience, that seems to have been true. But in 1970 Hershey began advertising and by 1980 was among the one hundred largest advertisers in the country with $42.7 million spent in advertising.

Hershey's reasons for advertising seem clear: they apparently were losing a share of their chocolate market to rivals Mars, Nestlé's, and others. There was an increase in consumer advertising by other firms, particularly with the television ads from Mars Inc. for their M&M's product: "It melts in your mouth, not in your hands." Mars was also doing very well with Snickers, 3 Musketeers, and Milky Way candy bars. Advertising was for Hershey, as for so many firms, a *defensive* strategy.

Despite the vast increase in advertising expenses, which may well have helped Hershey to hold its own against its rivals, per capita candy consumption declined sharply, from 20.3 pounds per capita in 1968 to 15.4 pounds per capita in 1980. The reason: the number of five-to-thirteen-year-olds declined from 36.7 million in 1970, 17.9 percent of the population, to 31.2 million in 1980, 13.7 percent of the population. A decline of 5.5 million people in the segment of the population most attached to candy could not but hurt sales. All the advertising in the world could not restore a decline of 15 percent in the size of the target audience for candy.[29]

There are some advertising efforts directed at increasing total or "primary" demand. Occasionally agricultural cooperatives advertise the benefits of eggs in general—or milk, or avocados, or beef. Even an individual firm, like Campbell Soup Co., may occasionally try to promote a whole category of products. Campbell's has 80 percent of the canned soup market, the kind of stranglehold few manufacturers ever attain. Campbell's has increased its share of the market about as much as it can and would like to boost total demand for soup. In 1981 it introduced an ad campaign designed to do just that; soup consumption per capita grew very slowly in the 1960s and 1970s and lagged behind increases in real income. With more working mothers and more fast food restaurants, fewer lunches are eaten at home and canned soup has been primarily a lunch-time food. But industry analysts were skeptical that the Campbell's effort would make any difference. There is little indication that efforts to change primary demand make much of a dent in the market. The milk campaigns, for instance, appear to have improved attitudes toward milk but milk consumption is still declining.[30] Most authorities agree with the conclusion of Neil Borden's classic study of 1942 that advertising helps expand demand when underlying conditions encourage growth and cannot overcome weak demand when underlying conditions are unfavorable.[31]

It may be that the sum of advertising for soft drinks and liquor helps account for the shift away from milk, fruit juice, and water. This seems to me a reasonable, though unproved, conclusion. Still, advertising by itself is not decisive. Coffee, unlike milk and water, is heavily advertised but its consumption has been declining steadily. Per capita coffee consumption has declined from 15.8

pounds in 1960 to 10.4 pounds in 1980. Advertising expenditures for coffee quadrupled from 1970 to 1980 while coffee consumption declined 22 percent. The National Coffee Association tested ads to boost the image of coffee in general in preparation for a 1982–84 campaign. The ads did not show any impact in test cities, according to an early report, but the campaign rolled out in the fall of 1983 with high hopes from the industry and serious doubts from industry observers.[32]

THE IMPORTANCE OF THE "HEAVY USER"

The logic of fighting for market share is simple. People who already use a product are the people most likely to use the product again. It makes sense to try to sway consumers from one brand to another, a rather modest task compared to the alternative strategy of trying to change consumer usage patterns altogether. In sales promotion, for instance, a firm can expect a 2 percent redemption rate on "cents off" coupons in a Sunday supplement or about a 6 percent return on "free-standing inserts" in Sunday papers, but a coupon for a product inserted in the product package will be redeemed about 18 percent of the time.[33] Obviously, the marketer's chances of stimulating a purchase are greatest when the potential buyer has already demonstrated an interest through a prior decision to buy.

There is a corollary to this: not only do advertisers typically orient their marketing to current users but they often direct their campaigns to current *heavy* users. In many product categories, a very small percentage of the population accounts for a very large proportion of total sales. In one of the early studies to report on this phenomenon, Dik Twedt, director of marketing research at Oscar Mayer & Co. used 1962 *Chicago Tribune* consumer panel data to show that, for instance, half of beer-drinking households consume 88 percent of all beer, half of cola-drinking households drink 90 percent of all cola, half of cake mix households consume 85 percent of all cake mixes, half of shampoo-using households use 81 percent of all shampoos. If one examines the "heavy user" group as a percentage of total (user and nonuser) households, then 17 percent of households consume 88 percent of all beer, 39 percent of households consume 90 percent of all cola, 37 percent of households consume 85 percent of all cake mixes, and 41 percent of households consume 81 percent of all shampoos. For some products, the figures are as extreme as they are for beer: 21 percent of households consume 89 percent of all bourbon, 16 percent of households consume 86 percent of all canned hash.[34] The catsup business would be cut by 40 percent were it not for families that use a bottle or more every week. One marketing professor polled his class on catsup and found that the average student used about a bottle every six months but that "heavy users," generally eating in dormitories, consumed a bottle every two days.[35]

The focus of advertising on users and heavy users does not suggest that advertising is ineffective; it suggests only that advertising is designed to affect people who are already committed to a general product category. They are encouraged to switch brands or to consume even more of a brand to which they are devoted. The AT&T "Reach Out and Touch Someone" ads, for instance, tried not to convert people who rarely call long distance but to get the regular long distance users to pick up the phone more often.[36] If this is how advertising works, then advertising may be very consequential for business without its power to persuade being a great deal more than a power to remind.

One form of advertising famous for its effectiveness is catalog and direct response advertising. Direct response is advertising usually conducted by mail but sometimes utilizing television or print, whereby a return of coupons or a phone call are the only ways for the consumer to act on the ads. Generally, in this kind of marketing strategy, advertising is the sole communication with the consumer. The consumer learns of the product *only* through advertising. Sales results, then, can be taken as a direct measure of the effectiveness of the advertising. And what is the record of direct marketing?

It depends. Whether the ad "pulls" or not depends on the product, the execution of the advertising, and—very importantly—the quality of the "lists." Direct marketers take great pains to compile or buy mailing lists that will include high percentages of the people known to be in the market for the advertised good or known to have purchased the same or similar goods in the past. Again, there is a concerted effort to talk to the already-converted. The power of advertising, Leo Bogart has argued, is that it may have an ability for "rather quickly motivating or activating the very small number of people who may already be potential customers, and who are, albeit at some remote level of sub-awareness, receptive to a reminder of what the advertiser wants to tell them."[37]

This is the rule. But there are significant exceptions. If a new industry is developing—say, in recent years, the home computer industry—*all* markets are new markets and there is a prodigious effort to seek new customers. Or, if an industry is stagnant, as the hard liquor industry has been, there may also be strong efforts to entice new customers.

ADVERTISING AND THE AFFLUENT CONSUMER

Advertising also tends to follow affluence. It is possible that the growth in sales or per capita sales that so many products have experienced in the past thirty or forty years is best explained as being a result of the general rise in disposable consumer income and the concurrent growth of consumer credit. This growth, it can be argued, has caused both the increase in product sales and the expansion of competitive advertising. Median family income, in constant 1979 dollars, grew from $10,008 in 1950 to $13,774 in 1960; to $18,444 in 1970; to $19,661 in 1979. Real income nearly doubled, then, in a generation. Families earning more than $20,000 in 1979 dollars rose from 15 percent of all families in 1955 to 22.4 percent in 1960; to 40.3 percent in 1970; and to 49.1 percent in 1979.[38] No wonder people bought more things and no wonder advertising began to compete more actively for consumer attention.

More money would have been spent by consumers in the past generation whether advertising had existed or not and whether advertising had expanded or not. Just as advertisers see product usage or heavy product usage as good indicators of future use, so they recognize affluence or rapidly growing affluence as good indicators of future consumer spending. They put their money where consumer money is.

The task of estimating the effects of advertising on sales, particularly aggregate sales of a product category rather than an individual brand, then, is difficult at best and very likely impossible. Sales may lead to advertising as much as advertising leads to sales. Some third factor may stimulate both advertising and sales —product quality, for instance, or rising consumer income. Even if advertising does promote sales, it may do so in ways that are significant to business but do not correspond to the notion of social critics that advertising persuades people to buy what they do not want or need. Advertising may redistribute consumers among brands rather than stimulate increased consumption of a product category and may particularly redistribute people who are already committed "heavy users." Indeed, advertisers organize their budgets and design their marketing strategy to place as little weight as possible on the persuasive powers of advertising. Businesses seek to speak to the already-converted consumer.

All of these realities of business practice are part of what is called "marketing." This is a philosophy, an ideology, and an orientation to business that seeks to distinguish itself from old-fashioned selling. Business leaders speak of the development of the "marketing revolution" or the "marketing concept" as a matter of transcendent significance. In this view, *selling* is a practice millennia-old but marketing is the opposite of selling. Selling, according to one leading text, is "trying to get the consumer to buy what you have." Marketing is "trying to *have* what the consumer wants." The text writers continue: "Selling focuses on the needs of the seller, marketing on the needs of the buyer."[39] Another textbook says: "Let us begin with a fundamental marketing axiom: Demand is almost never created. It can, generally, only be discovered and exploited. Perhaps this is the single most important concept that the student of marketing can come to understand."[40] Versions of this dictum are common coin in the advertising agency office as well as in the business school classroom. Karen Shapiro found in her ethnographic study of ad agencies that throughout the business "people remind each other that you cannot sell something that people do not want."[41]

Peter Drucker, the leading popular philosopher of American business management, emphasizes marketing as "the distinguishing, unique function of the business." Like others of a marketing-orientation, Drucker rails against an engineering emphasis. "The typical engineering definition of quality is something that is hard to do, is complicated, and costs a lot of money! But that isn't quality; it's incompetence. What the customer thinks he is buying, what he considers value, is decisive—it determines what a business is, what it produces, and whether it will prosper." The transformation of the American economy since 1900, Drucker says, "has in large part been a marketing revolution."[42] And this consists of a change in attitude among more and more American businesses:

> . . . fifty years ago the typical attitude of the American businessman toward marketing was "the sales department will sell whatever the plant produces." Today it is increasingly, "It is our job to produce what the market needs." However deficient in execution, the attitude has by itself changed our economy as much as any of the technical innovations of this century.[43]

For Drucker, marketing is "antithetical" to selling, beginning not with the product but with the consumer's wants. For him, "the aim of marketing is to make selling superfluous. The aim of marketing is to know and understand the customer so well that the product or service fits him and sells itself."[44]

Obvious as all of this may sound, it is *not* always obvious in business. Marketing professors and market researchers and other evangelists of the marketing philosophy delight in pointing to failures of businesses that have not been sufficiently marketing oriented. A textbook failure is Hollywood in the 1950s. If the studios had seen themselves as serving an "entertainment function" for consumers rather than as producers of full-length movies, the marketers argue, they would not have ignored television and would have weathered its competition much better than they did.[45] Naturally, the marketing evangelists more often point to failures of a nonmarketing orientation than to successes. Volkswagen in the 1950s and 1960s was very proudly a nonmarketing company, employing Doyle Dane and Bernbach's original advertising to sell a product whose selling point was its engineering and its unwillingness to compromise Spartan serviceability.

Within corporations, marketing-oriented executives see themselves pitted against engineering or product-oriented leaders, on the one flank, and finance-oriented leaders, on the other. The marketing-oriented executives see both a focus on the product and a focus on the bottom line as ultimately shortsighted; they believe that attention to the consumers, who they are and who they are *going* to be, is in the long-term best interest of the company. The marketing literature is not populist but is sometimes pseudopopulist; it is not the voice of the people and it cares nothing for enhancing the autonomous, rational choice of the people, but it insists that decision makers should anticipate what the people will want. Of course, "want" is narrowly conceived. Marketers are not greatly interested in what people with modest disposable income want. Such people are disenfranchised in the marketing world. Marketers are not interested in people's desires if they cannot be met by commercially profitable commodities. A desire for urban public space is not considered but a demand for a new high-rise condominium is. Nor are long-range desires considered: an interest in leaving a nontoxic environment to our children receives less attention than desires for consumer goods whose manufacture produces a by-product of toxic waste.

Marketing, then, an ideology and a philosophy, a general perspective on business practice, is oriented to learning the expressed or elicited needs and desires of consumers with disposable income for commercially viable products. It does not take the product for granted but may involve designing the products or modifying the products. While some products are motivated by engineering developments, others, when marketing-oriented executives have their way, are initiated by businesses that see a "hole" in the market and prescribe the attributes of a product that a research and development staff should create. Advertising agencies, too, may get into this act, urging upon clients certain types of rethinking or redesign of products.

Two kinds of extreme situations may clarify why, for business, marketing is the general problem of which advertising is but one feature. Usually, advertising and sales are correlated although, as I have suggested, it is not clear what this correlation signifies. But sometimes advertising and sales are not correlated and these cases are especially instructive. Sometimes there are substantial sales of a product without advertising and sometimes there is substantial advertising with little or no sales. A sampling of these anomalous cases should provide insight into what role advertising plays in sales or, to put it another way, what factors besides advertising have a powerful effect in selling.

Sales Without Advertising

Sometimes new products get off the ground with little or no advertising. In one form or another, they advertise themselves and word-of-mouth commendation proves sufficient for commercial expansion. A recent example is the Snugli, a cloth pouch for carrying infants on front or back. The Snugli grew out of Ann Moore's desire to carry her baby close to her body as she and husband Michael had seen people do when they were in the Peace Corps in West Africa. The early sales of Snuglis came simply from the exposure the contraption received as Ann Moore rode her bike around Denver, Washington, Kansas City, and other places the Moores lived. She would tell people who asked where she got the Snugli to write her mother in West Alexandria, Ohio, since she had made Ann's and was happy to make more. After a year, her mother, Lucy Aukerman, had more business than she could handle and involved neighbors in the Dunkard German-American religious group in the business. In 1966, two years after the first Snugli, Mrs. Moore sold two or three Snuglis a month, with "each new sale typically generating another five or ten orders a year." In 1968, the *Whole Earth Catalogue* wrote favorably of the Snugli and sales grew from fifteen a month to twenty-five. By 1972, the Moores sold three hundred a month and the business, run as a hobby, incorporated and Michael Moore began attending to it full-time. The business grew again when *Consumer Reports* in 1975 rated the infant carrier the best soft carrier available. In 1976 Snugli hired its first national sales force and in 1979 moved from exclusively cottage industry, homemade production to a machinemade factory model. Snugli is now a $4.5 million a year sales business, with advertising. But it was already a success that justified advertising because it was a quality product, in tune with the times, that had spontaneously attracted attention and caught on.[46]

Probably the most successful consumer products to turn to a mass market in the past fifteen years have never been advertised —marijuana and cocaine. This is not to say they do not find their way into the mass media. But they are a stupendous success, today a multibillion dollar business, growing at a rapid rate without the aid of advertising on either a wholesale or retail level. In 1980 street sales of cocaine have been estimated at $30 billion, marijuana at $24 billion. That is about the same as the total spent in 1980 in all media for all forms of advertising.[47]

Various novelties, counterculture products, and illegal products can succeed ably without advertising. Some products designed for very small markets—say, scholarly books—can make small returns on the most minimal advertising budgets. Other products for very small or esoteric or elite groups also depend in only small ways on advertising—the sales of race horses or sailboats, for instance, do not depend heavily on advertising. Some mass market products may do well with little advertising. Historical romance paperbacks initially gained their widespread popularity with little advertising.[48] Products that embody a distinctive technological advance may sell more on the basis of news stories than advertising. In 1983 a "sponge" contraceptive called "Today" sold out so quickly in the Western states where it was introduced that distribution to other states was delayed until production could catch up to demand.[49]

Generic products, introduced first in France in 1976 and in 1977 in this country, spread quickly as a non-advertised category of goods. They were designed to combat the growth of discount or "no-frills" or "box store" outlets that had sprung up and competed successfully with standard supermarkets during the inflationary 1970s. In the space of a few years, generics have become standards in the supermarket repertoire. Overall, they account for just one or two percent of supermarket sales (figures vary depending on whether one counts total dollars or total weight or total units). And their success rate varies for different categories of goods. With some purchases, people seek only to "satisfice," that is, to arrive at a "good enough" rather than a "best" choice. When people seek a satisfactory rather than an ideal product, they may try a generic good. This is especially common in non-food categories. "God never said a paper towel needed to drink up two cups of (spilled) coffee. Normal requirements call for a paper towel to wipe up a spill or dry bacon. There is a changing value system in terms of what it costs for such frills," says Robert Wunderlee, vice president of Pathmark supermarkets.[50] In general, people tend to favor generics where they do not believe there are pronounced or significant quality differences between brands.[51]

The reason for whatever success generics have had can be attributed to the inflation of the late 1970s and early 1980s and the growing budget-consciousness of many consumers. Consumers are buying more economical foods, avoiding luxury items, switching to house brands and generics, and responding more to special discounts. But it is not clear how to interpret the relative success of generics. If they are taking business away from house brands, which do little advertising, then their success indicates only that consumers who buy by price continue to buy by price and that most other consumers stay loyal to national brands. If generics are taking business from the national brands, however, it suggests that in a bad economy consumers can forgo their loyalties to branded and advertised goods. It appears that generics have "cannibalized" from both brand names and house brand or private-label brand goods. At any rate, their success is but a more striking version of the continuing success of the unadvertised (or modestly advertised) private-label products of the supermarket giants. Overall, private-label goods account for a sixth of supermarket sales. In some areas—health and beauty aids—their market share is very small (about 4 percent) but in other areas, like frozen and refrigerated foods, it represents more than 25 percent of supermarket sales. These are all products that have entered the American supermarket and the consumer's pantry without hoopla; they sell because they have a low price.[52]

One of the greatest advertising campaigns, by all accounts, the greatest campaign, according to many, was the Doyle Dane Bernbach campaign for the Volkswagen. One would not want to take anything away from the originality of that campaign or to doubt that it made a difference in popularizing the Volkswagen and legitimizing it as a part of American culture. But its role in affecting sales is not as self-evident as it may appear. Since 1954 VW had been selling handily "without advertising, without big deals, without fat trade-in allowances and with only four hundred dealers," as *Popular Mechanics' 1957 Cars Fact Book* put it.[53] And it sold without any of the consumer-consciousness that the marketing wizards would have recommended. It was an engineer's car, "an honest piece of machinery," as *Popular Mechanics* said. Not until 1958 did VW place a few ads through the J. M. Mathes agency. While these ads may not have attracted many buyers, they attracted the attention of media representatives who wanted to sell ad space to VW. The VW executives, however, knew at that time they were already unable to keep up with the orders pouring in—why should they want to advertise? When Carl Hahn came to oversee all American operations for VW in 1959, and decided to embark on advertising, it was not to spur sales but to protect VW against the imminent manufacture in Detroit of compact cars.

Volkswagen invested heavily in advertising for the first time in 1959. By that time, VW car and truck registration in the United States had grown from 30,928 in 1955 to 55,690 in 1956; to 79,524 in 1957; to 104,306 in 1958; and 150,601 in 1959. These advances represent gains of 80 percent, 43 percent, 31 percent, 44 percent, and 27 percent respectively. The increase of 27 percent or 41,000 cars in 1960 also made it a banner year—perhaps accounted for in some measure by advertising—still, less than either the percentage or absolute growth of the previous year. This was followed by two years of modest growth, two years of enormous growth, and several years of modest growth.[54] Brilliant as the ad campaign for VW was, it is clearly an instance where investment in advertising followed an upward sales trend of a quality product. The ugly little car was selling like hotcakes when Doyle Dane Bernbach created its campaign. The campaign caught the crest of a sales wave.

Advertising Without Sales

If products can succeed, for a variety of reasons, without being advertised, products can also be advertised without succeeding. The most celebrated failure of advertising and promotion was the Ford Motor Co.'s Edsel. The Edsel appeared on the market in 1957 with more promotion and fanfare than any consumer product had ever received. Ford expected to sell 200,000 Edsels in its first year. When production was halted just over two years later, only 109,000 cars had been sold. There have been any number of explanations for this abysmal failure, now a part of business history and the name Edsel a synonym for failure in the American idiom. Some blame the design, some the name. Others suggest that it was simply the wrong time—about two years too late—to introduce a medium-priced car into the market. Still another explanation is simply that very few new models had successfully entered the market from the 1920s until the 1950s and that the error at Ford was not in trying but in believing so strongly that their careful planning could not fail.[55]

Edsel was a new product and the fact is that many new products, massively advertised or not, do not succeed. Estimates on what percentage of new products fail vary drastically, but all of them are high. The very lowest figure I can find suggests that 23 percent of newly introduced products fail. This is the result obtained in a Booz, Allen, and Hamilton study of seven hundred major American companies. Of new products introduced between 1976 and 1981, 77 percent were still on the market at the time of the 1981 study. This, of course, is a very liberal measure of success, especially for the newer products in the survey. When success was judged by the responding company's own criteria, of 13,311 new items introduced, 35 percent were deemed to have failed. (This figure is consistent with a 1963–68 study that found a 33 percent failure rate. Both figures deal with new products liberally defined—most of these products were additions to or revisions of existing product lines rather than "new to the world" products. Presumably "new to the world" products would have a notably higher rate of failure. When success is more stringently defined, failure rates are higher. A 1980 Dancer Fitzgerald study of 5,125 new supermarket products used $15 million or more of retail sales as a "success" threshold and found only 12 percent success.)[56]

The most commonly cited figure in the business world is that 80 percent of new products fail. Andrew Robertson lists estimates ranging from 77 to 90 percent failure rates.[57] As Robert Buzzell and Robert Nourse point out, however, it is not clear where the 80 percent figure comes from or what it means. What counts as a "new" product and what counts as a "failure"? In their own study, Buzzell and Nourse examined 127 "distinctly new" food products introduced between 1954 and 1964. They found that 40 percent of the new products they looked at failed. When they examined what made the successful products successful, they were most impressed with the high success rate of "pioneering new products"—those that had "substantial, visible differences from existing products in taste, form, preservation, or other physical attributes."[58] As for the effects of promotion, they are skeptical. They find that the highly successful products have much higher promotional budgets, on the average, than other new products, but they suggest that this is most likely a result of early good sales leading to increased promotion. This is the feedback problem I have already discussed—that sales produce advertising as much as advertising produces sales. They note that at least one heavily promoted product can be found in each level of success, including "very unsuccessful," and so they conclude that "a high rate of promotional spending does not guarantee success."[59]

The Edsel is an unusual case of a widely advertised product that dies in that we *remember* it. Many new products that are widely advertised and do not sell slip quickly from the collective memory of the public and of business. Philip Morris, Inc., regarded as a tough and powerful marketing company, was enormously successful with Marlboro cigarettes in the 1950s and Miller beer in the 1970s. But it failed with Clark gum and Personna razor blades and its Cambridge 100s (low-tar cigarettes) have only a .2 percent share of the market after two years. Seven-Up lost market share after Philip Morris bought it in 1978. It may be too soon to tell if its "caffeine free" campaign will change that.[60] Another successful marketer, the Gillette Co., failed with Lady Gillette, a shaving cream for women, and similar products from Johnson & Son, Inc., Clairol, Inc., Alberto-Culver Co., and Colgate-Palmolive Co. also fizzled.[61] Remember the paper dress? It sold very well at first and for a time demand outstripped supply. It was introduced in 1966 by Scott Paper Company and by 1967 there were a number of manufacturers and the paper dress seemed to be a growing fashion. One manufacturer predicted that "Five years from now 75 percent of the nation will be wearing disposable clothing." Another claimed that "by 1980 disposable apparel will become a serious threat to conventional clothing and will account for at least 25 percent of the dollar volume of the giant garment industry."[62]

It never happened. What some observers believed or hoped was a sales trend was only a fad, and what people apparently liked in the paper dresses was nothing much more than their novelty. Certainly, the advertising and promotion (and the free media coverage that the paper dress generated) made a difference in its sudden spurt of sales. But what matters, if an industry is to be sustained, is not so much that people purchase as that they repurchase, and no one repurchased paper dresses.[63]

The famous Proctor & Gamble Co., perhaps the most eminently successful marketer of all, has had its share of failures. In 1968, they decided to enter the lucrative snack-food arena with a new kind of potato chip, Pringles. They turned potatoes into a dehydrated mash, then cut the dehydrated potatoes into uniform chips that could be stacked and sealed in cans the size of tennis-ball cans. This was inventive engineering and novel packaging, but many consumers thought the product tasted bland. Further, Pringles seemed to represent processed foods when "natural" foods were on the rise; rivals pointed out that Pringle's contained preservatives and additives—most potato chips do not. By 1981, reformulated Pringle's was trying again, but in the meantime, the product had lost $200 million.[64]

Not only do some products come and go quickly, despite promotional spending, but whole industries with considerable advertising behind them can disappear from the scene. It should not surprise us to know that the advertising for buggies and carriages did little to help the industry survive after the Model-T was on the road. It may be more surprising to think about less obvious cases. Why, for instance, did the market for men's hats collapse?

Between 1964 and 1970, the men's hat industry declined so sharply that the two leading manufacturers, Hat Corporation of America and John B. Stetson, were both forced to close their operations and sell their brand names and inventories to more diversified companies. How could a major element in the apparel industry simply disappear? It is not easy to know. The industry tended to blame matters on a change of fashion precipitated by President John Kennedy's hatless style. There was special concern about what he would wear to the inauguration (he wore a top hat) and there was continuing anxiety (for hat manufacturers) throughout his tenure. Kennedy did not create a trend but symbolized something already in the air. The *New York Times* suggested the problem might be the general casualness of the post-war years, beginning with a hatless vogue among college students right after the war. As early as 1949, Champ Hats inaugurated a campaign "to combat hatlessness and increasing general carelessness in dress among younger men." Men were going without undershirts, garters, ties, and other traditional apparel. Probably more important, the 1950s and 1960s were the decades of the move to the suburbs. People rode in cars much more often. Not only are hats awkward in cars and likely to be knocked off or set askew as one gets in and out of automobiles, but with automobile travel people are less often walking or standing out in the cold, thus decreasing the protective function of the hat. At the same time, there were changes in men's hairstyles. If any celebrity were responsible for the decline of the hat, it would probably be not John Kennedy in 1960 but the Beatles in 1963, heralding a move among younger men—and then older men—toward longer hair. Not only are hats more difficult to wear with long hair but, more to the point, hair styles become matters of great concern, a focal point of men's fashion-consciousness, not something they would want to hide (or muss) under a hat.

Whatever the reasons for the basic style change, there seemed nothing the hat industry could do to buck it.[65]

Liquor sales provide another curious case. While sales of beer and wine are growing and while sales of some hard liquors have continued to thrive, there has been a downward spiral of other hard liquors over the past two decades that no amount of advertising seems to have been able to halt. As with the case of the hat industry, there is no well-established explanation for the facts—only the disappointed companies and salesmen in the liquor business, face-to-face with a trend they cannot change or even, to any large extent, understand.

In the past several decades, the quantity of beer consumed has increased—from 24 gallons per capita in 1960 to 34.9 gallons per capita in 1980. The consumption of wine has grown from 1.3 gallons in 1960 to 2.1 in 1980; it hit a high of 2.5 in 1977 and has hovered around 2.1 from 1978 to 1981. The consumption of distilled spirits has also grown, from 1.5 gallons in 1960 to 2.0 in 1980; this figure has not changed from 1976 through 1981.[66] Within the distilled spirits market, slow growth overall has been a combination of growing popularity of some spirits—notably vodka, and very rapid sales decline among the traditional leaders—the domestic whiskeys. Whiskey sales decreased from 74 percent of the distilled spirits bottled in the United States to 44.6 percent from 1960 to 1982. The decline has been disastrous for parts of the industry. A famous bourbon distillery in Kentucky was sold in 1980 to Agferm, an alcohol motor fuel company.[67] The question within the liquor industry is: What has caused the sharp decline in sales of whiskeys? Why should the bulwark of the American liquor industry have plunged so precipitously in the past decade?

As in explaining the decline of the hat industry, so also there does not seem to be any consensus about the decline in whiskey sales. Vague sociocultural generalizations are all that remain to industry analysts when basic economic indicators are of no avail.

"Experts" cite a variety of factors. Most point to increased liquor consumption by women and, to a lesser extent, increased consumption by newcomers to alcohol, like young adults. Women, it is assumed, are more inclined to mild and sweet forms of liquor than are men. This observation has been used to explain the rise of vodka and premixed cocktail sales.

In addition, the general population, following the lead of women, has a new interest in diet and health. By 1981, low-calorie soft drinks made up 19 percent of all soft drink sales and light beers 13 percent of the beer market. By the midseventies, white wine had begun to outsell the martini at men's business luncheons. Within the wine category, red wines that far outsold whites in 1960 are now themselves dwarfed by white wine sales. In 1960, 74 percent of wine sold was red; in 1970, 50 percent; and by 1982, 23 percent.[68] "Light" wines have entered the market and sweeter, more casual wines seek a mass market. Riunite wine, for instance, disparagingly called a "lollipop" wine by some, accounted for nearly a quarter of all imported wine in 1980 and promoted itself in soft drink style: "The refrigerator, not the wine cellar, is the place to store Riunite, right next to the orange juice, beer and soft drinks," according to Riunite's marketing director.[69]

Price is another factor in the decline of whiskey sales since the lighter, less alcoholic liquors tend also to be cheaper. In a recession, this may make a big difference.

Finally, milder liquors seem more appropriate since drinking is increasingly a social activity that everyone engages in for convivial purposes, rather than being primarily a male activity aimed at getting drunk.[70]

All of these factors contribute to an explanation but none of them has helped the liquor industry learn how to buck the trend toward light, sweet, and white. The best response seems to be, "if you can't beat it, join it," and so some manufacturers have introduced "light" versions of their standard beers or wines while some distillers have bought wine companies rather than risking their all with whiskey. Heublein owns Inglenook, National Distillers owns Almaden, and in 1983 Seagram bought Coca-Cola's Wine Spectrum.[71]

If we are to attribute power to advertising in affecting the sales of goods, we are clearly going to have to acknowledge limits to that power, too. The question becomes: How best can we conceptualize the role of advertising *compared to* the role of other forces in affecting product sales?

This is a large problem and I want now to narrow it in a way that should prove useful. Product sales, as we have seen, may be affected by a great many large social and demographic factors. The declining birth rate following the "baby boom," for instance, had a marked effect on candy sales in the 1970s. Advertising could not change the trend—there were simply fewer of the relevant people available to advertise to. Any explanation of large trends in product sales will be obliged to take into account large social factors such as birth rates, the participation of women in the labor force, the changing size of households, the changes in amount of disposable income, the consequences of recession on total spending, the effect of the automobile on people's style of life, the status consciousness of different social groups, and so forth. Any model of consumption will necessarily be multicausal, and among these many causes advertising will have pride of place only in unusual circumstances. Any critical understanding of the American disposition for material pleasures should be no less canny than the marketers' own understanding of it. This requires that advertising be seen as but one factor interacting with and building from a host of others. Indeed, it means that there is what I would call an *infrastructure* to consumer behavior, a set of conditions necessary to the maintenance of a given level or type of consumption: conditions, however, that are rarely noticed (until they change) and are only sometimes within the power of a manufacturer or advertiser to control.

Nothing here is meant to suggest that advertising does not work, only that the *kind* of advertising that is most controversial, national consumer goods advertising, does not work *the way* the lay person generally assumes. The task is to identify what work advertising does. Advertisers use advertising as one way of coping with the ever uncertain world of changeable consumers and wily competitors, but they hedge the bets they place on it. They put advertising money behind products with already demonstrated popularity. They direct advertisements to populations already using the same or similar products, already known to have large disposable incomes, and often already known to be heavy users of the advertised good. These are all ways to maximize the value of advertising by assuring that it reaches and affects the people most likely to be consumers of the advertised product or its rivals in the same product category. These strategies all minimize risk but they do little to help the advertiser know the value of its advertising—they actually stand in the way of adequate measurement of advertising effectiveness.

If, normally, businesses expect advertising to be but one marketing tool among many and if they generally hope that it will help redistribute consumers of a given product category among the brands of that category rather than shifting consumers' buying patterns toward a new range of products, then it is difficult to argue that advertising is a prime mover in directly creating a culture of consumption. This says nothing of advertising's general impact as an art form and a symbolic system—its general role in shaping consciousness and providing a framework for thought and feeling. That is a vital matter I will take up later. Here I speak only of advertising's specific power to sell specific goods, and that power is clearly limited.

But how limited—or limited under what circumstances? I will take up that question in chapter 3 by examining the role of advertising from the consumer's viewpoint. In the next chapter, however, I want to examine the issues from the perspective of another key actor: the advertising agency. How does the agency come to terms with the uncertainties of the advertising business in creating advertising campaigns?

2

What Advertising Agencies Know

WHILE some advertisers create their own ads, most advertising today comes out of advertising agencies. These have become big businesses, especially in the past decade. In 1983, there were fifty-four American agencies with gross income over $15 million. Sixteen agencies had income over $100 million, and the four largest, Young & Rubicam, Ted Bates, J. Walter Thompson Co., and Ogilvy & Mather all had more than $300 million in gross income. (These four each had more than $100 million in income outside the United States—American ad agencies are powerful international institutions.) The four top agencies each had total billings of more than $2 billion. Young & Rubicam, J. Walter Thompson, and Ogilvy & Mather each employed more than seven thousand people, Ted Bates Worldwide, McCann-Erickson Worldwide, Foote, Cone & Belding and BBDO International more than four thousand. Overall in 1982, the gross income of American agencies was $6.51 billion, based on billings to clients of $44.2 billion.[1]

The largest of the agencies are located in New York, though a few, including the eighth largest, Leo Burnett, and ninth largest, Foote, Cone & Belding, have Chicago headquarters. And many of the larger New York agencies have branches in Los Angeles, Chicago, and other locations. But it is "Madison Avenue" that looms largest in the folklore of advertising, though few of the biggest agencies are actually located there today. If Wall Street is one image of American capitalism—dark, gray, granite—cold, calculating—Madison Avenue is its upbeat counterpart—steel and glass, jazzy and fast-talking, more cynical than serious, more pressed than pressuring, grinning but tense. This is where ads are made.

Most criticism of advertising is written in ignorance of what actually happens inside these agencies. Recent studies of other institutions in what has been called "the culture industry" should lead us to be wary of pronouncements about cultural products that are ignorant of the process of cultural production;[2] and that seems fitting in this case, too. Agency personnel are to some extent guarded about their work; they do not want to discuss confidential matters and they anticipate that inquiring academics or journalists are likely to be hostile. Still, the advertising world is far from a secret society or even a private club. One can take a look inside.

In this chapter, I want to show what kind of thinking guides an advertising campaign. What do advertising workers know or think they know about the products they advertise, the consumers they advertise to, and the effectiveness of their own ads? What assumptions do they have about the nature of goods, the psychological makeup of consumers, and the persuasive powers of words and pictures that affect how they make ads? The last chapter dealt with what advertisers know about advertising and the next chapter will discuss the place of advertisements in the "information environment" of a consumer; this chapter concerns the information and assumptions advertising agencies bring to bear on their work.

I will address this topic by examining how an agency plans, executes, and evaluates an advertising campaign. Of course campaigns will differ across agencies, across clients, across products, and across executives within a single agency. What I present is a very schematic "ideal-type" rendition of the kinds of considerations that normally engage an agency in designing a campaign.

The advertiser and the agency must answer four questions to launch an advertising campaign:

1. What is the product (and what, if anything, makes it distinctive)? This means that the advertiser and agency must also know what are *rival* products.
2. Who is the audience or group of consumers most likely to be interested in the product?
3. Through what media can this target population be most efficiently reached? (An idea about which media to use often guides a campaign from early on, although the actual "media buying" generally is the final step in setting up the campaign.)
4. Strategy—what kind of advertising appeal will be most effective? and execution—what art and copy will best do the job?

On each question, the agency brings expertise to bear in creating an ad campaign: learning about the product, learning about the market, learning about the media, and creating the art and copy of the ads themselves. Some of these areas correspond to divisions within an agency. Agencies typically have a creative division, a media or media buying division, and a research division. Separate from these departments is account management. An account executive is in charge of coordinating the agency's work for a given product for a given client. An account executive may have charge of half of a major account or up to two or three or more different accounts at one time. It is his, or often, her job to act as liaison between the client and the ad agency. Within the agency, the account executive organizes the planning of the campaign, bringing together people from the relevant divisions and setting up the plan of work.

The creation of an ad campaign is not a rational, linear process directed by a single intelligence. The account executive is not a "boss" but an agent for the agency, a go-between, a negotiator in arriving at an ad campaign that pleases the client. An agency's income derives not from sales of advertised goods but from the amount of advertising it places in print and on the air, regardless of the effectiveness of that advertising. By tradition, the client pays the agency 15 percent of the total billings for air time and newspaper and magazine space bought for the ads. Today, a variety of other compensation systems are also in use, but the 15 percent solution is still taken as the standard.[3] The agency thus benefits directly from convincing the client that advertising makes a difference; its income is proportional to the client's faith in the power of advertising.

The agency may not have an easy time convincing the client to believe in advertising, in general, or in that agency's work, in particular. As the previous chapter indicated, it is very difficult for businesses to gauge the effectiveness of their national advertising. They can rarely know the independent impact of advertising on sales and even proxy measures that rate the memorability of advertisements are not notably reliable. Since advertising is the most visible and one of the most easily manipulated elements in a manufacturer's budget, agencies are hired and fired with some frequency. The owner of a baseball team may not know why the team did not win, but he or she can feel decisive and efficacious by firing the manager. Advertisers can do the same, often with less justification, with their agencies. Nothing makes headlines more regularly in the advertising trade press than account switches. In 1981 McDonald's Corp. switched its $75 million account from eleven-year partner Needham, Harper & Steers to Leo Burnett Co. BBDO lost Vicks Health Care to Young & Rubicam and Campbell Soup Co. to Backer & Spielvogel; Young & Rubicam lost Eastern Air Lines' $45 million to Campbell-Ewald but gained United Vintners Inc.'s $20 million from McCann-Erickson. And so on. "It's a game of musical chairs," according to O. Milton Gossett, chairman of Compton Advertising. "What's most distressing is that, in most cases, those agencies have done a very creditable job."[4] Yet Eastman Kodak Co. has been with J. Walter Thompson for fifty years. The average relationship between agency and client lasts eight years, ten years with the largest agencies. Account shifting is time consuming; it requires the client to start over in educating a new agency to its way of doing business. Account switching may be initiated when there is a change in the client's top management or when some key advertising personnel move from their home agency to set up an agency of their own and then take some of the old clients with them. Whatever the sources of account switching, their frequency and unpredictability add an element of uncertainty to work that is tense and high-pressured in any case.

The vulnerability of the agencies, even the most powerful and profitable, to the whims of clients, arises in its most embarrassing form when prospective clients demand that the agencies make "spec" presentations. In 1982, for instance, Hallmark Cards, Budweiser Light, 7-Up, Sears corporate, Sears apparel, Taco Bell, Coors Light, Avis, and other major accounts—a majority of the largest accounts seeking agencies that year—hired agencies only after speculative creative work was presented. Hallmark asked Foote, Cone & Belding, its agency for thirty-seven years, to compete with three other finalists in preparing two finished and tested thirty-second television commercials with a third in storyboard form with finished music. Hallmark paid each finalist $100,000 for this effort, but that fell far short of the actual expenses. (Young & Rubicam won the account.)[5] These practices do not please the agencies. David Ogilvy writes: "The worst way for a manufacturer to pick an agency is to invite speculative presentations. The only thing this measures is the agency's willingness to divert its best brains from the service of its *present* clients to the pursuit of *new* ones."[6] But this did not prevent the agency Ogilvy founded, Ogilvy & Mather, from trying its hand in the Hallmark presentations and others as well.

Even when a prospective client does not base selection on speculative presentations, finding a proper match of agency and advertiser can be arduous—especially for the agency. When General Foods decided to add a fifth agency for some of its products in 1979, it appointed a committee to study the field. (Large advertisers commonly employ several different agencies for different product lines.) The committee narrowed the list to six large agencies and chose from among them on the basis of the agencies' written responses to a set of questions—responses that were hundreds of pages long. The questions asked for details on the finances of the agency, other clients, the addition or loss of clients in recent years, new product introductions, a balance sheet, organization and personnel of the agency, personnel training and development programs, and the philosophy of the "creative process" and the role of the agency and role of the client in that process.[7]

Keeping in mind that the creation of an ad campaign is a process, a negotiation between a client and an agency and not a well-ordered set of procedures guided by a single mind, I will nonetheless try to offer a schematic view of what kinds of knowledge (apart from the very crucial knowledge about the personalities and character of the client company) are brought to bear on making an ad campaign. The agency must find information or hunches or routines to respond to the questions: What is the product? What is the market for it? Through what media can we reach the audience? And what kind of advertising copy and art will best appeal to the target population? Both praise and criticism of advertising often picture the ad industry as almost omniscient in its understanding of how to reach deep into the consumer heart and mind. A recent popular book within advertising circles is subtitled, "The Battle for Your Mind," and the implication of this and more critical works is that advertising relies on a precise science of persuasion.[8] This is not so—although there are some sophisticated tools in advertising for gathering market information and a well-developed body of factual knowledge to guide advertising practice. But what kind of knowledge is this and how does the agency bring it to bear in actually creating an advertising campaign?

The Nature of the Advertised Product

Suppose that United Airlines has just hired a new agency. United in 1981 spent $79 million on advertising. It was the nation's eighty-first largest advertiser.[9] To serve United well, the agency's staff must learn something about the product—not just United, but commercial air travel in general. (Conceivably, alternate forms of transportation might also deserve study if trains, cars, or buses are often options for air travelers.) The agency quickly discovers that United uses the same planes as the other major airlines; essentially United offers the same thing that rivals supply. What, then, can it advertise?

United can emphasize some features that are distinct, and it does so. It has more widebody aircrafts than other airlines. It serves a number of key destinations with more frequent service than other airlines, and its advertising emphasizes schedule frequency on these routes, or low fares, or features of life in the destination city. United advertising keys on Hawaii because United is the leading carrier there. Sometimes United focuses on special services that make it to some degree distinctive, such as its "Ocean to Ocean" special entrees, wine, and linen napkins on transcontinental flights.[10] If United did *not* offer something distinctive of this sort, the agency might urge United to develop itself as a more distinct alternative to other airlines. The agency may try to find something about the client's product that makes it unique or special, some aspect of the product that can be the basis for what advertising executive Rosser Reeves dubbed the "unique selling proposition."[11]

With most products, each brand has some unique feature. But with a number of widely advertised products, there is no significant difference from one brand to the next. Detergents are largely the same. Toothpastes are largely the same. Most beer drinkers cannot tell their own brand from a rival in blind taste tests. Most cigarette smokers cannot tell one brand from another within a range of the same type of cigarette.[12] If products do not differ materially, they may nonetheless differ or be made to differ in *attributed* qualities, or "image." If consumers believe a product to be distinctive, this belief in itself may become a product attribute. If, thanks in large part to effective advertising, Campbell's "MM-mm Good" soup takes on the image of wholesomeness more than other soups or if consumers come to expect courtesy and graciousness from "the friendly skies of United" or if people regard Marlboro as a "real man's cigarette," then the product has a distinctive brand image that any new advertising campaign will want to exploit.

There are conventional, common-sense differences among

product types that affect advertising strategy. Industrial products are handled differently from consumer goods. Among consumer goods, "durables" tend to differ from "nondurable" or repeat-purchase products. To some extent the product dictates the ad campaign: not only how much will be spent, but also how it will be spent. With "search goods," for instance, products like clothing that a consumer can evaluate reasonably well prior to purchase, advertisements will generally offer a good deal of factual information. Advertisements for "experience" goods—products that can be judged only by actual use (the taste of tuna, the effectiveness of a deodorant)—are more often "lifestyle" or "affective" in their approach.[13]

The dictates of types of products can turn into prescriptions for advertising agencies. Foote, Cone & Belding has developed a classification of goods relevant to advertising content. Goods are either "thinking" or "feeling" goods and consumers have either "high involvement" or "low involvement" with them. This leads to a four-fold table as follows:

	Thinking	*Feeling*
High Involvement	car, house, furniture	jewelry, cosmetics, apparel, motorcycles
Low Involvement	food, household items	cigarettes, liquor, candy

Advertisements for high-involvement, thinking products emphasize information and may be characterized by long copy. Ads for low-involvement, thinking products will just provide a reminder—these are products consumers buy by habit. Ads for high-involvement, feeling products emphasize mood, image, or emotion. Ads for low-involvement, feeling products emphasize the satisfaction of personal tastes. There is a tendency for this type of product to shift up to the high-involvement, feeling category—the consumer's economic investment is slight but his or her ego involvement may become very high.[14] Indeed, other ad executives refer to these as "badge" products that express a person's public self and in which people have a psychological investment.

Knowing the product means more than understanding its engineering features. It means understanding how the product compares to its competitors. The advertising agency and its client must study not only the product and its target audience but also the products that rivals offer the same or similar populations. Advertisers orient their marketing strategies as much to one another as to a concept of who the consumers are. In the pages of trade journals like *Advertising Age,* stories about new ad campaigns or new product introductions are more likely to mention rival firms than to profile likely consumers.[15] The trade journals are replete with discussions of "positioning" a product in a field of products. In stories in *Advertising Age* in 1981, for instance, a new General Foods campaign for Master Blend coffee is pictured as an effort to displace Procter & Gamble's leadership (with Folger's) of the regular ground coffee market. Master Blend was to be "positioned" as an economical ground coffee, "battling" Folger's and Hills Bros. Coffee's "High Yield." (All this, of course, while coffee consumption continued its long-term decline.) Coca-Cola introduced "Ramblin' " root beer to New York, encouraged that the root beer category did not have a clear-cut leader. Kentucky Fried Chicken introduced a television campaign, "We do chicken right," to distinguish itself from competitors McDonald's, Wendy's, Ponderosa, and Burger King that had all introduced chicken dishes to their menus. Heublein introduced "American Creme" to "go up against" Bailey's Irish Cream. At least nine other marketers were seeking a niche in the "category created and dominated by Bailey's." Heublein's aim was to "control the low end of the category."[16]

According to the prevailing wisdom in marketing, another key factor in advertising strategy is what stage of the "product life cycle" the commodity is in. When a product is new, the job of advertising is to stimulate a new demand, to lead the consumer to "trial" of the product. When the product is established and is part of a "growth" market, advertising's job is less to get consumers to try the product than to get them to prefer one brand among many. When the market has reached "maturity," emphasis may shift toward retaining retail outlets, maintaining shelf space, and emphasizing marginal product differentiation. So a product is defined, from a marketing perspective, not only by its physical attributes or its consumer benefits, but by the degree of maturity of the market in which it competes, and the nature and intensity of competition in the market. These factors affect what kind of advertising is possible or desirable.[17]

The result is that investment in advertising differs sharply across industries. In 1982, United Airlines spent 1.3 percent of total sales on advertising. This was very close to American Airlines' 1.5 percent and TWA's 1.8 percent. Leading automobile manufacturers spend less as a percentage of sales—General Motors' $549 million in advertising represented .9 percent of sales and Ford also spent .9 percent of sales. In contrast, drug and cosmetic industries are typically very high investors in advertising. Richardson-Vicks's $12.9 million represented 11.6 percent of sales, Sterling Drug 7.8 percent, and Miles Laboratories 6.7 percent.[18]

According to marketers, products succeed only if their manufacturers know the territory of competition and the cognitive terrain that the array of competitors maps for consumers. Businesses fight their rivals to take advantage of existing or changing consumer patterns and tastes. This means, of course, that they must know something about those elusive consumers.

The Target Audience

Clearly, the agency must understand not only the product but its likely audience. To return to United Airlines, the agency must know who flies in commercial airplanes. There is data to help the agency. Seventy-four percent of all American air travel expenditures come from professional and managerial heads of households. Only 63 percent of adult Americans have ever flown in an airplane and only 25 percent of the adult population flies in a given year, a figure largely unchanging in the period 1971–77. Thirty-eight percent of air travel expenses are for business, the rest is for visiting friends and relatives, sightseeing, and tourism. Most air travel is done by people aged thirty to fifty with family incomes over $25,000, and this is the main target group for airline advertising.[19]

This data may provide an agency a good deal of useful information. The agency will note that a very small percentage of the population—and an identifiable group with predictable media habits—accounts for the vast majority of expenditures on air travel. Most of these air travelers are men but this will be changing as more women enter the business and professional world. A Newspaper Advertising Bureau study found that a quarter of business travelers are women.[20] And women may have different attitudes and different needs in air travel. This is what the Leo Burnett Company which, in fact, handles the United account, considered a few years ago. They conducted "focus group" research on professional women who travel often by air. They asked these women what they liked and did not like about airplanes, air travel, and airline promotion and advertising. While this research could not substitute for quantitative data, the agency might have found it very helpful. Especially for the "creative" department, qualitative research has special value: "The words of the target audience as spoken in these research sessions provide the most valued information for creatives who are trying to learn how people should sound in the commercial."[21]

The focus group has been in vogue in market research the past decade or so. It is simply a group discussion in which a trained leader talks with a group of consumers to learn about buying habits, responses to new products, or views on competing products. Like other fashionable research tools in advertising, it has both proponents and detractors. It is cheap and quick, but its results are hard to generalize. Mary Tuck, a British marketing consultant and lecturer on management, observes that in the rare case where someone has tried to establish if results from one focus group are comparable to those from another, the findings are negative. She concludes that "most mass commercial activity in group discussions is not research at all. It is a comfort mechanism for decision makers. Its sociological function is to provide hypotheses or confirmations which spread the responsibility for action."[22] In its place, however, focus group research has been very useful for agencies. It is not so driven by weighty and often wrong-headed pseudo-Freudian theory as was "motivational research" in the 1950s and not so lifeless as the reports on the demographic characteristics of various types of consumers that still comprise the main research in advertising. It keeps the agencies in some kind of personal touch with the man and woman on the street, provides a source of ideas, and even offers a reservoir of words, phrases, and colloquialisms to inspire the creation of ads.

In any event, an agency is likely to employ both quantitative research and some kind of softer research like the focus group in learning about the target audience. The quantitative research may become very sophisticated. Basic data will include the age, sex, income, race, and region of consumers. It may also go beyond this to demographic *projections*. Marketers need to know not only who the target population is today but who it is likely to be tomorrow. It is important for advertisers to know, for instance, that the population age twenty-five to forty-four, sixty-two million in 1980, will be seventy-eight million in 1990; the population age fifteen to twenty-four, forty-two million in 1980, will be only thirty-five million in 1990. A soft drink advertiser, then, would be well advised to orient advertising less to teenagers and more to adults establishing families and careers. Not just the age distribution but the household distribution of population is changing. The number of households is growing but the number of persons in each household is declining, from 3.14 in 1970 to 2.80 in 1980 to an anticipated 2.60 in 1990. The number of single-person households has grown enormously—from 17 percent of all households in 1970 to 23 percent in 1980 to an expected 26 percent in 1990. This suggests to the wise marketer that there will be an expanding market for convenience foods, for packaging to suit the needs of single people, and so forth.[23]

Quantitative data may also be detailed enough to begin to put together profiles of likely consumers for a product, profiles including a variety of "lifestyle" factors. J. Walter Thompson reported to its dog food client Liggett and Myers that the target population for dog food sales was the thirty-five to forty-nine-year-old female age group in families where (in 1971) income was over $10,000, there were school-age children, and the wife did the family supermarket shopping. Liggett and Myers commissioned a more psychologically-oriented market study which added that household pets were increasingly treated as "a member of the family" and that the pets were especially important for housewives, giving them more to do and providing them with another focus of affection. The study found that it is "primarily women who receive emotional support and satisfaction from their pets."[24]

Audience research may indicate not only who uses products but how people use products and on what occasions. Bill Ross of J. Walter Thompson argues that there are not so much different types of consumers to appeal to but consumers with a repertoire of "occasions" and "needs." The market researcher's job, in this view, is to identify the occasion or situation-specific desires of the consumer.[25] Research that helped inspire the Miller High Life campaign, one of the more celebrated advertising campaigns of the past decade, not only reported that a very small percentage of the population drinks a very large proportion of all beer, it also demonstrated that about two-thirds of all beer consumed in the United States is consumed at home and that two-thirds of beer is consumed between 4:00 P.M. and 8:00 P.M. This latter information was important in developing the Miller campaign with the theme, "It's Miller Time: when it's time to relax, one beer stands clear; if you've got the time, we've got the beer." That campaign often featured a sunset in its different television commercials, emphasizing the appropriateness of Miller to late afternoon and early evening.

Agencies may be involved not only in survey research and focus groups but in in-home use studies even before full-scale test marketing. In such studies, perhaps two hundred or three hundred families would receive free samples of a new product for home use. After a period of use, families are polled on how they liked the product and whether they would be likely to buy such a product. The amount of research and the kind of research that an advertiser and its agency employ will vary by client, by product, and by agency. Certain agencies are well known as being research-intensive (Grey Advertising is one of these). Certain clients are famous for meticulous attention to research and testing

(Procter & Gamble, for instance). Advertising in certain product areas tends to rely more on research than in others; cosmetics advertising, for instance, does not rely on research very much. As one executive told me, "Working on cosmetics, we never researched anything. It's more exciting, seat of the pants, you use your own judgment."

Just how useful market research is to creating an ad campaign remains open to question. "Creatives" in an agency are by reputation hostile to research. "Research," the famous ad man Albert Lasker said, "is something that tells you that a jackass has two ears."[26] William Bernbach, a more recent hero among creatives, is supposed to have been no more awed by research. According to legend, a research report concluded that his slogan for Avis, "We're number two, we try harder" was un-American and would fail with Americans who like being number one. Bernbach is supposed to have responded: "Get some other research."[27] Milton Gossett, president and chief executive officer of Compton Advertising, noted the faddishness of market research: "First we had a voice-pitch analysis. Pupil dilation is 'out,' eye excitement is 'in,' and now we have brain-wave arousal. It's interesting but . . . we use research like a drunk uses a street lamp, for support, not for illumination."[28] One copywriter in a large agency told me, "We get lifestyle studies from the research department, long and dull profiles of audiences. But most of it is pretty obvious. There are three kinds of Cutlasses. Cutlass Supreme is the basic Cutlass—kinda new, kinda young, and kinda not anything else. Cutlass Calais is sporty—bucket seats and maybe a T-handle floor shift. The driver in the ad might wear gloves, it's for the tentative macho types. Then there's Cutlass Supreme Brougham, the elegant version, and the ad will show it in front of a fancy hotel with a doorman." Research, he suggested, was not necessary to figure this out. On the other hand, many people in creative work have developed increasing respect for their research associates down the hall. One creative director told me, "Any creative person who's any good in this business loves to get facts. You get better advertising results if you know a lot about what you're trying to communicate."

Does research on consumers provide agencies a general view

of what motivates the consuming public? Do agencies have an image of the audience they generally try to reach? Critics sometimes believe that Madison Avenue takes consumers to be rather weak and deplorable bundles of fears, anxieties, and desires that need only be tapped to unleash a flow of spending. Industry talk of locating "hot buttons" to sell a new product, be it underwear or home computers, is the kind of language that confirms critics in their view. Yet the sometimes racy and often hyperbolic language of the agencies does not actually represent their activities very well. "Shop talk" in any business tends to be cynical and funny, designed to create comradeship and deal with tension. Advertising workers sound almost saintly when discussing the consumer compared to what one can hear when physicians talk about patients or, for that matter, when university professors talk about students.

When social scientists examine the image of an audience held by the writers of television dramas, journalists at newsweeklies, television news reporters, or others who produce materials for large audiences, they are frequently surprised to discover that their subjects have relatively little knowledge of their audiences, and almost no systematically gathered information about them.[29] One would imagine ad agencies to be different. They must depend on a precise view of the target population, a sound understanding of what the interests of potential consumers will be. If anyone outside the professional worlds of psychology, psychiatry, and the social sciences would have a sophisticated view of the human personality, social reference groups, the dynamics of sex, race, class, and region, it would be marketing and advertising people. But what, then, is the agencies' collective vision of the American population? If the ad industry were to articulate a sociological or psychological theory of consumer behavior, what would it be?

It is a common view both in the advertising industry and outside that, once upon a time, ads were primarily informational, appealing to the rational consumer, but that ads in the twentieth century have become increasingly persuasive, oriented to a nonrational, impulse-driven consumer. For instance, it is generally argued that nineteenth-century advertising made little or no use of "sex appeal." Authorities often cite Albert Lasker's remark that J. Walter Thompson's early twentieth-century ad for Woodbury soap, "The skin you love to touch," was the beginning of open sex appeals in advertising. But even a cursory look at nineteenth-century advertising suggests this is nowhere near the truth. The nineteenth-century ads showed no bathing beauties, perhaps, but the ads did not hesitate to picture Greek and Roman sculptured nudes or robed women of alluring countenance. "Sexual titillation was an established attention-getter from the earliest days of national advertising," Jackson Lears writes. "Long before the turn of the century advertisements were serving up breasts and thighs. By 1910, an electric sign advertising corsets showed a young woman dressing and undressing atop Times Square."[30]

Not only was sex used to sell products in early advertising, but advertisements did not become markedly more sexual as time went on. One thorough content analysis indicates that sexuality plays a relatively small role, overall, in magazine advertising. For instance, in every decade of this century, except the 1920s, magazine ads made more appeals to family values (nurturance, companionship, having a home) than to sexuality (erotic relations, personal vanity, and sexual attractiveness).[31]

Where, then, does one get the view that advertising has become increasingly sensitive to human emotions and impulses rather than to human reason? In part, this simply reflects the changing rhetoric of the advertising business itself. The professional literature in advertising, as historian Merle Curti has shown, shifted over time from seeing human nature as rational to seeing it as emotional. Curti examined the trade journal *Printer's Ink* from its 1888 beginning to the 1950s. He found that from 1888 until 1910, the majority of comment in *Printer's Ink* took human nature to be rational and self-interested. From 1910 until 1930, the majority of comment accepted that human nature is essentially nonrational. The majority of experts took human beings to be emotional, believed that the language and methods of applied science could be used in advertising, and took advertising to create desires rather than to provide information. By the 1950s, advertisers wrote more about satisfying rather than creating desires, but continued to accent the emotional aspects of the consumer.[32]

It would be a mistake to draw too much from the foregoing about advertising practice in general. What advertising people say in their trade journals about "human nature" may have little bearing on their actual work. The trade literature is bound to be more pretentious and more in search of comprehensive visions, justifications, or ideologies than is actual advertising practice. In practice, it seems to me, there is no overall view of human nature but, instead, a common-sense understanding of the relationship between people (or certain kinds of people) and certain kinds of products. Further, I do not think that advertising practice has been sharply influenced by any particularly powerful ideas or theories about human nature but by a few fundamental shifts in the demographic profile of consumers, the character of clients, and the technical possibilities of the media.

There have been changes in American advertising in the past half or three-quarters of a century and they are consistent, in general, with a move toward viewing the consumer as driven by emotions, not cost-benefit calculation. According to Richard Pollay's content analysis of two thousand print ads from ten leading magazines, 1900–1980, ads have become less informative. They are more focused than they used to be and emphasize fewer bits of information presented more dramatically. The information-richness of magazine advertising reached lows in the 1940s and 1960s and has increased in the 1970s—but still not to the level of the early decades of the century. On the other hand, if total information has decreased, advertising has constantly emphasized rational benefits of products in the appeal it makes to consumers. Pollay finds that practical product attributes have been promoted far more than any other product quality in every decade. The second most-often-cited benefit in the 1970s was low cost, although newness and uniqueness outdistanced low-cost in the 1960s. Newness, uniqueness, and technical qualities were mentioned more often than low-cost in the 1950s.[33]

From 1900 to 1950 there was increasing emphasis in advertising on stressing consumer benefits rather than product attributes. This was consistent with the "marketing" emphasis that focuses on what the consumer wants rather than on what the product provides. There was also growing emphasis on emotional rather than logical rhetorical strategies. These trends, however, reversed themselves in the 1960s and 1970s—there has been, as Pollay says, a "subsiding sizzle" in advertising.[34]

So the evidence is somewhat contradictory about the trends away from informativeness in advertising—it depends on what one measures and by what means one does the measuring. To the extent that ads have progressively turned toward the emotional rather than the informative approach, the reasons for change have had little to do with the application of psychology and the behavioral sciences to advertising, much to do with a few notable marketplace changes that have altered the world in which the advertising agency operates.

First, advertisers came to note that women, not men, were their primary audience. Literature in marketing still refers to the consumer as "she." It may have been less a changing concept of human nature than a changing concept of who consumers are that accounts for the tone of the trade literature. Popular conventional understanding saw men as rational, women as emotional. The recognition of women as consumers thus legitimated an emotional rhetoric in advertising. While reference to women as the purchasing agents of the American family suggests a rational, budget-conscious person—and this image continued to influence advertisers—advertisers also believed in the emotional vulnerability of "the little woman."[35] (In advertising, as elsewhere, ideology is often two-sided, flexible enough to provide rationale for almost any practice that might come along.)

Second, and even more important, if the concept of the audience was changing for the ad agency, so was the nature of clients. There were more clients and there were more of them within a given product category. Advertising *had* to change, ads had to become more differentiated. With more competing ads, there was more incentive to come up with something distinctive and memorable. This in itself may account for the decreasing informativeness of advertising; the aim has become increasingly to grab the viewer's attention with a few eye-catching words or pictures; telling the whole story of the product is less important. Ads have become, through the years, more like *USA Today,* less like the *New York Times.*

The typical American supermarket offered nine hundred items for sale in 1928, three thousand in 1946, nearly eight thousand by 1970.[36] The growing number of consumer goods and brands not only puts a premium on advertising that will achieve some distinctiveness but also makes it hard for a consumer to know his or her own needs. That is, people have needs for food and household cleaning products, but they experience them in the context of solutions that the world, especially the commercial world, offers. Needs, as William Leiss argues, become "ambiguous" in a high-intensity market society.[37] There are more alternatives within a product category available and there is a rapid growth and differentiation of product categories. Further, an efficient distribution system, refrigeration, and improved storage facilities in stores and in homes make more of these brands and product categories *simultaneously* available. The result is that people deal every day with more uncertainties about what they want and need. With question and choice forced upon them, they have more occasion to be reminded of just how unsure they are. It may be that the ambiguity of needs with respect, say, to household cleaning products is not a serious matter. If the consumer's needs become ambiguous, he or she at the same time may develop a certain indifference to them, and much of advertising is lavished on products to which people feel relatively indifferent. At the same time, people confront many more self-conscious choices among products than they used to and are thereby regularly reminded not only that they have a delicious freedom of choice (within a given and generally unquestioned range) but that they may not have a firm grip on what criteria of choice matter or should matter to them the most. In a high-intensity consumer society, the daily bread becomes a cafeteria; the staff of life one once could lean on becomes a set of choices to make among white, whole wheat, rye, or sourdough, toasted or untoasted, butter or margarine.[38]

A third factor in the changing nature of advertising has been, of course, the changes in the media available for advertising; technological changes in printing, photography, reproduction, color, and later the development of television enabled and required new kinds of advertising appeals. Up until television, art directors in ad agencies were technicians or illustrators or, as they were dubbed, "wrists" who carried out the ideas developed by the copywriters. Creative directors I spoke to in New York remembered getting into the business in the 1950s when art and copy were separate departments. Still today, creative directors tend to come from writing rather than art backgrounds, but since television, art directors have contributed more centrally to the conceptualization of ads.[39] As the possibility of elaborate and effective visual presentation has enlarged, the importance of the visual relative to the verbal has grown, even in "print media" like magazines. Ads with little or no written message are reasonably common now but would have been unknown fifty or sixty years ago. It would be a mistake to identify "reason" with words and "emotion" with pictures, but it is surely true that new possibilities for the visual in advertising have stimulated the development of emotional, affective, or "mood" advertising.[40]

Advertising makes use of a highly sophisticated set of practices for gaining the consumer's attention and interest. But this has less to do with impressive psychological theory, which simply does not exist in advertising, than with a conviction of the emotional vulnerability of women, an intense competition among more and more products and more and more ads that forces agencies to explore more rococo means of manipulation, and an increasing emphasis on the visual media, on images rather than words and the creation of moods rather than the telling of reasons.

The result is that advertisements have only the most happenstance and eclectic theoretical foundation; they are not based on any serious understanding of people's attitudes about worldly goods. Despite efforts at "psychographics" which, here and there, have proved useful guides for advertising, the most consistently used and efficient criteria for describing consumers are the most psychologically blunt—demographics. What is the sex, age, marital status, race, religion, region, income, and labor force participation of the target consumer? This is the most easily collected data and it is the data most easily translated into decisions about what media will be likely to reach which prospective buyers (see next section). It is the most consistently employed kind of data in advertising work. Add to this the fact that the most evidently successful advertising is still advertising that abandons all efforts at psychological manipulation and just tells people that the product offered is on sale or has a low price. Even in nonprice advertising, it remains the advice of many advertising authorities that *providing information* is the best "come-on" an ad can have. David Ogilvy reports that magazine ads that have some "news" have a higher readership than ads that do not provide new information.[41]

Advertising operates not with an image of the consumer but with a concept, usually rooted in common sense, of a person-product relationship. Agencies do not take consumers to be either rational *or* emotional. It all depends on the product and the circumstances. Some products are taken to be emotional ones, notably cosmetics and perfume. A product like clothing, however, is more difficult to predict. Women's fashion marketers may hold that consumers "want something more colorful and emotional," "they want romance." On the other hand, fashion marketers who sense a conservative mood among women will argue just the opposite—that women want quality and durability for their fashion dollar. Whether consumers are regarded as "emotional" or "rational" varies with the product, the time, and the circumstance. Whether consumers are taken to be traditionalists or seekers of novelty varies similarly. Marketers of the "wet/dry shaver" noted that American men like high-tech products but that only 25 percent use electric shavers. Why? Because American men are traditional and cannot give up the "feeling of wetness" they connect with shaving. At the same time, marketers are convinced of people's love of the novel, and so Envoy sports shoes promoted their model as "the only shoe in the world with pockets." One does not have to read the advertising trade literature very long to find that consumers are characterized as rational at one time, impulsive at another; individualist and then again conformist and status-conscious; skeptical about advertising—and then relatively gullible; seekers of novelty and also followers of tradition; interested in cost and then again willing to overlook cost for status or quality. Advertising practice employs a vast array of notions of the consumer and ideas of human nature in an utterly ad hoc and opportunistic way. Whatever frightful characteristics one may attribute to the American advertising industry, consistency is not one of them.[42]

The absence of a systematic sociology or social psychology of consumption in advertising enables agencies to freely adjust their advertising campaigns—and the rationales for those campaigns—to the particular tastes and biases of an individual client, to the idiosyncrasies of a specific product and market, and to the exigencies of a historical moment, whether a period of recession or expansion, conservatism or venturesome activity. This opportunism is unlikely to change and, even as techniques of testing advertising effectiveness or pretesting advertising copy become more refined, the chances of a theoretical understanding of consumption grow no greater in the advertising business. Most consumer research is proprietary. It has very limited goals and a very narrow focus and it often concentrates on product categories where the stakes for business are high but the interest of consumers low. As consumer researcher Morris Holbrook has put it, most research is devoted to the psychology of "products about which consumers really just don't give a damn." He writes:

> Yes, we can build multiattribute models that predict preference toward toothpaste; we can generate complex multidimensional spaces that represent perceptions of cigarettes; we can construct devilishly clever procedures that trace the acquisition of information on cereal brands; we can—with our bare hands—construct mighty regression analyses that relate detergent usage to 300 separate life-style variables. In short—when it comes to the factors of least importance to the consumer's emotional, cultural, and spiritual existence—we excel.[43]

Advertising workers speak sometimes with contempt of consumers, sometimes with respect. They speak sometimes on the basis of computer print-outs, sometimes on the basis of intuition. They speak sometimes of consumers in general and sometimes apply their remarks only to consumers of certain types in certain contexts. The language in which they discuss the consumer changes with fashions in psychology and research methods, but the highly variable evaluation of what moves consumers is guided by an understanding of why people seek out different goods that does not differ notably from the common-sense understandings by which most people operate. From time to time, pop psychology codifies these implicit understandings in one or another caricatured version. The advertising industry, in its quest for assurance that it has a knack or a science, will often pick up the marketing version of one or another of the pop psychologies. Thus popularized Freudian psychology begot "motivation research" in the 1950s and the popular characterization of different "lifestyles" cross-cutting class lines has more recently begotten "market segmentation," "positioning," and "values and lifestyles" models of the consumer. Any of these codifications may offer some guidance for a time but all of them seem fated to fade back into an eclecticism of common sense.

Media Buying

Suppose United's mythical new agency has come to understand the product, commercial air travel, and has data, or at least hunches, on the nature of the target audience. The next question is how best to reach this audience. Specifically, in what medium or combination of media should ads appear? The task is to learn what kinds of people in what numbers attend to the different available media, primarily radio, television, newspapers, and magazines.

Most airline advertising is local, often in print, because most airlines have local or regional markets. United, as the largest airline and one of only a few with national coverage, is the leader among airlines in network television spending. Even at United, however, most advertising dollars are spent on local media. In 1982, United spent 9 percent of its budget on local newspaper advertising, 22 percent on spot television advertising, 40 percent on network television, 23 percent on radio, and 6 percent on magazines. Most airlines spend more heavily in newspapers. American devoted 37 percent of its advertising budget to newspapers, Delta 54 percent, and Eastern 42 percent.[44] ("Spot" advertising is advertising purchased station by station rather than bought in one transaction for a whole network. With spot advertising, a business can concentrate on radio and television stations in a particular region or with a particular demographic cast.)

The various media, of course, want to do what they can to attract the advertiser's dollars. (For a measure of their success, see table 2.2.) They try to demonstrate by a variety of measures that they are the best outlets for the advertiser's purposes. The most significant number they present to a potential advertiser is their cost per thousand (CPM), the cost of an ad per one thousand audience members reached. The lower the CPM, the more people who will see the ad per dollar spent to buy advertising time or space. But this is not the only consideration. A medium may boast to advertisers that it can reach a larger total number of people than other media—network television, of course, can often make this claim. Or a medium may argue that, though it does not reach the biggest audience, it has the *best* audience in terms of some desirable audience characteristic like high average annual income.

TABLE 2.2

Estimated Annual U.S. Advertising Expenditures (in millions of dollars)

	1935	*1940*	*1950*	*1960*	*1970*	*1980*	*1982*
Newspapers	761	815	2,070	3,681	5,704	14,794	17,694 (27%)
Magazines	130	186	478	909	1,292	3,149	3,710 (6%)
Television	—	—	171	1,627	3,596	11,366	14,329 (22%)
Radio	113	215	605	693	1,308	3,702	4,670 (7%)
Direct Mail	282	334	803	1,830	2,766	7,596	10,319 (15%)
Business Publications	51	76	251	609	740	1,674	1,876 (3%)
Outdoor	31	45	142	203	234	578	721 (1%)
Miscellaneous	352	439	1,180	2,408	3,910	10,891	13,261 (20%)
National Advertising Total	890	1190	3,260	7,305	11,350	29,815	37,785 (57%)
Local Advertising Total	830	920	2,440	4,655	8,200	23,735	28,795 (43%)
Grand Total	1,720	2,110	5,700	11,960	19,550	53,550	66,580

SOURCE: Adapted from data prepared for *Advertising Age* by Robert J. Coen, McCann-Erickson, Inc.

With respect to air travel, *Time* magazine puts out research that shows that, among magazines, it is the best spot for airline ads. According to a 1979 study, 46 percent of "frequent flyers" read *Time* while only 31 percent read *Newsweek,* 12 percent *Reader's Digest,* and 10 percent *Playboy.* Besides, *Time* announced to prospective advertisers, *Time* publishes different editions with the same editorial content but different ads. One edition, *Time Business* went to more than 1.5 million business executives who in 1978 took three or more air trips. *Time A+* (no longer available) went to six hundred thousand high income subscribers, 69 percent of whom took three or more air trips in 1978.[45]

What could *Newsweek* say to snatch United ads away from *Time?* The response is the sort that appeared in a full-page *Newsweek* ad in *Advertising Age* in 1981, headlined, "Nobody Stretches Your Media Dollar Like *Newsweek.*" *Time* may have had more high-income readers but *Newsweek* would give the advertiser more such readers per dollar of ad expenses. The CPM for readers with incomes of $25,000 or more was $3.84 for an ad in *Newsweek,* considerably cheaper than the $4.93 for *Time* or the $5.19 for *U.S. News,* according to the *Newsweek* figures.[46] (*Newsweek,* like *Time,* publishes special demographic editions—one for executives, one for high-income executives, and one for women.)

The competition is not only within media but across media. Clearly, no newspaper, radio station, or magazine can compete with network television for the sheer size of an audience. Nonetheless, these other media take potshots at the limitations of television advertising. *Cosmopolitan* tells the readers of *Advertising Age* in a full-page ad that if an airline or resort advertises only on television, it will miss the "*Cosmopolitan* world traveler." Only 5.8 percent of women eighteen to thirty-four are in the daytime television audience for an average half-hour but 16.9 percent of this group read *Cosmo;* only 3.9 percent of women watching daytime television took a foreign trip in the previous five years compared to 26.7 percent of the *Cosmo* reader group.[47]

Newsweek commissioned research on television commercial viewing habits. The *Newsweek* study examined television viewing habits in a sample of more than two thousand households. It found that, on average, only 62 percent of American adults remain in the room with the television during commercial breaks in a television program. Of those who remain in the room, many are doing things besides watching the commercial. Only 22 percent of the total audience remain in the room, just watching. The others are reading, talking, engaged in household chores, or involved in other activities. The higher the income of the audience, the more likely they are to be engaged in other activities if they remain in the room.[48]

In 1963 a newspaper survey found that only 23 percent of television viewers telephoned could name the product on the last television commercial they had just seen. A 1965 study by the American Newspaper Publishers Association found that 18 percent of prime-time adult viewers could name the last advertised brand (plus 14 percent who were able to name some brand advertised earlier in the program). Even studies without such biased sponsors find only modestly higher figures. Since television commercials have become shorter and more numerous, recall figures have declined substantially to as little as 7 percent in a 1981 study.[49]

The nontelevision media try to whittle away the faith of the advertising community in television. Since the big competitor, after all, is not television as a technology but television networks as an outlet for advertising, they have been assisted in recent years by the growth of the cable industry. With the advent of cable television and pay television and the growing popularity of independent television stations running syndicated network situation comedies, the networks have been losing their grip on the audience. With some cable stations appealing to specialized tastes and demographically distinct audiences, the possibility of "narrowcasting" arises to compete with broadcasting in television. Narrowcasting has been very successful in magazines and radio as special-interest outlets in those media have increasingly taken advertising dollars away from general-interest publications and stations. In network television, the loss of audience during the day has been greater than the loss in prime time, probably reflecting the increasing number of women working outside the home.[50] The networks deny that there has been an erosion of their audience. The Television Bureau of Advertising answered a *Reader's Digest* ad campaign that claimed television audience slippage by noting that 38.6 million households watched prime-time television in 1981–82 compared to 38.5 million five years earlier. Small consolation at a time when the total number of American households has also increased and the average *size* of a household has decreased so that the Television Bureau's figures actually indicate that network television commands a smaller percentage of all households than earlier and perhaps an actual decrease in the number of people represented in those households. Of homes tuned to television, 78 percent are watching one of the networks rather than independents or pay cable stations, but BBDO research projects that it will be 65 percent by 1990.[51]

The growing popularity in the 1980s of remote-control devices for televisions has led both *Reader's Digest* and the Magazine Publishers Association to develop advertising campaigns that suggest that these "zapping" devices, used to switch channels when a commercial appears, diminish the power of television advertising. Several studies suggest that less than 10 percent of television ads are zapped, but with remote control devices now in about 25 percent of all homes and a standard accessory on a third of all new television sets, it is clear that these gadgets represent a potentially serious concern for television advertisers.[52]

Television remains an advertising medium of special power, despite the best efforts of magazines, newspapers, and radio to demonstrate otherwise. The special quality of network television advertising—primarily, that there is a very limited amount of prime-time advertising opportunity—makes it especially potent. If cable grows the way some optimists predict, the power of television advertising will be more like that of radio, but more likely than not, there will long be a special aura to network television advertising.[53]

Radio, probably the least glamorous of the media, has been changing rapidly in the past decade and making itself known to the advertising community. Radio promoters emphasize the importance of high "frequency" in advertising. It is too expensive for most advertisers to maintain high frequency on television, but one can supplement a television campaign with more frequent radio messages. Radio listening has grown faster than other communication media since 1960. Heavy radio-listener households have higher incomes than heavy television-viewer households. And different radio stations have very different audiences and so can attract advertising seeking highly specialized audience segments. Even classical music stations, with very small audiences, can attract advertising since their audiences are generally very affluent and so are a good bet for certain prestige advertisers.[54]

Different media rely on different kinds of research. *Parade* magazine cites consultant Alven A. Achenbaum's notion that because multiple exposure is a key to effective advertising, the most effective advertising will be advertising in a medium that appears regularly and frequently—say, for instance, a weekly magazine. *Parade* offers advertisers a multimedia presentation showing how a small ad budget can be stretched for maximum impact, arguing that "media shock" and "image overload" have led consumers to screen out a good deal of the television advertising they see. And why should that lead one to *Parade?* Well, think of "an environment that is peaceful and receptive . . . the environment of a special day . . . a special time: Sunday morning," and "it wouldn't be Sunday without the Sunday paper," with which, of course, *Parade* is distributed. Generously, the *Parade* presentation also mentions *TV Guide,* Sunday metro supplements, and other weeklies as places where the same theory of advertising would lead an advertiser.[55]

Not all media promotions are so benign. Magazines as well as radio stations go up against each other with elaborate presentations to potential clients. One of the most clever bits of research was done by Yankelovich, Skelly, and White for Triangle Publications' *Seventeen* magazine. Ordinarily, *Seventeen* uses consumer panels of several thousand teenagers to find out their views on cosmetics, fashion, skin and hair care. In this instance, they surveyed women thirty to thirty-four to find out what brands and products they used and when they began using them. They found that 41 percent of the sample used the same brand of mascara they began using in their teens, 37 percent the same packaged cheese, 34 percent the same mouthwash, 33 percent the same nail polish, and 29 percent the same perfume. For potential advertisers, *Seventeen* made it clear that it pays to get consumers when they are young.[56]

As in other areas of advertising, research in media is controversial. What, for instance, is the meaning of magazine circulation? *Paid* circulation is one thing but magazines are read by many more people than the number who buy them or subscribe to them. There is "pass-along" readership that magazines would obviously like to be able to claim—or some magazines. In 1979 one research organization tried to revive interest in "primary audience" research, believing that the people who actually pay for the magazines spend more time with them and are more influenced by the advertising than pass-along readers. Some magazines expressed interest, but others observed that only magazines with high circulation and low reader-per-copy usage would have a vested interest in such research. Primary audience research had been abandoned years before so that magazines would have bigger numbers to show to agencies and advertisers in trying to fight television for the advertising dollar.[57]

There is controversy, too, regarding the basis on which a firm should buy advertising space. In 1980, R.J. Reynolds Tobacco Co. decided to abandon the traditional "cost per thousand" method of buying magazine space. Instead of placing ads according to the cost of reaching one thousand readers, Reynolds decided to pay greater attention to *which* readers its ads reached. The recalibration reduced Reynolds's magazine spending by $20 million a year. Ads in many general magazines were cut back. Ads in *Business Week* increased—because of the "good profile" of *Business Week* readers and because *Business Week* was able to provide the kind of information about readership that Reynolds sought.[58]

An agency would like to know much more than it does about placing ads in the media. Take, for instance, the simple question:

How often should an ad be repeated? It is not, it turns out, a simple question. An Association of National Advertisers study suggests that a single exposure of an ad has little or no effect. Two exposures will have an effect. So will three. More than three within a four-to-eight week period increases effectiveness but at a declining rate. That would be useful information were it not for the qualifications that follow. First, the effects of frequency vary on television ads (the subject of the study) depending on what part of the day the ads are shown. Second, the effects of frequency vary from one product to another. Third, the effects vary from one brand to another within the same product category. The report concludes that each brand "should receive experimentation designed to determine its own frequency-of-exposure response function." In short, the study offers *no* general information about frequency.[59]

Rosser Reeves has claimed that "a great campaign will not wear itself out,"[60] but others hold that ads lose effectiveness after a time, that there is "television commercial wearout."[61] There are no reliable generalities about this; advertisers and their agencies operate by hunch, by taste, by level of anxiety. United Airlines, like many other companies, takes a middle position, holding to a theme for many years ("Fly the friendly skies of United") but ringing changes upon it from time to time ("People who fly for a living fly the friendly skies").[62]

Placing ads in different media requires considerable expertise because the media world changes rapidly. Keeping abreast of those changes is a chief task for the media department in an agency. Agency media departments follow all the latest developments in print and electronic media and sort through the changing and conflicting claims and data about audiences the media present. Still, media buying is the most cut-and-dried, go-by-the-book part of the advertising business. But it could not be handled by a computer. Expertise is important but personal relations, in this as in other parts of the business of advertising, are very important, too. A good media buyer has good relations with people in the media and can parlay these into good positioning, say, opposite editorial material rather than opposite other ads in a magazine.

The Creative Process

Finally, there is the most famous and fabulous part of the advertising agency's work: creating the art and copy for the ads themselves. This is not the place to detail the creative development of an ad nor to document the way in which a television commercial is altered as it goes into production. The latter is especially well discussed in Michael Arlen's *30 Seconds.*[63] My focus is on the knowledge brought to bear on advertising work. What do the people who make ads think they know about what kind of ad to make? How do they arrive at what they think they know?

There is no science at this stage of advertising work. The premium in the ad world is placed not on the technician or researcher but the person with a creative flair. It is not even possible to simplify very much the approaches to creative work. One marketing text suggests that there are three schools of advertising: the "brand image" school that seeks to present a riveting, emotionally powerful image for a product (David Ogilvy can be taken as the guru of this school); the "logical presentation approach" of Rosser Reeves that seeks a "unique selling proposition" for each product; the "visibility school" that believes the main task in advertising is to get the public's attention—through humor, bizarre visuals, anything that will grab.[64]

But workers in the agencies rarely think in terms of "schools." Their assumptions about what makes for successful (and that means profitable) advertising are infrequently explicit and often become visible only when some innovation or departure from traditional practice lays them bare. For instance, in the late 1970s blue jeans manufacturers began to advertise on television. Howard Goldstein, president of the Howard Goldstein Organization which created the Jordache jeans commercials, was the first to use television. "I told everybody to go into television three or four years ago. They said it would never work."[65] Using television to advertise clothing was unheard of in advertising circles. However, Jordache did so, successfully, for some years before other apparel manufacturers decided to try the same thing. Russ Togs, Inc. advertised only to the fashion trade through 1980. In 1981 it spent $1.5 million in television advertising to the consumer. Executive vice-president Joel S. Grey said, "Our goal is to sell the stores and reach consumers. Print can't do it compared to the reach of TV." Roxanne Swim Suits Co., Harve Bernard, Stanley Blacker, Inc., BonJour International Ltd., and the International Wool Secretariat all moved to television advertising.[66]

This change was seen, at first, as unthinkable—you just don't advertise clothes on television. You advertise to the trade, to the buyers, and they control what goes into the retail outlets. In fact, of course, manufacturers have used advertising for decades to speak over the heads of middlemen directly to the consumer, going back to Nabisco soda crackers and Quaker Oats at the turn of the century. Why did it take apparel manufacturers nearly a century to learn the lesson? Because there are important differences in the marketing of different products; business people take pride in their experiential knowledge of a particular industry and they know that a lesson in one field does not necessarily transfer to another. When a change occurs, it is experienced as a blow to deeply held, if seldom stated, convictions about how "the business" *has to* operate.

The most celebrated break in advertising tradition was the ad campaign for Volkswagen. "In the beginning," writes Jerry Della Femina, "there was Volkswagen."[67] According to Walter Henry Nelson's rather too glowing account in *Small Wonder: The Amazing Story of the Volkswagen,* advertising copywriters in the 1950s were interested only in one another's opinions, not in ad effectiveness, and they regularly condescended to the public. But VW abandoned the conventional effort to associate its product with sex, wealth, sunsets, and romance. The effort was to provide "honesty in advertising," and that meant, as one VW official said, not only not telling lies, but "facing up to what people regard as your shortcomings. One of our ads said our station wagon had 'a face only a mother could love.' Well, that's the way people felt about this vehicle, so why not face it?"[68]

One of the most famous ads in the VW series of consistently interesting and appealing ads was the one with the simple headline, "Lemon," and the familiar picture of a Volkswagen. The copy explained that the pictured car was a lemon, one of the rare ones, and that it had a defect caught by one of 3,389 inspectors. This was not the kind of advertising anyone had ever used for a car before. It had been unquestioned that one did not acknowledge weaknesses or problems in a product and it had been unquestioned that humor doesn't sell.[69]

Volkswagen opened the door to humor and self-mockery in advertisements—or so one might imagine. But the rules and myths in advertising are product-bound. That is, the fact that one could use humor in an ad for a small foreign car did not convince anyone that humor was acceptable for other kinds of products, or even, as it happens, for other kinds of automobiles. An executive at J. Walter Thompson responsible for the Schlitz Light account pointed to the use of humor in Schlitz Light and other beer commercials and said that humor in light beer ads had been frowned upon until the late 1970s. "Like so many of the rules in our industry," he went on, "they all stand until someone proves them wrong."[70] It is more subtle than that: they all stand until someone does something different to make people notice they were abiding by an unacknowledged rule in the first place.

The content of advertisements is subject to industry-wide conventions, to particular agency traditions, to the will or whim of clients, and to general trends and fads. In 1980, the *New York Times* reported the revival of the use of animal images in advertising: Borden's Elsie the Cow; RCA's fox terrier, Nipper; Nestlé's hound, Farfel; NBC's peacock; and Bon Ami's chick were all resurrected. The *New York Times* quoted an executive vice president at BBDO: "You can generate more awareness per ad dollar with a symbol that still lives in people's minds than you can with something new. This is a recession-inflation tactic." In fact, this is rationalization, not explanation. The executive probably had not the faintest idea whether or not what he said was true. If it were true, it should have raised serious questions in the minds of clients whose advertising dollars in the previous decade had not generated as much awareness as had been possible. The *New York Times* also quoted the tongue-in-cheek statement of advertising man Jerry Della Femina: "Americans are disillusioned with spokespeople. You can buy Reggie Jackson and Cheryl Tiegs, but you can't buy Elsie, Nipper, and Farfel. They're not being paid. They're obviously doing it out of love and because they believe in the product."[71] The particular animal symbols re-employed were not all replacing spokespeople; there is no indication that the vogue of spokespeople is declining. Wheaties discontinued its use of Bruce Jenner as a celebrity endorser because, according to the *Los Angeles Times,* research had shown that "people don't use a product on the basis of a big name athlete or movie actor endorsement."[72] Research shows lots of things and dozens of major advertisers act on just the opposite assumption.

On most key creative matters, there is no more consensus than there is on the question of using celebrities. Should ads be hard sell or soft sell? There is simply no agreement. One creative director told me, "I like the idea of pleasing people. In the midst of all the junk on TV, the advertising is better than the shows. It's a matter of pride with me. Advertising is filled with people who want to do good work. This may be because it's a public business. If we do something terrible, we're going to be embarrassed." A Marschalk Company study reports that a third of consumers may be prompted by an obnoxious ad to buy a rival product. But another creative executive observed that "Mr. Whipple" has been a very effective commercial for Procter & Gamble's Charmin toilet paper, even though most people hate the ad.[73]

Should ads be informational or emotional? Reeves stresses that a consumer should be given a logical reason to buy, what he calls a Unique Selling Proposition, a notion that has guided work at Ted Bates since the 1940s.[74] But many others emphasize more affective advertising and the role of "brand image." Of course, which style is in favor depends in large part on what the product is. But even within a product category, there is not consensus. On liquor advertising, Eugene Novak, creative director at Rumrill-Hoyt stressed information: "You can't give consumers enough of it." But John Chervokas, another creative director, says that consumers should not be given a logical reason for buying liquor: "In the post-Ogilvyan era, I think long copy, as far as taste, feel and smell goes, isn't necessary. If I'm a consumer buying a $10 bottle of scotch, I don't need to know the whiskey is aged in charred barrels or that 'God's sun showered down on the grain.' "[75]

In 1982 the *Wall Street Journal* noted a trend toward more emotional and outright sentimental commercials, following perhaps from the success of the AT&T "Reach Out and Touch Someone" campaign begun in 1979. There seemed to be more "frisky puppies, cute children and doting parents" in television commercials. People grew tired of the hard sell, according to Jerry Siano, creative director at N. W. Ayer: "Irritating people to get their attention is the wrong way of developing a relationship with your customer." At the same time, Bayer switched from a sentimental to a straight, hard-sell commercial when the first approach failed. And Foote, Cone & Belding tested a set of "thinking" and "feeling" commercials and found them equal in memorability.[76] The prevailing view in market research seems to be that factual messages work better for technical products like cars and stereos, and emotional or evaluative messages for products like cigarettes or cosmetics where qualitative attributes are more important.[77] But there are more exceptions here than rules and a good marketing idea seems to make rules rather quickly dispensable.

Creative directors condemn the conventionalism of American advertising. "There's a pressure to be safe, to look like everybody else," one creative director told me. Creative director Eugene Novak calls liquor advertising "lazy." He, like others in the business, refers to it derisively as "bottle and glass advertising." Ad executives find it relatively easy to persuade clients that this conservative approach is acceptable; selling something more daring is harder. The result is that liquor advertising "is awash with ads that depict the bottle and anywhere from one to nine glasses."[78]

The trade literature of advertising endlessly bemoans tradition-bound advertising. At the 1980 meeting of the American Association of Advertising Agencies (4As), "the unchallenged premise was that not only has U.S. advertising grown worse over the past ten or twenty years—depending on the speaker—but that the creative work is increasingly dictated by clients, those who pay the bills."[79] As always in such settings, the creative experts called on agencies to take more risks and dare to stand up against clients for more adventuresome advertising.

Not everyone in the business cares for advertising art or cleverness for its own sake. The editor of *Advertising Age* wrote a cutting column about well-known ad man George Lois. Lois had complained that *Advertising Age* was "the enemy of those of us who believe advertising can be an art, not the silly science your trade journal insists that it stay." Editor Rance Crain responded that good advertising "should in some loose way be related to the merits of the product." Lois, he complained, felt that all products in a category are really about the same and that "the only difference between them is the advertising." For Crain, in contrast, most products really do have some identifiably different features that should be emphasized. He then lampooned one after another of Lois's failed ad campaigns—for Spiedel digital watches, for REA Express, for Subaru, for Cutty Sark. All of these campaigns lasted only briefly and prompted a change in ad agencies. For Crain, "product-unrelated advertising" is neither effective nor, he implied, morally sound. Crain concluded:

> Mr. Lois talks about the creative revolution that we ignored. The real revolution, I'm convinced, is in a new assessment of the worth of advertising and a consequent realization that effective advertising means providing meaningful and genuinely helpful information to consumers. What Mr. Lois and others have consistently failed to understand is that advertising simply does not exist as a pure art form, any more than capital expenditures or research and development or any other management tool exist all by themselves. The chief job of advertising is to persuade and inform consumers. That lesson was ignored in the last creative revolution, and it is being applied in the latest revolution that is ignoring Mr. Lois and his colleagues.[80]

It seems far-fetched for either Lois or Crain to talk about revolutions; there have only been fads and fashions, and none of them pervasive in advertising's creative work. Doyle Dane Bernbach (DDB) in the 1960s was widely recognized as the fountainhead of change and creativity in contemporary advertising. It was "an incredible collection of people," one creative director told me.

"They discovered or rediscovered a natural, honest way of talking to people." DDB had an impact on advertising, but for all the plaudits they received for their Volkswagen ads, none of the other automobile advertisers followed suit. DDB is also renowned for the Avis rent-a-car "We try harder" campaign (1962–67). The campaign emphasized that Avis was the second largest rent-a-car firm (unnamed Hertz was number one) and that because it was only second, it had to "try harder" to serve consumers better. The campaign apparently made a difference for Avis. Three years after the campaign began, Hertz still was number one, three times larger in revenue and five times larger in number of vehicles, but its airport business had dropped from 60 to 50 percent of the market while Avis had climbed from 30 to 40 percent.[81]

The Avis campaign should have demonstrated the value of comparative advertising though, admittedly, theirs was unusually graceful and clever comparative advertising. But the usual torpor of the advertising industry was unaffected. Not until the Federal Trade Commission (FTC) officially encouraged comparative advertising in 1971 did changes begin. The FTC's intention was to make advertising more genuinely informative to consumers. Comparative advertising had been held back by both informal and written agreements within the advertising industry and the media. The networks rejected commercials that referred to competitors other than as "Brand X." But by 1972 all networks repealed their bans on comparative advertising and in 1974 the 4As announced new, more liberal guidelines.[82] By 1978, various other self-imposed restrictions on comparative ads were dropped. The FTC persuaded the federal Bureau of Alcohol, Tobacco, and Firearms to lift its restrictions on comparative advertising for alcohol, freeing the way for comparative "taste tests" for beers.[83] Still, within the advertising industry itself, doubt about comparative advertising persisted. Ogilvy & Mather declared that comparative ads "exacerbate the problems of the advertising industry by increasing negatives toward those product categories where a number of brands are naming names—decreasing both the believability and clarity of the advertising."[84] Other agencies believe no such thing. Only in 1980 did Ogilvy &

Mather acknowledge that comparative advertising might be effective and joined in their growing acceptance.

One source of conservatism, in the view of agencies, is the need to please clients. I heard many stories at the agencies I visited about the aesthetic insensitivity of clients (not the agency's own clients, of course, but other agencies' clients). A second source of conservatism is the need to make ads that score well on copy testing. Before an ad is put on the air or in print, it is generally tested on sample audiences or in test markets. Most agencies contract with market research firms for copy testing, the most widely used being Burke Marketing Research. Burke tests commercials by telephoning people (from their thirty regional offices) the day after a commercial has been shown. They keep calling until they reach two hundred people who viewed the program on which the commercial was aired; this may take up to five thousand phone calls. Burke prepares a report of their findings; the emphasis is on the "related recall score." This is the percentage of respondents who saw the relevant program and could recall at least one substantial element of the ad in question.[85]

Day-after-recall scores measure what a person can consciously remember and verbally report when given a product or brand cue. "It does not measure attention, intrusiveness, or impact of the test ad," as Joseph T. Plummer of Young & Rubicam observes. Plummer argues that the test is appropriate only for certain types of commercials—"highly structured commercials with a strong product substantive claim." But it is less apt for advertising that has a more diffuse, emotional appeal. Foote, Cone, & Belding claims that "mood" commercials (for which they are well known) do well if viewers see them a few times but that they do not fare well on recall in single-exposure tests like those of Burke.[86]

This is not the only problem. There are serious questions about the statistical reliability of the tests. It is also becoming more difficult to judge what the tests mean with a growing clutter of ads, changing television formats and programming, the cable-induced fragmentation of the television audience, and the problems in day-time telephone interviewing when more and more women are out of the house working.[87] Further, there is the constant reminder that the tests, at their best, measure only ad memorability, not product sales. Douglas Banik, vice president of research at the Advertising Research Foundation, complains, "I've never seen scientific evidence linking high test scores with ultimate success in the marketplace. A lot of tests simply measure memorability. Does that have anything to do with sales persuasiveness? It might be true, but it hasn't been proven—not to me."[88]

There are alternative testing methods. The most common alternatives to on-air recall methods such as Burke's are "forced-exposure" methods where, for instance, consumers are brought to theater-laboratories in shopping centers where they are questioned about products and brands before and after viewing commercials. Other testing methods also compete for the agency's research spending. One organization shows commercials on televisions placed at supermarket check-out counters and questions shoppers about them as they leave the store. A number of organizations choose not to *ask* consumers anything, doubting the value of verbal responses, but measure physiological response in some way—brain waves or galvanic skin response or eye movements during commercial viewing, or analysis of voice pitch as the viewers talk about the commercials after viewing them.[89] At Young & Rubicam, there is interest in the use of tests of physiological responses in line with theories that emphasize the non-verbal side of successful advertising. Plummer suggests that successful ads may be ads that "reward" the viewer immediately, providing entertainment, news, a scene with which the viewer can empathize, or communicating respect for the viewer in tone and approach. Young & Rubicam is seeking ways to evaluate viewer "reward."[90]

"Creative" workers tend to be hostile to copy testing. One agency copywriter told me that creative departments are reluctant to send out for testing any ad with a baby in it because ads with babies *always* score best in copy testing and the creatives do not want to draw and film babies full-time. An advertising man in San Francisco, Robert Pritikin, argues that not only are copy testing methods fallible; the better the ad campaign the worse it will do in copy testing. He wrote:

> . . . a great campaign is usually an innovation. The first or second exposure to an innovation always causes people to recoil and withdraw. . . . It's repeated exposure that makes the person comfortable, and *then* it becomes a blockbuster. Years ago, when they introduced the eye-patch man for Hathaway—I mean, what they're doing there is exploiting a guy who's blind in one eye to sell shirts. Well, on the surface, the average person would see that and respond negatively. . . . Research is a tidy, scientific approach, which shouldn't even be applied to advertising—which, at its best, is an art form.[91]

This is not just one disgruntled man talking, although one of my respondents found this quotation "egregious bullshit." In 1982, the *Wall Street Journal* published a list of the year's twenty-five favorite commercials, a list that a testing company, Video Storyboards, came up with from thousands of consumer interviews. Of the twenty-five, J. Walter Thompson had seven on the list. Of these, four were never copy tested before being run. Chief executive officer at J. Walter Thompson, Burton J. Manning, who began on the "creative" side of the business, seemed particularly pleased. "The tide is turning. Chief executive officers don't want test scores, they want judgment. And it's turning because they've found out it's an illusion that they could prove with numbers that they're right. What was supposed to be an aid to judgment has turned out to be a substitute for judgment."[92]

A new testing method may offer significantly better information. BehaviorScan is a research technique developed by Information Resources, Inc. of Chicago. In four test markets, 2,500 households have agreed to identify themselves by number each time they buy something at the local supermarkets. The supermarkets have scanning equipment for purchases so that a record of each household's transactions can be kept. Further, all participating households have cable television and ads can be placed on cable exposing the whole sample or certain subsamples to particular ads. Participants know that they may see test ads but they do not know which ad is a test. Adtel, a division of Burke Marketing, offers similar services, having pioneered split-cable techniques in the 1960s and adding the use of Universal Product Code (UPC) equipment and identified panelists in three test markets in 1980. The potential for discovering the effects of particular ads on sales among particular demographic groups would seem to be enormous, though it is still not clear how this retrospective data could be usefully translated into guidelines for the creation of new ads and new campaigns.[93]

Normal copy testing examines the memorability or influence of whole ads. Some advertising research seeks to learn what *aspects* of an ad play a role in effectiveness. The results are not startling. With print ads, bigger ads are more effective than smaller, color more effective than black and white, ads with pictures better than those without, short copy better than long copy. But where advertisers might like to have more solid results, there are none. Sex, humor, and fear as elements in ads are neither regularly effective nor ineffective. Nor is there a consistent relationship between whether consumers *like* an ad and whether they can remember it or eventually buy the advertised product.[94] Charles Ramond concludes his review of advertising copy research:

> The safest conclusion is that copy research, like medicine, will remain an essentially clinical discipline, its best practitioners being those who have walked the wards long enough, mastered the few diagnostic principles, and perfected an effective bedside manner with their creative colleagues.[95]

None of the general philosophies of advertising—be it "brand image" or "positioning" or "Unique Selling Proposition" (USP)—gives very much guidance to artistic execution or, for that matter, very much *emphasis* to it. The philosophies of advertising are marketing and copy writing strategies, not media-conscious or visually oriented strategies. Richard Rich, the copywriter who created successful and notable campaigns for Alka-Seltzer in the 1960s, Benson & Hedges 100 in the 1970s and the Wendy's "hot-n-juicy" campaign that began in 1977, emphasizes the importance of a striking visual gimmick. He offers as a test for advertising, WIWIJ—"Will it work in Japan?"[96] (If there is little in the way of coherent philosophy to guide the advertising artist, there seems to be none at all to direct the writer of advertising music, though the lay person knows that a memorable jingle may keep a product name in one's mind for a long time. Not until 1983 were awards for excellence in advertising music established although awards for art and copy had been handed out for decades.)[97]

Ideas for copy or art do not derive from a philosophy. Creative workers tend to say that a good, intuitive understanding of human nature is what matters most. A creative director told me, "The best people I know are intuition people. A feeling for other people, an ability to empathize, that's what matters. I don't know anything now, after twelve years in the business, I didn't know when I began, except some technique. Advertising is not an art but a highly developed craft." If ideas for ad campaigns come from any identifiable place, it is from the culture of advertising generally. Agencies eagerly peruse the work of other agencies. What Trevor Millum writes of British agencies is true in America as well: "The world is inward-looking. A great deal of attention is paid to other agencies' advertisements, other magazines, especially colour supplements and other media."[98] This is mocked, but epitomized, in the quotation I saw posted in one advertising executive's office, from Woody Allen: "There is no question that there is an unseen world. The problem is, how far is it from midtown and how late is it open?"

The Finished Product

In the end, what has the advertising agency produced?

In the end, the agency rarely knows. Advertising workers can know, more or less, if their ads are memorable by the conventional but unsatisfactory tests now used. They can know—and this above all else they *must* know—if the client is pleased. But chances are that neither the client nor the agency will ever know very much about what role the ad has played in sales or profits of the client, either short-term or long-term. Perhaps the most quoted line in the business is one attributed to various people ranging from F.W. Woolworth to Lord Leverhulme: "I know that at least half of my advertising money is being wasted. My problem is—I do not know which half." Some are even more despondent. Gus Priemer, director of advertising for Johnson & Son, Inc. (Johnson Wax) says, "Fifty percent is a substantial understatement of what is unproductive today." He estimates that, in television advertising, 85 percent of advertising dollars are wasted.[99] "Executives go on the assumption that advertising is doing something, just like praying or going to church is doing something," Priemer says. But advertisers do not know what their ads are doing. "Advertisers spend as much as they can afford to spend. They don't ask how much is needed to do the job." And advertisers generally accept "substitute evidence" for the real evidence of ad effectiveness.[100]

Skepticism on the part of a client, no matter how justified it may be, makes the life of the advertising agency difficult. The agency must constantly balance the possibilities of great gains that would come from a successful, unconventional campaign against the relatively low costs that would come from continuing a conventional campaign that is neither notably successful nor unsuccessful. There is an argument among scientists about what function the white and silver plumage of the herring gull may have. One side says the plumage is a kind of camouflage, making the gulls look something like the sky and allowing them to approach fish unseen. Another side says that the plumage is designed to make the gulls conspicuous, not inconspicuous, to help gulls see one another from a distance to allow them to gather together in places where food may be momentarily abundant.[101] The character of advertising is, in a sense, like the plumage of the herring gull. On the one hand, every ad must be conspicuous to do its job. It must attract the notice of the consumer and score high on memorability on tests. On the other hand, if it is *too* different, and then fails, its failure will be widely noted. It therefore is likely to adapt some camouflage so that, even if its rewards may not be enormous, the possibility for grim failure are much less, and the capacity to justify and rationalize the ad, in the event of failure, are much higher.

In the advertising trade literature, while there are ritual reminders and pep talks that advertising is good for business, news stories that remark on the sales success or failure of products do not typically highlight the role of advertising. If they do, advertising still seems to play a relatively small role. One story in *Advertising Age,* for instance, explaining the slow sales of Nestlé's line of low-fat, low-starch, low-sugar foods, "New Cookery," in its test marketing in Erie, Ft. Wayne, and Fresno, emphasized "price resistance." Consumer response in middle-income areas was cool while in affluent areas sales were relatively good. In another story, an explanation of the twenty-year decline in the cigar industry placed emphasis on the public perception of cigars as offensive, on laws restricting cigar smoking in public areas, and on the image of the cigar in the movies. Advertising was cited as a factor in that the cigar companies tend to be resigned to their dwindling market and are not financially strong enough to use advertising or to introduce new products to stimulate growth.

In a third case, a decline in market share for Sara Lee frozen baked goods was explained primarily by two factors: that a recession always hurts frozen goods and that Entenmann's Bakery Inc.'s fresh baked goods had aggressively expanded nationally and hurt Sara Lee. The story *also* mentions, but does not emphasize, that Sara Lee's ad budget was declining. Another story focused on the worldwide decline in the sale of instant cameras, and Polaroid Inc.'s troubles in particular. The reasons cited for the sharp decline in the total market were an economic downturn combined with the continued high price of the instant photograph, double that of conventional photographs. A problem for Polaroid, in particular, though advanced a bit more gingerly as an item of major import, was that Polaroid's new Sun line is technologically complex and that its advantages may be harder to communicate to consumers.

These stories are typical. When the advertising industry examines a product's success or failure, rarely does it attribute major responsibility to advertising. If advertising is not a major cause of marketing failure, what is? The advertising industry seems to believe just what many economists believe: consumer income determines product success or failure. A bad economy or some other decline in consumer real income is often cited as a cause of product failure. The size of the target population also receives frequent mention. The American military has lost "market share" of high school graduates but is also troubled because the total pool of graduates is declining in the 1980s; the stagnant German detergent market may be related to a declining birth rate in Germany; sporting goods sales are down because the "baby boom" generation is beyond the classroom and so sales to schools and leagues have declined. A third factor mentioned is government policy: in 1977 Congress revoked its generous G.I. Bill program of educational benefits and made the military less able to compete for the eighteen-year-old male population; a judicial decision on airport car-rental franchises brought Hertz more competition; a government-ordered recall of Firestone tires hurt the company's reputation and sales; government regulations have restricted cigar smoking in public areas and hurt sales.[102]

This is consistent with the findings of advertising research. As Charles Ramond, editor of the *Journal of Advertising Research,* concludes, in a set of "principles" about the relationship of advertising and sales, *"Advertising's effect on sales is always less than that of population, income and other environmental variables."* That is the first principle he lists. The second is equally notable: *"Advertising's effect on sales is almost always less than that of other marketing forces.* Product quality, distribution, price differentials and changes, and other promotions have almost always been found more sales-effective than advertising weight, copy or media."[103] Grim words for the advertising agency. But these are conclusions the advertising agency is already well aware of.

In the end, advertising workers still operate amid high anxiety and great uncertainty. They move on, worrying about the accounts they may lose, scanning the changing media scene to place ads where, for the right price, the right people will be exposed to the right appeal. Many are glad to be in a field where they can see their own contributions in the finished product. As one executive wrote me, "Advertising's *not* a science; it's an art. And that means it's made by individuals, not by rules. That means I can make a difference." At the same time, it is not easy to know what difference the product itself makes in the world. The same executive wrote, "The *worst* that I can do will not hurt anyone . . . the best will provide little bits of pleasure to millions of people." Two others I interviewed independently used the same metaphor: "Advertising is not brain surgery"—either in difficulty or in importance, and this seemed to provide some solace. As often as advertising workers point with pride to the most visible successes of their industry—the Volkswagen campaign or Miller Lite or Arm and Hammer baking soda or Marlboro—they take refuge in the view that their work is probably incapable of causing much harm. But they worry, as professionals, about the collective tedium created by the multitude of unimaginative campaigns. "I think advertising is mostly pretty awful," one creative director told me, echoing the views of most of the people I spoke to. "Creative breakthroughs don't come along very often. When they do, it's a shock."

3

The Consumer's Information Environment

THE EFFECTIVENESS of advertising depends on the amount and kind of product information available to consumers. How prominent is the place of advertising in the consumers' field of information? How does the ad for Brand X compare to the ad for Brand Y? And how do both ads compare to the range of other information, some of it from noncommercial sources, that enters into consumers' buying decisions?

Most consumers come to an advertisement with background experience of advertising, of products, of getting and spending in general. (This is less true of children and some other groups I will discuss at the end of the chapter.) The normal adult consumer has a lifetime of informational resources and a complex cognitive makeup to bring to any new advertisement. Consumers operate in an "information environment" that includes the following resources:

1. The consumer's own information from personal experience with the product or related products.

2. Word-of-mouth information about the product or related products from family, friends, or acquaintances.
3. Information in the media about the product or related products that is not paid advertising. Some of this information will be planted by the public relations efforts of commercial companies and some of it will be independently generated by government reports, consumer groups, journalists, and other noncommercial agencies.
4. Information available through formal channels of consumer education, especially the school system, credit institutions, and other agencies.
5. Advertisements for rival products and also advertisements for unrelated products, the "clutter" of advertising in general.
6. Skepticism about the credibility of the medium in which the ad is placed.
7. Skepticism about the credibility of advertising in general.
8. Information from nonadvertising channels of marketing.
9. Price. This is a special case, and an especially important one, of a nonadvertising channel of marketing.

In this chapter, I will examine each of these sources of consumer information. Second, I will show that businesses develop marketing strategies sensitive to the multiple sources of information available to consumers. To see advertising as but one factor in a large array of information sources is not an insight or invention of social science but is part of the practical, daily concern of businesses selling consumer goods. Third, I will suggest that the influence of advertising is relative to the information environment; advertising will be more successful the more impoverished the consumer's information environment. This view has implications for public policy that I will spell out at the end of the chapter.

This perspective is only in the loosest sense an "information-processing model" of consumer behavior. I do not for a moment assume that cognitive rather than affective elements dominate consumer decisions. Nor do I assume the consumer always actively seeks out information to make a purchasing decision. I ask simply what kind of knowledge a consumer normally brings to a buying choice. That knowledge may include facts and figures about a product but it may also include the emotional responses or social approval of friends or neighbors. Advertising, the news media, friends and family, and the consumer's own past experience with products provide *grounds for decision making,* be they emotion laden or not, and that is what I mean here by information—the knowledge or feeling that *informs* and leads to a decision.

Sources of Information

PERSONAL EXPERIENCE

It is widely accepted in the advertising industry that getting people to buy something *once* is not the aim of most advertising. "The key question," as A. S. C. Ehrenberg argues, "is whether people continue to buy something *after* they or their friends and neighbors have used it."[1] With most goods people buy, including most widely advertised goods, people have direct experience of the product by having used it. They generally have direct experience of several brands of the same product, either because they regularly stock several brands (drinkers of Coca-Cola are very often *also* drinkers of Pepsi) or because, in the past, they have tried other brands. They also have the experience of family, friends, and neighbors who have related their experience with different products. "The average housewife," Ehrenberg argues, "is far more experienced in buying her normal products than the industrial purchaser buying an atomic power station. She is also far less likely to make a mistake."[2]

From this, Ehrenberg develops the proposition that advertising works, when it works, not by creating new needs but by reinforcing "already developed repeat buying habits." Advertising is *defensive* and seeks to prevent consumers already largely satisfied with a brand from switching to other brands: "The consumer does not have to be persuaded to think of his habitual brands as better than others, but has to be reinforced in thinking of them as at least no worse."[3]

One of the reasons this can work is that people tend to be more attentive to advertising for brands they already use than for other brands. They may want to learn more about the product they own; they may want information to help them defend their choice of products among their acquaintances; or they may be seeking peace of mind, preventing what has been called "cognitive dissonance" by finding reasons to justify actions that they have already taken. People not only attend to ads for their own brands, they also tend to give them greater credence. A 1953 market study conducted interviews with 2,298 car owners. It found that, in general, 38.6 percent claimed to believe in automobile ads, 25.8 percent expressed flat disbelief, and 35.6 percent were skeptical or doubting. When asked specifically about ads for the make of car they presently owned, however, 77.9 percent expressed belief, only 10.3 skepticism, and 11.8 percent disbelief. An earlier study showed similar results for cigarettes. Where, in general, 20 percent expressed belief in cigarette ads, 60 percent expressed belief in cigarette ads for their own brand.[4]

The advertising industry's aphorism that "good advertising kills a bad product" justifies advertising workers, convincing them that they cannot do real harm to consumers. It is a plausible rationalization; it is likely to be true in many cases. For the maxim to make sense, it is not necessary that people be able to distinguish the relative merits of two brands of dish detergent or paper towels and then compare the results to the advertising claims. It requires only that consumers be able to determine for themselves if the brand they bought does an adequate job. Consumers will often not know if a product, per dollar, maximizes their utility. But does the product serve their needs at a price that seems to them reasonable? That is something people can and do determine.

Consumers' own experience with products does not always speak truly to them. People develop unreasonable attachments or antipathies to products they have tried adventitiously. A medication that once seemed to work will be bought again, even if the recuperation, in fact, was not affected by it. If one gets stuck with a "lemon" of an automobile, one will not buy a car of that make again even though the experience of others suggests that the manufacturer makes reliable cars. The influence of personal experience on buying decisions need not always be rational, but it is almost always going to be powerful.

PERSONAL INFLUENCE

When Bubble Yum entered the New York area market in 1977, the rumor quickly spread that it contained spider eggs. Life Savers, Inc., the manufacturer of the gum, took out full-page newspaper ads denying the rumor.[5] General Foods resorted to full-page ads, too, to combat the rumor that their candy, "Pop Rocks," exploded in the stomach and caused cancer.[6] In 1978 McDonald's sales in the Southeast were noticeably affected by rumors that McDonald's added red worms to its hamburgers to increase their protein content. In Detroit, K-Mart was hurt by rumors that a woman was bitten by a snake that had hatched from eggs laid in the packing case in which her Taiwanese-made coat, bought at K-Mart, was packed.[7]

The most astonishing rumor of this sort affected the giant Procter & Gamble in 1982. Rumors spread, especially in the Bible Belt, that Procter & Gamble was linked to satanism. The Procter & Gamble symbol of a crescent moon with a man's face facing a group of thirteen stars was said to be a satanic symbol. The rumor began slowly but after two years, in the spring of 1982, led to some twelve thousand telephone calls a month on Procter & Gamble's toll-free lines. Some shoppers threatened boycotts of stores carrying Procter & Gamble products. Procter & Gamble salesmen in stores were accosted and there were reports of air being let out of tires and cars being sprayed with shaving cream. Procter & Gamble would not say what effect the rumors had on sales but a spokesman acknowledged that the rumors are "a major distraction to conducting business." The company initiated lawsuits against several individuals identified as spreading the rumor.[8]

These are extreme and bizarre instances of a much more common phenomenon and the most important source of information for consumers outside their own experience—the experience of family, friends, neighbors, and acquaintances conveyed by word-of-mouth. In communications research, there is a long tradition of interest in word-of-mouth communication or "personal influence," as it is called in the classic study by Elihu Katz and Paul F. Lazarsfeld who studied consumer decisions among women in Decatur, Illinois, in 1945. Earlier studies of voting behavior had found, to the surprise of researchers, that personal influence made more of a difference than the mass media in determining voting patterns. Katz and Lazarsfeld chose to study personal influence in greater depth, taking as their starting point "the idea that persons, and especially opinion leaders, could be looked upon as another medium of mass communication, similar to magazines, newspapers, and radio."[9]

Katz and Lazarsfeld identified a great many changes of opinion among the women they studied—in opinions on fashion, politics, movies, and household goods. They found that 58 percent of these changes came about "without involving any remembered personal contact, and were, very often, dependent upon the mass media." But in the other 42 percent of cases, respondents recalled specific conversations with another person related to the opinion changes.[10]

Moreover, results indicated that when personal influence was a factor in decision making, it was more often than mass media influence, the decisive factor. For instance, in opinion changes regarding brands of household products, 38 percent included some remembered personal influence; in 15 percent of the cases, this personal influence was judged by the subjects the most important factor in decision making. While mass media exposure was also very high in these decisions, the *effectiveness* of this exposure was relatively low. Thirty percent of decisions involved radio advertising and 30 percent newspaper advertising, but radio was the most important influence on decisions in only 8 percent of cases and newspaper ads in 2 percent of cases. In other areas of consumer decision making, mentions of the mass media as being factors continued to outnumber mentions of personal influence, but again, personal influence was more "effective" in influencing the decisions than the mass media.[11]

Katz and Lazarsfeld offer a simple and sensible explanation of why personal influence should be more effective than media influence, even when it is not more general than the mass media:

> Formal media will influence mainly by representation or by indirect attraction, that is, *by what they tell.* People, however, can influence both this way and by *control.* People can induce each other to a variety

of activities as a result of their interpersonal relations and thus their influence goes far beyond the content of their communications.[12]

Not surprisingly, the most important personal "influentials" are intimates of the consumer. For married women in the sample, 64 percent of the "influentials" came from within the family and the most influential person was the woman's husband. For single women, parents were the leading influentials, although friends were also important.[13] (As an advertising executive working for a large personal-care products manufacturer told me, "There is brand loyalty. Your mom's probably the greatest influence in your buying habits.")

A second reason personal influence is especially powerful is that so much of consumption is related to social "reference groups." People want to buy things that their family, friends, and neighbors will approve of. Television advertisements may give the impression that anyone who buys Brand X will be the envy of friends and neighbors, but this impression is a poor substitute for the readily available direct opinion of friends and neighbors. People do not make all purchasing decisions with regard to a local social group. One study found that people's reference groups influenced their choice of cigarettes, cars, and beer at both the product level and the brand level. That is, their decision to consume the good *at all* and their decision on brand of good to consume were both made with a reference group in mind. People's consumption of instant coffee, black and white television sets, and air conditioners related to the reference group at the product level only, influencing them to buy but not influencing their choice of brand. In other areas—furniture, clothing, magazines, and soap—the reference group influenced the choice of brand but did not affect the decision to buy *some* brand of the product in the first place.[14]

Another study divided the world of goods into four categories and found that some categories of goods are more likely to be influenced by reference groups than others. William Bearden and Michael Etzel characterize goods as publicly consumed luxuries (like golf clubs), privately consumed luxuries (trash compactor), publicly consumed necessities (wristwatch), and privately consumed necessities (toilet paper). They find that a reference group will influence purchases strongly at the product level on luxury goods and at the brand level on goods that are consumed in public. Publicly consumed luxuries, then, are influenced by reference groups at both the product and brand level.[15]

A third reason for the power of personal influence in consumer choice has to do with the fact that every purchase is at least in a small way a risk. It is an investment of time and money one risks for a return. If the consumer does not always count on being rewarded, he or she at least hopes not to be injured. For larger expenditures, people tend to canvass friends and neighbors before leaping ahead though, for the shy or socially isolated, confidence in a retailer or a brand name may substitute for this kind of activity. Where the purchase involves some degree of physical risk in consumption, people are especially careful—assuming that they view the matter as a market transaction rather than happenstance or family tradition. The middle class, to some extent, has come to view the choice of a physician as a market transaction—one can "shop" for a doctor. Still, most people take physicians as family heirlooms, handed down from one generation to the next, or else take the fact that a person is a licensed physician as a guarantee or seal of approval—which is, of course, exactly what the medical profession intends. Where consumers view services or commodities as goods with risks attached (say, power tools or automobiles) or purchase commodities whose very object is safety (say, infant car seats or smoke alarms) they are likely to shop with some care and seek guarantees from manufacturers, from the counsel of trustworthy salespeople, or from the experience of friends.

Physicians themselves are one source of counsel and the influence of physicians on consumer choice is well known. McNeil Consumer Products (a division of Johnson & Johnson), the manufacturer of Tylenol, campaigned hard with the medical profession, not only with the public at large, after the Tylenol murders of 1982. According to McNeil's research, 80 percent of Tylenol users had begun taking Tylenol at a doctor's suggestion.[16] When I asked students in my class on advertising to write about a product to which they were "brand loyal," several women mentioned particular brands of soap and said that their doctors had assured them that the brand was the best for sensitive skin. They were somewhat taken aback to discover that each was loyal to a different brand, though all had subscribed to their brands on the advice of physicians.

Consumers may be uncertain about their objectives in buying a product, they may be uncertain about which products or brands will maximize or "satisfice," in Herbert Simon's coinage, their enjoyment, and they may be uncertain about what adverse consequences may follow from purchasing the product (or failing to purchase it). The consumer will perceive more risk the more that is at stake, financially or otherwise, and the more uncertainty exists about possible unfavorable consequences. One tradition of consumer research views all consumer purchases as instances of risk taking and examines the strategies consumers develop to reduce risk.[17] In general, the higher the perceived risk, the more the consumer will seek an array of information before making a decision to buy. At the same time, some information-*limiting* strategies may also be risk reducing. Brand loyalty, I think, is less likely to be an irrational attachment to a product or its image than it is a simple, rational solution for minimizing risk by buying a known and personally tested product.

Not only do people who know they are taking risks seek information, but those who *have taken* risks are often eager to supply information to others. When people buy uncommon, very expensive, and "all-or-nothing" goods—like foreign cars—they are especially willing to be voluntary salespeople for the product among their friends.[18]

The Katz and Lazarsfeld study has been criticized for overemphasizing personal influence in decision making. It was conducted before television became an influence in American culture. Further, the study examined only one target group—adult women—and so cannot be taken to provide information on, say, the relative importance of the mass media and personal influence on young children.[19] Despite the study's omissions, its logic remains persuasive—that personal influence is often more effective than media influence because persons not only "tell" but "control." Recent surveys come up with consistent findings. A Whirlpool Corp. study in 1983 asked people what their most reliable source of product information was, and friends were cited most often (23 percent), with another 15 percent citing relatives and only 6 percent listing advertising.[20] The "talk of the town" is a vital influence on consumer decisions. People take into account not only their own experience when they decide to buy something, but the experience of the people they know best, the people they trust most, and the people whose high opinion means most to them.

INFORMATION IN THE MASS MEDIA BESIDES ADVERTISING

Consumers are surrounded by product information that does not come openly from commercial sources and may not stem from commercial sources at all. In 1968–1970, for instance, anti-cigarette advertisements sponsored by health groups appeared on television. This preceded the 1971 ban on television advertising of cigarettes. For several years pro-tobacco and anti-tobacco ads ran concurrently. The effect is not easy to determine, of course, although one statistical analysis concluded that the tobacco health scare had more effect on cigarette sales than did cigarette advertising. The tobacco companies were worried enough to recommend a voluntary ban on broadcast commercials if, in return, the government would grant antitrust immunity for the action and would drop plans for stronger health warnings.[21] When Congress finally adopted the ban on cigarette television advertising, consumer groups lobbied for it, the television networks lobbied against it, and the tobacco manufacturers sat on the sidelines. Michael Pertschuk, chairman of the FTC under Carter, believes that the ban may have actually helped the cigarette industry. Television advertising was increasingly expensive and the anti-smoking commercials seemed to have some effect. Moreover, the visibility of television advertising, while perhaps a commercial asset, was a serious political liability; the ban "removed from public consciousness the most visible goad and stimulus to government regulation; the ubiquitous presence in the home of the cigarette commercials."[22]

The news media may provide a great deal of information about a product when the product becomes the subject of political conflict or social interest regarded as "newsworthy." The media disseminate information about commercial products in a number of ways. First, they cover products that make news. The news media paid considerable attention to Rely tampons (Procter & Gamble) when research indicated that Rely tampons apparently were connected to a marked increase in the incidence of toxic shock syndrome. The press covers the recall of products or other government actions related to products.

Second, the news media provide a critical function with respect to certain products. Reviewers of films, theater, concerts, books, restaurants, and personal computers act as intermediaries for consumers. Some consumers, of course, never examine the critiques in newspapers or on television. But for others, the critics are a vital source of product information. For the commercial production of books, films, records, and other "culture industry" products, the role of these media gatekeepers is especially important. A product may be critically successful without gaining popular appeal and a product may gain commercial success without critical acclaim, but attracting the notice of the media is vital and favorable notice is better still. A damning review in the *New York Times* can kill a Broadway play.[23]

Third, the news media are a prime target for public relations efforts of manufacturers. Public relations and advertising are both marketing functions for firms. In some respects, they are difficult to distinguish. Corporate image advertising is hard to distinguish from public relations. It has the same aim public relations does—not directly to sell a product, but to aid the firm indirectly by promoting its reputation with the public or with significant segments of the public. In other respects, however, advertising and public relations are very different business functions. Advertising is publicity that a firm pays for; public relations seeks publicity that does not require payment to the media for time or space. Not surprisingly, then, the media found the development of public relations early in the twentieth century to be a dangerous and unsavory practice.[24]

Public relations has two advantages over advertising from the firm's perspective. First, it does not cost money. It may cost to hire a public relations agent, but when the agent places an item, it is placed as news and not paid for as advertising. Second, if an item appears as news, it has a legitimacy that advertising does not have. Consumers discount or discredit advertising, to some extent, because they know it to be a message from an interested source. A news story is not so easily discounted.

During World War II, the De Beers diamond manufacturers, through their ad agency, N. W. Ayer, placed misleading stories about diamonds in the news media, suggesting a growth in the diamond business at a time when the business had come to a standstill.[25] In 1980, Philip Morris began a series of public opinion surveys on a variety of topics, aiming to get their "Merit Report" (named after their cigarette) quoted in the media as news so that Merit cigarettes could gain greater visibility. In its initial year, the campaign successfully gained media coverage in nine Southeastern test cities.[26]

Some companies make their way into news columns more indirectly. In marketing sports equipment, the use of a product by a leading athlete can help sales. In 1960, a French skier on Rossignol skis surprised the world by winning a gold medal in the winter Olympics. Rossignol Ski Co. was quickly swamped with orders. After that happy accident, Rossignol has taken pains to see that it keeps happening. Rossignol contracts with more than two hundred champion skiers from eighteen countries to use Rossignol equipment exclusively. These skiers act as a kind of on-going product testing institution and whenever they win competitions or are photographed on skis by the news media, they spread the Rossignol name and image.[27]

Public relations may focus on media institutions besides the news media. Getting a product mentioned or pictured in a film is often a boon to sales. (In contrast, network television limits the mention of brand name goods on its programs.) In the 1930s and 1940s, De Beers increased the role of diamonds in Hollywood films, just as cigarette manufacturers saw to it that leading actors and actresses smoked cigarettes in movies in the 1920s. De Beers's public relations efforts led a film's title to be changed from *Diamonds Are Dangerous* to *Adventures in Diamonds.* The De Beers campaign also managed to introduce a scene about selecting a diamond clip and bracelet for Claudette Colbert in *Skylark* and helped get Merle Oberon to wear $40,000 worth of diamond jewelry in *That Uncertain Feeling.*[28]

In 1982, the producers of Steven Spielberg's film, *E.T.*, contacted the Mars candy company to see if they would like their product, "M&M's," to be included as the candy that cements a friendship between the extra-terrestrial creature and the young boy, Elliott. Mars was not interested. Unbeknown to Hershey, the producers substituted Reese's Pieces, a Hershey product. Before release of the film, Hershey was contacted and asked if it wanted to put money behind a tie-in promotion of the film and the candy. Hershey liked the film, put up a million dollars, and sales of Reese's Pieces jumped 70 percent the month after the film's release. Two months later, more than eight hundred movie theaters carried Reese's Pieces, though none had done so before.[29] In this instance, what eventually became promotion in a fairly conventional sense began as the largely accidental placement of a product in a nonadvertising communication setting.

It is not usually so accidental. There are now businesses that specialize in placing products in movies. The best known is Associated Film Productions (AFP), a company organized in the late 1970s that by 1982 had more than fifty clients and one hundred fifty brand name products it represented. For an annual fee ranging from $25,000 to several hundred thousand dollars, AFP promises to place its clients' products in at least five feature films. Through product placement of this sort, Bertolli olive oil appears in *North Dallas 40,* Wheaties in *Rocky III,* Milk Duds in *The Formula,* a Nikon camera in *Hopscotch,* Coca-Cola in *Missing,* Blue Diamond almonds in *Arthur,* and a Dynavite exercise machine in *Being There.* In the latter case, AFP recommended enlivening a rather dull scene with the president of the United States, played by Jack Warden, by having him ride the exercise machine in the Oval Office. While it was Robert Redford's friendship with August A. Busch III that got Michelob featured in *Electric Horseman,* Anheuser-Busch Inc. is one of AFP's most important clients. AFP not only places Budweiser and other Anheuser-Busch products in feature films but works to keep these products out of films or scenes in films of questionable taste. Mercedes-Benz of North America Inc., likewise, is happy to loan its automobiles to film producers but insists that the "bad guy" not drive them.[30]

Even without public relations, commercial products are often the focus of news media attention. The media function as gatekeepers to cultural products and reporters of newsworthy events. Legitimate news coverage is especially important, particularly in eras when political actors who, by the canons of conventional journalism, must be covered, are taking active roles as consumer advocates. In the 1960s and 1970s, the legitimacy gained by Ralph Nader, other consumer advocates, and the ecology movement brought consumer issues into the newspapers, television news, and magazines. (It is worth recalling, however, that it took Nader years to attract media attention and that only General Motors' decision to spy on him enabled him to break into the spotlight.) Concern with consumer issues strengthened the hand of sympathetic legislators and federal officials in the Congress, the FTC, the Environmental Protection Agency (EPA), and other bodies. A widespread concern with health, for instance, gave legitimacy and attention to the Senate Select Committee on Nutrition and the "shock" of its chair, George McGovern, when he learned that the fiber content of ITT Continental Baking Co.'s Fresh Horizons bread was sawdust. ITT explained that it used a highly refined cellulose powder derived from wood, rather than flour, to keep calories down—but sales plummeted.[31]

There is an institutional bias in the media toward commercial enterprise because, first, journalists are fundamentally accepting of the capitalist system, and second, businesses are active on their own behalf with public relations information.[32] But there is also an institutional bias against business in that "bad news" tends to be more interesting and "newsworthy" than good news. When a tire is recalled, salmonella found in a canned good, a realtor or car dealer indicted, or a tampon connected with a deadly disease, it makes the newspaper. And people tend to remember it. Negative information about a product is more memorable than positive information.[33] To the extent that people are risk avoiders rather than pleasure maximizers in their consumer behavior, then negative information, however slight, may have more lasting impact than positive information, however alluring.

Of course, this is not always true. The media provide a good deal of information in straight news stories that people take as models for their own behavior, and this may have very salutary effects for certain products. When President Reagan started publicly using a hearing aid in the fall of 1983, the demand for hearing aids increased across the country.

Not all mention of products in the media can be classified as positive or negative. There are also expressions of ironic or ambivalent attitudes to material goods. This is especially the case with jokes. But jokes, even as they ridicule a product, may contribute to its celebrity. One advertising creative director spoke of the importance of developing a "visible theme line" for a product and added, "I would pay thousands to have a pickup on it by Johnny Carson or have it mocked in a cartoon in the *New Yorker*."[34] Even mockery can be legitimation.

FORMAL CHANNELS OF CONSUMER EDUCATION

School systems offer consumer education as part of standard academic curricula. When students learn in arithmetic how many apples they can buy if they have three quarters and two dimes and apples are fifty cents a dozen, they learn not only arithmetic but also the elements of unit pricing. In social studies or geography, students learn what products are produced in abundance by what countries and states, and so they can develop the background information that New Zealand is expert in the production of lamb, England woolens, and the Netherlands chocolate. Fresh fruit comes from Florida and California, apples from Washington, potatoes from Maine and Idaho.

Some classes are more directly concerned with teaching students consumer skills. Students may learn about nutrition, vitamins, and the importance of a balanced diet in classes in health or home economics or physical education. Some school cafeterias will serve the football team a "training meal" the day of a game, so the players, instructed directly, and others, who can learn by observation, see what kind of foods are best for sustained energy. Students may also learn directly about products that schools themselves employ. Apple Computer Inc. encouraged legislation in California to provide tax advantages to corporations that donate microcomputers to educational institutions. In 1983 Apple began shipping $21 million worth of computers to almost all the nine thousand public and private elementary and secondary schools in the state. Not only will students thus have access to computers, they will develop familiarity with Apple computers and Apple software.[35]

Besides the important influence of the school system in teaching students about consumption, there is also instruction regarding how to read the media, including advertisements. Recently, there have been curricular innovations in "television literacy," with courses or parts of courses designed to make students more informed and critical viewers of television programming and advertising.[36]

Outside the school system, other agencies are engaged in formal consumer education. This includes government agencies that produce informational bulletins for consumers and for specialized groups of consumers, like farmers. It includes government and other social service agencies involved in social welfare. Hospitals and doctors' offices, formally and self-consciously or informally and haphazardly, instruct clients in nutrition, exercise, the use of prescription drugs, the use of over-the-counter drugs, and so forth. Banks and savings and loans and credit unions instruct borrowers not only in the purchase of credit but in the purchase of automobiles (for example, by making "blue books" available to customers) or other major items. Private institutions like the Better Business Bureau handle consumer complaints and provide consumers information about the business practices of local concerns, consumer rights under law, and grievance procedures. There is also an extraordinary range of consumer information available in books of etiquette, financial planning, do-it-yourself guides, car repair manuals, "helpful household hints" in newspapers and women's magazines, travel guides, and expensive handbooks on how to travel cheaply or where to order free goods and booklets.

Fred Hirsch has observed that the plethora of consumer information from consumer groups as well as from commercial groups reinforces citizens in a tendency toward individualistic calculation. He notes that the press and consumer periodicals pay "increasing attention to management of personal finances, including advice on tax avoidance: fully rational on the individualistic calculus, but also likely to discourage and erode feelings of social obligation."[37] This is a legitimate point; consumer information designed to combat commercial influence nonetheless generally adopts the presuppositions of commercial sources. While it may thus help citizens to become more intelligent and informed consumers, less subject to the impulsive appeals of advertising, it makes them no less—and very likely more—embedded in a consumer mentality. This is not true of *all* consumer information. Much of the ecology movement and the informational organizations it has spawned appeal directly to people's concerns about other people and about future generations. Still, much consumer information does not lead people to be other-regarding but more intelligently self-regarding.

This is an appropriate place to observe that the different sources of consumer information are not independent of one another. For instance, the mass media and formal channels of education play a more active role in situations where personal experience is less likely to be relevant. Philip Nelson's analysis of the difference between "search" goods (where consumers can learn a lot about goods by shopping) and "experience" goods (where knowledge of the product comes only through use after purchase) finds that institutions like *Consumer Reports* devote much more attention to experience goods than to search goods. They also devote more attention to durables, purchased rarely, than to non-durables, purchased often and therefore more likely to be goods with which consumers have prior experience.[38] Newspapers and magazines that provide consumer guidance generally attend to goods purchased rarely or only once—movies, books, and restaurants. Among restaurants, expensive restaurants are more likely to be reviewed than sandwich shops. Affluent consumers patronize both but they can more easily afford to treat the sandwich shop than the posh, candle-lit restaurant as a search good.

ADVERTISING FOR OTHER PRODUCTS

Part of the information environment for an advertisement is all the other advertisements around it and all the products they advertise. The plethora of products and product messages makes the salience of information about any one product or brand harder to establish. Consumers may be confused when they try to shop among the more than twenty-eight thousand nationally advertised branded products on sale in the United States. A BBDO study found that 40 percent of the people they surveyed believed that the number of products available makes shopping more difficult. Consumers felt that there are "too many" brands of cigarettes, dry cereal, alcoholic beverages, and cough remedies. Only with cars and canned vegetables did as many as 10 percent of respondents believe there to be "too few" brands available.[39]

There are a great many products. There are also a great many messages about them, creating "clutter," as the advertising industry calls it, which makes it difficult for any single ad to be noticed.

With advertising in print, the amount of space available is, in principle, infinitely expandable. And an advertiser may try to break through the clutter of ads by simple expedients, like buying a larger ad space. With television advertising and through government regulation, there is a strict upper limit to how many ads can be shown. There are only twenty-four hours in a day and, by industry custom, only so many minutes per hour, depending on the segment of the day, that can be devoted to advertising. Expedients to gain greater attention relative to other ads are difficult to discover in broadcast advertising.

The problem of clutter in television has grown significantly since the standard ad was reduced in length in the 1970s from one minute to thirty seconds. Now twice as many ads are shown in the same length of time. Advertisers may seriously wonder just how much the consumer is able to absorb. As I have indicated, television ad recall has declined from 18 percent in 1965 to 7 percent in 1981. John O'Toole, chairman of Foote, Cone & Belding, complained, "The reason is obvious and its name is clutter. The most dramatic change that occurred during that period was the switch from one minute to thirty seconds as the standard commercial. That was in 1971–72. It may be the single worst decision in the history of network broadcast."[40]

Obviously, marketers are especially sensitive to that part of the information environment made up of messages from direct competitors. There is even an appropriate jargon for this. A company may be interested not only in the share of the market its product attains but in the "share of voice" its advertising achieves. A company's "share of voice" is the ratio of advertising dollars spent on its product to the total advertising expenditures for all brands in the same product category. General Foods, for instance, in its unsuccessful effort to make "Cycle" dog food a marketing success, set a "share of voice" goal in its early marketing.[41]

The vast number of advertisements to which Americans are daily exposed makes the chance of any single ad attracting attention rather remote. This is the most obvious element of the problem of clutter. But there is a second element: the more consumers are exposed to the shrill cries of advertisers hawking their wares, each one claiming to have the best, newest, most convenient brand of whatever it happens to be, the more consumers are likely to develop a certain level of skepticism toward all advertising. Consumers will then look for clues outside the ad itself for indications of the credibility of the ad.

SKEPTICISM ABOUT THE ADVERTISING MEDIUM

Different media inspire different degrees of confidence in consumers. Advertisers recognize that the credibility of an ad will be heightened or discounted to some extent depending on the context in which the advertisement appears. In one study of consumers in a small, Southwestern city, 68 percent of respondents said they believed that the most misleading ads are to be found on television. Only 12 percent cited newspapers, 7 percent magazines, and 6 percent radio.[42] There are many reasons an advertiser might want to select television as the medium for advertising, but a cautious advertiser will be concerned that consumers may "discount" television advertising more readily than they would print ads.

Not surprisingly, this kind of information greatly interests advertising sales directors at magazines and newspapers. The Magazine Publishers Association commissioned a 1969 survey of young people fourteen to twenty-five and found that respondents consider magazines, including the ads in magazines, to be more believable than radio or television. Fifty-one percent found television advertising "annoying" but only 13 percent were annoyed by magazine ads. Forty percent held television ads to be deceptive; only 26 percent felt the same way about magazine advertising. Similarly, a Newspaper Advertising Bureau study in 1981 found that 68 percent of respondents regarded newspaper advertising as "believable" or "very believable" while only 39 percent felt the same way about television (52 percent for magazines, 59 percent for radio, and 25 percent for direct mail).[43]

There are differences in degree of credibility not only among media but within the same medium. Any reader of *Advertising Age* will be familiar with the advertisements directed at the advertising community from various newspapers, magazines, and other media, each claiming to be the best location to place an ad. While some of the media stress the number of people they reach, or the affluence of their subscribers or viewers, or the cost effectiveness of an ad placed in their publication, some also stress their high "credibility" with readers. *Seventeen* magazine, for instance, claims that its readers are loyal and faithful and it advises potential advertisers, "Because she believes in us, she'll believe in you."[44] An ad for a money market fund in the back of the *National Enquirer* will have less credibility than the same ad in the *Wall Street Journal.*

Understanding the information environment, then, is not just a matter of cataloging the sources of information available to consumers but recognizing the ways in which the quality of information in a given ad changes depending on context. An ad *competes* with other information sources for attention and, at the same time, *changes* as a unit of information itself, depending on its location.

SKEPTICISM ABOUT ADVERTISING IN GENERAL

If consumers discount advertising according to what they view as the credibility of various media for advertising, they also have a discount rate for all advertising, regardless of medium. The information environment is constituted not only by the varieties of information in it but by the weight consumers attach to the different sources of information. Information from personal experience with a product or information from trusted friends and neighbors tends to be weighed heavily. But advertising tends to be discounted. People recognize the difference between friends who talk about a product without having anything to gain monetarily by their talk (and, indeed, are as likely to suggest what brands *not* to buy as to recommend brands for purchase) and advertisers whose only purpose in advertising is financial gain. Evidence from experimental psychology suggests that consumers weigh negative information about a product more heavily than positive information where their personal investment in the product under consideration is high or where their decision to buy implies some kind of final commitment. Consumers also tend to place greater emphasis on negative information when they are harassed or pressed for time.[45]

According to a 1980 Yankelovich, Skelly and White study, 70 percent of Americans are concerned with the truthfulness or deceptiveness of advertising. At a time of antiregulatory feeling, 70 percent nonetheless favored more regulation of advertising.[46] In studies conducted by the 4As in 1974, 82 percent of people surveyed said they believed that advertising "often persuades people to buy things they shouldn't buy" (compared to 64 percent in the same survey for 1964). Only 41 percent felt that "in general, advertising presents a true picture of the product advertised." None of this skepticism, however, led people to seek major changes in the advertising world; 88 percent (up from 78 percent) believed "advertising is essential" and 57 percent (down from 74 percent) held that "advertising results in better products for the public."[47] A Philadelphia market research firm found in 1981 that most consumers think "new and improved" as a product description means only that the manufacturers "have found a way to increase the price." The research firm advised marketers to find a new and improved way to say "new and improved" but did not express confidence that consumer skepticism could be overcome.[48]

Advertising has what could be called a "coefficient of credibility," a coefficient less than one, by which the believability of an advertisement is multiplied. The coefficient varies over the life cycle—children are more trusting of ads than adults. It may vary over time; the coefficient of credibility is lower in some historical periods than in others. Skepticism about advertising has shown some increase from the 1960s to the 1970s, according to 4As survey data.[49] It will certainly vary according to the media environment in which the ad is placed.

All of this is important, but not all-important. For one thing, there may be a "sleeper effect" in attitude change. One set of studies in social psychology suggests that people are more influenced by high-credibility than by low-credibility sources but that the magnitude of the difference diminishes as time passes after the moment of exposure.[50] For another, as I will suggest later, it may not be necessary for people to *believe* advertising claims for the advertising to be effective.

INFORMATION FROM NON-ADVERTISING MARKETING

Commercial firms have many ways to promote their products besides advertising, as I have already shown. The importance of advertising relative to other marketing efforts varies from product to product. With some products, advertising makes up more than half of total marketing expenses. This is the case with drugs, perfumes, cosmetics, razors, chewing gum, liquor, and some other products. In some other product lines, even where total selling costs are high, advertising costs are nonetheless modest. For instance, with breads and cakes, selling costs as a proportion of sales are fairly high—28.6 percent, but media advertising is only 2 percent. With vacuum cleaners, selling costs are 25.2 percent but media advertising is only 3 percent; with calculating machines, marketing costs are 22.1 percent of sales but advertising costs are just 2.8 percent.[51]

Some nonadvertising strategies are within the hands of the advertiser, like morale of the sales force and promotions. Others are in the hands of retail stores and salespeople. It is important for the consumer that not only goods but stores (and not only stores but individual salespeople) have reputations that they want to maintain and that consumers, therefore, can come to trust. Consumers gain a great deal of information from the simple fact that their trusted local camera shop does or does not carry a certain brand or line of goods, that their local mechanic does or does not speak well of a certain make of car, or that Sears stands behind the power tool or hiking boots they just bought. The salesperson in the clothing store or stereo equipment store may be very free with comparative product information. This is also to be distrusted, sometimes, but less so the more clear it is that the store can profit from a long-term relationship with the customer. The retailer, then, provides the consumer with information additional to, and sometimes counter to, that provided by manufacturer advertising. An analyst of the tire industry offers a good example in downplaying the potential of a new Firestone ad campaign in 1981:

> Most tires are sold by independent tire dealers that carry four or five lines. The consumer may come in wanting a Firestone, but go out with a Phoenix or some other brand he's never heard of. The tire dealer is the ultimate determiner of what gets sold. Goodrich got all kinds of attention for its clever "we're the guys without the blimp" campaign, but did it sell them more tires? I've been following this industry for fourteen years, and I've learned that advertising doesn't mean diddly-squat.[52]

PRICE

One of the most important things a consumer knows about a product is its price. Price is not an intrinsic quality of the product. In classical economic theory, price is an index of relations of supply and demand. In practice, price is often determined more arbitrarily. Regardless of how a price is actually set, consumers take price to be crucial information in their decision to buy or not to buy. This is so in two respects.

First, consumers have limited amounts of money and a sense of how much they can budget for given items. If the price of a good is too high, the consumer cannot be persuaded by advertising or any other source of information to make a purchase. The product is "beyond the means" of the potential consumer. Of course, people will adjust their sights and decide that they can afford what originally they thought beyond them. Or sellers will find new ways of financing so that buyers can borrow or pay in installments. Even so, consumers often have in mind some upper price limit for a given purchase, and they will not go beyond it, regardless of other information. To the extent that this is true, price has a priority among the sources of consumer information. It has a pre-emptive power, pushing aside other possible decision-making sources. This suggests that one of the most important parts of the consumer's information environment is not what the consumer knows about the available products but what the consumer knows about him or herself. In particular, what do consumers know about their own ability to pay?

If price serves as an absolute limit on consumer spending choices, it serves also as an index of quality. People assume that the higher the price of a product, the higher its quality. The familiar rule of thumb is, "You get what you pay for." This is not a safe assumption. Studies of the relationship between price and the quality of hundreds of categories of goods evaluated by Consumers Union indicate that there is a .26 correlation between quality and price. In more than 20 percent of the product categories tested, there was a negative relationship between price and quality. For nondurable products, there was a negative relationship 35 percent of the time.[53] Nevertheless, people often take price to be an indicator of quality. "Ego-sensitive" products like perfume, silver items, and various gift items sell better at a higher than at a lower price. When there are known to be or believed to be large quality differences between brands, consumers will select higher-priced goods.[54]

This subjective valuation of price is well known to marketers and enters into their pricing decisions. Traditionally, price has been determined on a "cost-plus" basis. Manufacturers add up the cost of producing the product, overhead and depreciation costs, estimated marketing costs, and a margin for profit. The price of the good is then set to cover these costs. Modern marketers, however, regard such practice as being decidedly old-fashioned and engage in backward or "retrograde pricing." Price is based not on ascertained costs but on estimates of what consumers are willing to pay. This is what business schools now take to be more "enlightened" and marketing-sensitive practice. If research suggests that demand will be greater if a new product is "positioned" to attract more "upscale" consumers, then the product should be priced high. Sometimes, even if sales decline at higher price levels, the increase in price may offset the loss in volume. This was the case, for instance, when Heublein Inc. raised the price of Popov vodka 8 percent in 1980. Sales decreased and Popov lost 1 percent of its market share, but Popov profits grew 30 percent.[55]

Whether consumers take price to be a deterrent to spending or an index of product quality, price is a check on advertising claims. If ads boast of product quality and the product price is high, price serves as a second kind of advertisement, a promotional tool in its own right, an affirmation of quality. If ads claim that a product is top quality but it sells for a low price, consumers may be skeptical about the quality, though they may try it anyway, attracted not by ads but by price. In this case, price works against national consumer advertising. A low price on an unknown brand may undercut loyalty to a recognized product. But because of the subjective equation of lower price with lower quality, many marketers are reluctant to actively promote their products on the basis of price, with coupons or discounts or deals. They fear that such promotion, emphasizing low price, is ultimately destructive to the image and reputation of their product. Price competition is a last resort for marketers of national brands who seek instead to secure a "consumer franchise," a following of some segment of the public that will remain loyal even if it means paying a premium.

Advertisers' Response to the Information Environment

An idea of the consumer's information environment is part of the consciousness of the corporation and advertising agency as they plan their marketing. They must be aware of and ready to respond to each of the sources of consumer information I have reviewed. They do so either by incorporating an understanding of the consumer's information world into the presentation of their own advertisements or by adjusting marketing strategy generally to their knowledge of what consumers know.

For instance, marketers respond to the importance of consumers' personal experience with products in two ways. First, they may make personal testimonials central to their advertising. While some agencies may decide to attract consumer attention with celebrity endorsements, others use a "man or woman on the street" approach to emphasize that "real" people have used the advertised product and want to buy it again. At the same time, a marketer may respond to the importance of personal experience by abandoning media advertising or supplementing it with free samples or other special introductory offers that will allow consumers to try out a product themselves at little or no cost. Getting a consumer to *try* a product may be very important in breaking down resistance to a product category, in getting consumers to experience something novel or off-beat, or in breaking through loyalty to an old brand in product categories with high degrees of brand loyalty.

Advertisers are well aware, of course, of noncommercial information available to consumers in the media and in formal educational channels and they respond to it directly. This is most dramatic in the case of cigarette marketing. In 1952, only 1.4 percent of cigarettes were filter tipped, but by 1956, after the first major controversy over cigarettes and health, it was 29.9 percent. By 1979, filtered cigarettes were used by 91.7 percent of regular smokers. Responding to the more recent public concern regarding cigarettes, tobacco companies have shifted both production and promotion to low-tar cigarettes. In 1970 they spent 10.5 percent of their marketing dollars on low-tar cigarettes; by 1978 they spent 48.1 percent. (This outran the actual market share controlled by low-tar products, which was 3.6 percent in 1970 and 27.5 percent in 1978.) The battle for supremacy in low-tar cigarette sales is fierce. In June, 1982, the FTC responded to complaints from R. J. Reynolds Tobacco Co. that Brown & Williamson Tobacco Corp.'s Barclay brand contained more than the one milligram of tar it advertised. The FTC agreed with Reynolds that the unusual filter in B&W brands led to misleading readings on the FTC tar testing machine. The FTC asked B&W to move "expeditiously" to change its advertising claims.[56] Why all the fuss? Clearly, the medical findings of the relationship between cigarette smoking and lung cancer and other diseases has affected the general public. The percentage of *smokers* who agreed that "cigarette smoking frequently causes disease and death" grew from 52.2 percent in 1966 to 70.7 percent in 1975.[57]

Tobacco is the most celebrated field in which marketers have responded to information independently available to consumers, but it is one example among many. Automobile manufacturers redesigned their cars as well as their ads when consumers became more concerned about the high price of gasoline and the possibility of gasoline shortages after the 1973 gasoline crisis. Procter & Gamble voluntarily withdrew Rely tampons from the market after they were connected to cases of toxic shock syndrome, while manufacturers of other tampons and competing products changed their advertising to adjust to the new information available to consumers. Chrysler Corp's extensive corporate image advertising campaign was clearly a response to public perceptions of the company's troubles and public controversy surrounding the government's decision to provide Chrysler loans to cover its huge losses. Hitachi Sales Corp. of America and Mitsubishi International Corp. altered their advertising strategies when news of their industrial espionage hit the Japanese press in 1982. They canceled their ads in Japan, preferring to keep their names out of the public light until the storm of controversy died. One Mitsubishi executive said, "There is no admission of guilt by pulling [out] advertising. But when your name is linked to something like this, you are not going to flaunt it in front of everybody."[58] This is not just Japanese practice. It is common, for instance, for U.S. airline companies to withdraw advertising after widely publicized plane crashes.

Examples could easily be multiplied. Advertisers recognize the importance of competing and conflicting information to which consumers have access. They are well aware of and often directly responsive to the multiple sources of information that consumers use.

Vulnerable Consumers

The ideal consumer in the economist's hypothetical model of how a market economy should work has a great deal of information about products and the time, education, and ability to judge rationally the relative merits of competing products. This ideal consumer probably has at least a high school and more likely a college education, has the time and inclination to consult with friends and family and to go from store to store to compare products on any major purchase, reads a good newspaper regularly, knows the phone number of the local Better Business Bureau, and subscribes to *Consumer Reports* or is lucky enough to find the desired issue on the shelves at the public library.

Few people are like that. Still, large numbers of middle-class people at least are in a position to approach that ideal under ordinary circumstances. But not all consumers, not even all middle-class consumers, live in ordinary circumstances. When a group in the population is removed from a variety of information sources, it necessarily becomes relatively ignorant and thereby vulnerable to whatever information—like advertising—still gets through. I want to briefly discuss five groups whose situational or structural ignorance makes them unusually vulnerable to advertising: highly mobile people, highly immobile people, children, the poor, and many of the relatively poor and poorly educated people in the Third World.

People who have just moved from one neighborhood or community to another may have many information resources but they will be at least temporarily cut off from the information provided by personal influence—information gathered from trusted friends and neighbors. This is simply because it takes time to establish new friends and trust in new neighbors. Also, in a community where one has lived for some time, people establish relationships with certain stores and with salespeople or proprietors of some stores. These people can be relied on for good advice; they have a greater interest in preserving a relationship with a long-standing customer than in profiting from the sale of any particular good or line of goods. The person or family that has moved must seek to establish connections of this sort all over again. The newcomer is without many personal sources, then, and has many more buying decisions to make—not only about what to buy but about what store or shopping center to buy it at. In this circumstance, the newcomer may read and watch local ads more carefully and be influenced by them more strongly than he or she would be otherwise.

At the same time, the availability of national brands provides a protection for consumers who move to a new community. Most of the goods they will find in local stores will be the same goods they knew in their previous community. They will be more open to advertisements suggesting where to buy, but they will be able to rely on past experience for deciding what to buy. In this respect, national advertising serves as a form of consumer protection.

People are mobile not only in physical but in social space. As people age, they enter new situations to which they are strangers. To manage new roles, they require new information and find themselves without one key source of support—personal experience—in assimilating new data. This applies to newlyweds, to new parents, to the newly retired, to the newly bereaved. It applies to newly arrived immigrants or others who are not fluent in the dominant language. It applies with special force to teenagers who have a floating, unformed sense of their own selves. They may try on several selves for size and they are notoriously open to suggestions from peers, teachers or other adult role models, and the media. They often have encyclopedic knowledge of rock music, automobile styling, fashion, or other personality-related topics and products. They devour advertising and, while not devoured by it, may be more than usually susceptible to it while their identities are in flux.

The relatively immobile have a different problem. To the extent that elderly people, for instance, are confined by poor health to limited physical activity, they may find themselves more socially isolated than they once were. While they have a lifetime of personal relations to rely on, they may have a declining number of daily social contacts with friends and family. Most obviously, they will have less contact with workmates. They will thus have relatively less access to the incidental exchanges of information about new purchases, the incidental asking for and giving of advice about where to get a car repaired cheaply, what store has what shirts and blouses on sale, which movie theater has a "dollar night" on Wednesdays. Also, if the older person no longer drives a car or is reluctant to drive long distances, he or she becomes more dependent on local shops for buying. This limits the range of possibilities and restricts the chance to do comparative shopping. Catalog sales and other direct mail selling are ways in which advertising may help enlarge the elderly consumer's options.

If the elderly person becomes psychologically "disengaged," and consequently monitors the world less avidly through a variety of media, he or she will become relatively more dependent on the media still employed. This means, most of all, that television becomes relatively more influential. As elderly people read less of magazines and newspapers and spend more and more time in front of the television, the range of consumer-product information open to them narrows and the influence of television advertising may be relatively larger.[59]

The limits on physical mobility that apply in one way to the elderly apply in a different way to the poor. If the range of their shopping is limited by the distance they can walk or the convenience of bus and subway lines, they have fewer options than if they could shop by car. Their mobility in relation to goods is also limited because they have little opportunity to save money and, if they can buy on credit at all, they will pay a premium for doing so. Money begets money; having a cushion of comfort allows the middle-class person to budget more wisely, to wait for deals, and to shop for credit, all possibilities foreclosed to the poor person. If the poor person is also poorly educated, or simply does not have the money to afford newspapers and magazines, major sources of product information become unavailable. If the poor person comes from a poor family, he or she is not likely to have had as much personal experience with a variety of goods as a person from a more affluent family; inexperience feeds itself, too, and will lead to less than optimal purchasing decisions, decisions more reliant on advertising than decisions by a person with the wider experience with goods that affluence brings.

In some respects, however, advertising is not well adapted to exploiting the poor and may, in fact, be a protection for the poor consumer. The poor are disadvantaged as consumers most of all by not having much money. They are further disadvantaged, as Alan Andreasen argues, because they are collectively a poor market for business. The result is that stores in poor neighborhoods tend to be poorly managed, to have a small selection of goods, and to have a higher price per item to cover extra costs of doing business in economically depressed neighborhoods. All sorts of merchandising practices among retailers may discriminate against the poor, but national advertising is not one of them. Indeed, it can be argued that there is not *enough* advertising directed toward the poor. If advertising were more available to poor consumers, it might be useful to them as a resource against the relatively small shopping opportunities they generally have.[60]

For children, of course, and especially preschool children, many sources of information are unavailable. Any information that appears in the print media escapes young children since they are not yet literate. While they may see news on television, they are not likely to find it interesting or to understand it; it is much less available to them, much less directed to them, than is television advertising. Further, children have had very little personal experience with consumer products. As children grow older, they become skeptical of the claims made by advertising; by the sixth grade they have acquired a "global distrust" of advertising, as one researcher puts it.[61] While older children are very much like adults in their skepticism, younger children, especially preschool children, are more attentive to commercials than older children, do not discriminate between program content and commercials on television, and are relatively trusting of advertisements. They treat television more like a word-of-mouth medium than like a commercial mass medium.[62] They have little experience of the world or of products in it and have relatively few alternative information sources to depend on.

Further, one of the major information sources in adult consumer decisions is almost entirely unavailable to young children —price. Without knowledge of the disposable income of his or her family, or the efforts taken to acquire the income, the child has little sense of the barrier price provides against desire. Even when children are aware of price, it means much less to them than it does to an adult, who is able to compare the price to what it used to be, or to what it is likely to be (for seasonal goods), or to the price of rival products, or to the family's budget. The child desires in a conceptual vacuum; it takes time to develop the psychological structure of economic activity. Thus, without the mediating influence of economic relevance, the child is relatively more vulnerable to advertising.

Of course, since the preschool child has little or no disposable income, the amount of money that will be misspent because of children's avidly voiced wants for toys or cereals they see on television is of small account. Nonetheless, in family dynamics, the presence of television advertising directed to children is a serious problem.[63] There is no doubt that advertising to children belongs in a different category from other advertising and is, at best, morally suspect. The FTC's examination of children's television advertising, begun in 1977, concluded that advertising to children is inherently unfair, but it did not outline any feasible remedy. Voluntary curbs, stimulated by the threat of government regulation, have been proposed by business groups like the Network for Better Nutrition but they have not yet had great effect —nor much encouragement from the Reagan administration.[64]

Finally, people in the Third World are relatively more vulnerable than the typical American to advertising and marketing practices. This is so for many reasons. First, they are subject to all the limitations that poverty and illiteracy inflict on American consumers, too. Rates of poverty and illiteracy, of course, are very high in many Third World nations. Second, most people in most developing nations are in the position of the newcomer in relationship to American, European, or Japanese mass-produced goods. Neither the prospective consumers nor their friends and neighbors have very much experience with the goods that are suddenly flooding into their countries. Personal experience and the personal experience of trusted friends are both relatively unavailable to Third World consumers.

Third, most governments in the Third World do not have the infrastructure of consumer protection found in the United States. Weak as the Food and Drug Administration, the FTC, and the EPA may be, they do offer significant controls over the manufacture and sales promotion of at least some goods. Cigarettes sold in the United States must have a health warning printed on the packages, but American cigarettes sold in Latin America, for instance, are not obliged to do so and in fact do not.[65]

Products judged unsafe for American consumption are nonetheless "dumped" by American and multinational corporations in Third World countries. This practice has been widely reported on and documented. Milton Silverman, Philip R. Lee, and Mia Lydecker, for instance, have surveyed the marketing of drugs in the Third World. They find that many drugs withdrawn from American and European markets or never approved for use are widely available and widely promoted in the Third World. Often, in literature accompanying the drugs, the dangers or side effects are minimized and the claims of effectiveness wildly exaggerated. While Silverman and colleagues acknowledge that drugs have done much more good than harm in developing nations, they conservatively estimate that the use and promotion of drugs that are not approved for use or are approved only for very specialized use in the United States and Europe may account for ten to fifteen million cases of injury and one million deaths annually in the Third World.[66]

The marketing of infant formula in the Third World was one of the great scandals of the past decade. International health organizations first called attention to the problem in 1970. By 1975, most of the marketers of infant formula agreed to abide by a self-imposed code of marketing practices. But critics felt the code was too weak, and too rarely heeded, and the Interfaith Center for Corporate Responsibility (of the National Council of Churches) and an independent group, the Infant Formula Action Coalition (INFACT) kept up the pressure. When the World Health Organization arrived at a new code in 1981, this was a triumph for the activist groups, but their boycott of one of the marketers, Nestlé, continued until a settlement was reached with Nestlé in early 1984.

The issue was what one authority has called "commerciogenic malnutrition."[67] It is universally agreed that the best food for infants, under normal circumstances, is breast milk and that breast feeding should be encouraged wherever possible. Bottle feeding is recommended only where the mother, suffering malnutrition or for other reasons, is unable to feed the infant herself. Bottle feeding has been adopted in the Third World because of urbanization and the entry of women into the industrial work force. The popularity of bottle feeding among affluent families in the Third World is another important factor. Bottle feeding is taken to be a sign of Westernness or modern thinking, and poorer families emulate the wealthy. The association of bottle feeding with modern and Western ways has been accelerated by the distribution of formula through food aid programs and health services. It has also been promoted by a variety of marketing techniques. These have included direct consumer advertising and a variety of inducements to the medical profession in Third World countries to encourage them to push the use of infant formula.

Whatever the reasons for the use of bottled infant formula, the results have been tragic. There are indications from all over the world that infants have suffered from malnutrition and have died because they have not been breast fed. Ordinarily, manufactured infant formula is a nutritionally adequate substitute for breast milk (although it does not provide the contribution to the immunity system that breast milk does). But if directions for its use are not followed accurately, it will not substitute well. Because of the poverty and poor education of many of the users of formula in the

Third World, infants do not get appropriate nourishment. The formula is often diluted too much with water because the formula is *very* expensive for a relatively poor family and the mother seeks to make it last longer. Even if the formula is prepared properly, in many rural areas and even some urban areas, the available water is not potable and infants are unprepared to withstand the disease-carrying water.

The marketers of infant formula responded that they did not create the demand for bottle feeding in the Third World. Bottle feeding existed before the major marketing efforts and the bottles usually contained unnutritious combinations of water, sugar, flour, and root extracts. No doubt infant formula is a significant, though expensive, improvement on this. But there is no argument, even from the marketers themselves, that formula is superior to breast milk. The marketers all adhere, at least in principle, to the position that they should encourage breast feeding and offer formula only as a substitute when breast milk is unavailable or needs to be supplemented. But marketers have been lavish with free samples of infant formula to new mothers. In addition, posters, calendars, and booklets, and considerable assistance to the medical profession including the sponsorship of social entertainment at medical conferences and the provision of travel and fellowships are directed to encourage formula use. Doctors received free six-month supplies of formula for babies in their own families. One of the most controversial marketing techniques was the hiring of "milk nurses" who served in Third World hospitals and clinics and maternity centers. They provided assistance in health care, but their master was the food processing company that hired them and expected them to encourage mothers to try infant formula.[68]

Some of the infant formula corporations acted responsibly when confronted with irrefutable documentation of commerciogenic malnutrition. But even where the corporations, at the top, took steps to eliminate direct consumer advertising, to distribute information on the value of breast feeding, and to control marketing efforts to the medical profession more carefully, the competitive situation led to a gap between the humane pronouncements from corporate headquarters and the actual practices in the field.

There remains too much incentive for people lower down the hierarchy to cut corners to keep up with competitors.[69] Surely major corporations did not intend for Third World mothers to dilute formula too much or to use bad water mixed with formula or to use up their small earnings on feeding the baby. They intended only to sell formula. But under the circumstances of life in the Third World, which are changing only slowly, reasonable people must acknowledge what the consequences of infant formula use will often be. The powers of marketing here—through the medical profession as much as or probably more than through direct advertising—influence consumer choice. In this instance, infant deaths have been the tragic consequence of a system of competitive marketing.

Advertising and Information

To view consumer behavior as being the outcome of intentional or unintentional information gathering is commonplace. In economics, it has been stimulated by "Chicago school" economists aiming to show that advertising contributes to the consumer's information and thereby to the perfection of the market system. It has also served those economists who seek a new emphasis on time in economic theory and examine the "search" costs in consumer behavior. It is connected, as well, to the emphasis in the consumer movement on disclosure and control of deceptive practices.

All of these perspectives assume information to be a kind of product or commodity itself. If one takes information as process, not product, the issue may be reformulated. The problem of advertising arises only because of the establishment of marketed and mass-marketed goods in a world where, for a variety of reasons, "craft knowledge" has declined. Advertising cannot weigh heavily where people make their own goods or know enough about the manufacture of products so that they retain an expert knowledge or, as William Leiss puts it, a "craft knowledge" (implying some kind of intimacy as well as expertise). But craft skills and craft knowledge "atrophy in the expanding commodity environment."[70] Of course, there are many people with a craft knowledge of automobiles, for instance, or of materials used in a hobby—people active in hunting, fishing, sailing, and skiing often have expert and loving knowledge of the equipment they use. Yet people ordinarily have less intimate knowledge of the things they use than was true a century ago. The knowledge they have is qualitatively, not just quantitatively, different. Their knowledge is more product than process. With the exceptions noted, like cars, rifles, fishing rods, sailboats, and ski poles, the knowledge of goods is more often absorbed from advertisements, instruction manuals, service departments, and other people than from direct experience. For most people, this is the case with toasters, stereo systems, typewriters, toothpastes, and fruits and vegetables (unless one has a garden).

There is no returning to the world in which most knowledge was craft knowledge. Nor, I think, would many people want that world and all it entailed. People would not want the restricted range of experience that would be available if they could only make use of materials where they had craft knowledge. (Would one want to stop listening to Horowitz because one did not know how to play the piano? Or to stop flying in planes because the principles of aerodynamics were not second nature?)

It is only in the world where so much of our knowledge comes second hand that it makes sense to think of consumer decisions as arising from an "information environment." In this world, efforts like those of the FTC to improve the quality of information available to consumers have a rationale. Certain populations, for whom a range of information is relatively inaccessible, are especially vulnerable to the attractions of advertising. They are populations at risk. Their situation merits either much more serious self-regulation on the part of advertisers—which does not seem to be forthcoming, or more vigorous efforts by other institutions, including government regulatory agencies, to protect people who cannot protect themselves.

It is not possible to conclude as an absolute judgment that "advertising works" or that it fails to work. If the role of advertising in selling goods is to be understood, the important question is *under what circumstances* will advertising be *more or less likely* to make a difference. Advertisements are placed in a media environment where they have plenty of competition for the consumer's eye or ear. Some of the competing information will directly contradict the claims of an advertisement and may do so with a level of credibility that the ad cannot match. Consumers do not exist in a social or informational vacuum but employ a variety of resources, intentionally or by rote, to make decisions about products. Where consumers have personal experience with products or trustworthy second-hand information from friends or school or consumer groups or reliable salespeople, they will be relatively immune to the sales pitch of a commercial. Where these resources are unavailable, they approach the advertisement in greater ignorance and with greater vulnerability.

The capacity of advertising to persuade is *contingent* on the social and informational location of the consumer. It is also contingent on the nature of the product. There are product situations where advertising may have a special power, a kind of monopoly of influence. With "experience" goods rather than "search" goods, the consumer is less able to judge a product by testing it out personally and is more dependent on second-hand evaluations. Where the product is a new one on the market, no consumer is able to rely on personal experience or the experience of friends and neighbors to evaluate the product. With some products, like over-the-counter drugs, the consumer is not in a good position to judge the quality of a product even after having used it and may continue to buy a brand whose "success" was purely adventitious.

Advertising is also contingent, clearly, on the skill of the creators of the ad in exploiting the most appealing features of the product and keying into the public's tastes and moods. There is no science to guarantee that an agency, even with lavish budgets, will succeed in this work.

Despite all the limits to the power of advertising and despite all the barriers to ever *knowing* just how effective advertising is, American businesses share a general faith in advertising even when they couple it with specific doubts. The American public seems relatively accepting of advertising and appreciative of it, even when appreciation is tempered by a high level of skepticism about the veracity of advertising claims. The American cultural climate is hospitable to consumer goods and tolerant of advertising that is more pervasive and more intrusive than in any other industrialized country. The role of advertising in American culture cannot be finally understood if one looks only at the business of advertising narrowly conceived; it is necessary to explore more widely the romance of the commodity in American life and some of the sources of receptivity to a consumer culture.

4

An Anthropology of Goods

IN THE FACTORY we make cosmetics," Charles Revson of Revlon, Inc. said, "in the store we sell hope."[1] An advertising executive told me, "We've convinced the mothers of America that they're not good mothers if they don't serve Minute Maid." Another executive, referring to AT&T's "Reach Out and Touch Someone" campaign said, "Advertising turned that instrument, a physical inanimate object, into an instrument of the heart." These are the sorts of statements, no matter how hyperbolic or self-serving, that critics of advertising seize on as the inner worm of truth in the apple of the ad industry. As I have argued, advertising as a business tool is more complicated than such claims suggest and people are more simple, and sturdy, than these visions imply. If one is to arrive at an understanding of the modern passion for goods, an examination of advertising is an essential step but it is not the first step—as marketers know very well and as social critics should learn. The first step, it seems to me, is to gain an understanding of the role material possessions play in human lives not just in advertising-saturated societies but in any society. The next step is to try to understand the social forces that gathered in the past one hundred years to produce both the advertising industry itself and the infrastructure of a consumer society that called for and supported new attitudes toward goods and a new receptivity to advertising. Only then can advertising's role as a specific goad to sales and a general cultural encouragement toward materialism be viewed in its proper context.

This chapter will sketch in some key features of the role of material possessions in human social life—looking toward the ways our own relations to goods share something with the attitudes and practices of people in simple, nonmarket societies. The next chapter will outline the social forces that emerged in nineteenth-century America and gave rise to a consumer culture, including the institution of advertising. Chapter 6 will be a case study of the rise of cigarette smoking in the 1920s and an analysis of what array of factors created a change in consumer patterns as substantial as that one was.

The Concept of "Human Needs"

The common image of a primitive society is one of hunters and gatherers scraping a living from the savannah, surviving from hour to hour in search of food, spending their entire lives getting enough to eat. These creatures get along with the true basics of existence, not strikingly different from other animal species.

Such groups or part-groups have existed under extreme circumstances in advanced societies. The people who lived in Nazi concentration camps barely survived. True, their needs for survival were psychological as well as biological, but they were as close to the human edge of existence as any group has ever been. Primitive societies, however, were not and are not like that. Primitive societies, as anthropologist Marshall Sahlins has provocatively observed, are characterized not by a paucity of goods but by a paucity of needs. Hunters and gatherers do not often starve nor must they normally work hard to keep from starving. They typically have an abundance of food and they typically have more leisure time than most people in modern industrial societies. Our most ancient human ancestors, as best as we can tell from the simplest societies we find today, were "affluent." Hunters and gatherers today generally have ample caloric intake and acquire the food they need with just a few hours of work a day.[2]

Not only do the hunters and gatherers satisfy "basic" or "biological" needs easily, but perhaps the more vital point is that the needs they seek to satisfy, as is true of every other human society, are not strictly biological needs. People in any society we have ever encountered, or can even imagine, are biological and social at once. The infant's first sucking at the breast is an act both biological and social. From that point on, the infant will want to be not only a *living* person but a living *person,* a socially creditable being. No one becomes socially creditable simply by biological survival except infants. Infants often have nothing but food on their minds, wanting, when they are awake, to be fed. But adult human beings are not like that. Adults do not eat all day long and normally eat through an institutional complex unknown in the nonhuman world: the meal. Human biological functions, like eating, are culturally coded and socially organized. It is important in primitive societies as in industrial societies that people eat like human beings, not like animals. This requires adherence to certain social conventions for eating. In the American middle class, a person must eat a certain quantity of food so that it cannot be said that the person "eats like a horse," on the one hand, or "eats like a bird," on the other. More important still, one must retain a certain reserve about eating so as to acknowledge that the activity is one of eating a meal, not one of simply consuming food. Without that reserve, a person can be accused of "eating like a pig" or of failing to engage in the social activity of eating altogether by "inhaling" food. (Many people in American society regard an establishment that announces in neon, "EAT" or "EATS" as vulgar, and it is probably no accident that the English language has borrowed from the language thought to be most refined and civilized to describe a dining establishment as a "restaurant.")

The importance of making eating into a social and symbolic, a human activity, can be seen in extreme situations. In Alexander Solzhenitsyn's *One Day in the Life of Ivan Denisovich,* prisoners in the Soviet labor camp are fed only a thin gruel with some fish heads and tails thrown in. Ivan Denisovich, weak from malnutrition and overwork, nonetheless organizes his own ritual for eating. He takes off his cap before he eats. He refuses to eat fish eyes. This description is among the most moving and poignant in the novel. And why? Because here, in a society intending to animalize prisoners, Ivan continues to eat meals as he consumes food and so retains, literally, his humanity.

Even in the poorest societies and even in the most primitive human worlds, human needs and desires are culturally constituted and socially defined. Human needs are for inclusion as well as for survival, for meaning as well as for existence. For purposes of social analysis, the notion that there are basic biological needs that can be separated from artificial and created social needs does not make good sense. All needs are socially constructed in all human societies. What people require are the elements to live a social life, the elements to be a person.

But what, then, is required to live a social life? This, of course, will differ from one society to another. The requirements of personhood in different societies will differ, as both the philosopher of modern capitalism, Adam Smith, and the most trenchant critic of capitalism, Karl Marx, understood. Smith defined human "necessaries" as "not only the commodities which are indispensably necessary for the support of life, but whatever the custom of the country renders it indecent for creditable people, even of the lowest order, to be without."[3] He observes that a linen shirt is not "strictly speaking" a necessary of life. The Greeks and the Romans lived well without linen shirts. Still, he noted:

> . . . in the present times, through the greater part of Europe, a creditable day-labourer would be ashamed to appear in public without a linen shirt, the want of which would be supposed to denote that disgraceful degree of poverty, which, it is presumed, no body can well fall into without extreme bad conduct.[4]

Similarly, Smith held, leather shoes are a necessary of life in England for men and women. In Scotland, leather shoes are necessary for men but not for women—women can walk in Scotland without leather shoes and not be discredited. In France, leather shoes are necessaries for neither men nor women. Necessaries are things that custom or "the established rules of decency," as well as nature, have rendered vital for even the lowest ranks of people.

Smith's position has several important implications. First, for Smith, poverty is not a level of income. Poverty is relative to what a given society deems a decent standard of living. Second, Smith observes that no one, even the people in the lowest ranks of England, lives only on necessaries. Even the poor enjoy luxuries. This raises the possibility, although Smith himself does not say so, that one of the requirements of decent or creditable conduct is the ability to afford some things, whose nature is not specified, beyond the things required for decent conduct. That is, the creditable human being must have not only the things needed for decent life, but something extra, something superfluous or sentimental or luxurious. The human being, to be human, must show that he or she is not just an animal or brute, not just biological, and must in some manner make that nonanimal nature visible.

Smith sees very clearly that he lives in a class society. For him, the term "necessary" is not altogether relative. It is relative only to what the *poorest* creditable citizens require. An upper-middle-class professional may feel that he or she requires fresh ground coffee daily because, in that person's social circle, it would be discreditable not to have it. That does not make it a human "necessary" in Smith's view, not unless respectable poor people in the same community feel the same way. In American society, they do not. Freshly ground coffee is not a necessary. A television set in good working order, on the other hand, may well be a necessary. It is something taken to be a requirement for decent living even among the poorest creditable people in American society.

Karl Marx, like Adam Smith, understood human needs to be socially and historically produced. Human needs vary according to the physical conditions of the country and according to "the degree of civilization of a country."[5] In *Capital,* Marx holds that there are two kinds of consumer goods—consumer necessities and luxuries. True articles of luxury are items that only the capitalist class consumes. A consumer necessity is something that is in general and habitual use among the working class—like tobacco, whether or not it is physiologically essential to life.[6] This is consonant with Adam Smith's view of the matter. Like Smith, Marx fully appreciated that human needs are social and relative. In *Wage, Labour and Capital*, he wrote that an owner may find a small house adequate so long as other houses in the same neighborhood are the same size. Then someone builds a palace and "the house shrinks from a little house to a hut . . . Our desires and pleasures spring from society; we measure them, therefore, by society and not by the objects which serve for their satisfaction. Because they are of a social nature, they are of a relative nature."[7]

In the tradition of Thorstein Veblen, sociologists and cultural critics have thought it clever and damning to show of some social behavior that its function is to display status rather than to serve "basic" needs. But this view implicitly accepts the puritanical prejudice, which neither Smith nor Marx succumbed to, that whatever is not a fundamental material need is superfluous. The assumption is that people care about status only because they are vain, foolish, economically irrational, or in Veblen's view, industrially unproductive.[8] But that is not sociology, it is economistic ideology. The sociologists' studies of lifestyle in Newburyport or the meaning of living-room furniture in Detroit or the anthropologists' accounts of yam display in the Trobriand Islands or lace curtains in East London are all about essential attributes of human social life.[9] And one could go further to say that even so-called basic material needs satisfy only as they are mediated by social attributions. Except in the extreme case—the prison, say, or the military—people do not eat food that has no social meaning. There are jokes about "institutional food" or the "army mess" for good reason, and college food riots are not so bizarre as they seem: food out of the family context is very hard to digest. Marx saw what social scientists have too long ignored, the anthropological truism that things do not have value in themselves but only relationally, as part of a language of values, in a socially constituted and situated vocabulary of meanings.

Gifts and Materialism

American popular culture shares with American social science certain characteristic modes of explanation. Explanations for social phenomena tend to be materialist, rationalist, and individualist. Other things being equal, we prefer to assume that social phenomena are caused by the intentional actions of individuals operating in their own material self-interest. Social science, especially economics, tends to explain the world in such terms. And in the popular culture, Americans frequently explain their own behavior in the same terms. These explanations may be right, of course, but they come so readily, they are applied with such reflex-like quickness, that a skeptical observer is obliged to wonder if they do not cover up as much as they unveil.

Anthropologist Claude Lévi-Strauss, a pioneer of "structuralist" explanations for social behavior that have nothing to do with the autonomous will of participating individuals, offers a tale about gift giving in modern societies. In cheap restaurants in the south of France, small tables are set for two and, at lunch, when people pour out of the factories and offices and crowd the restaurants, strangers often sit opposite each other. Each person eats the food by him or herself but treats the carafe of wine set at each plate very differently: "Food serves the body's needs and wine its taste for luxury, the first serving to nourish, the second, to honour." One person lifts the carafe and pours the wine into the other's glass. The neighbor then reciprocates.

Why? Economically, nothing has happened—two identical items have been exchanged and consumed. But, Lévi-Strauss observes, "there is much more in the exchange itself than in the things exchanged." The gift giving "substitutes a social relationship for spatial juxtaposition."[10] And it sets in motion a set of mutual obligations for cordiality and conversation. When the two people at lunch do each other a favor, they demonstrate, and must continue to demonstrate while together, their adherence to what Alvin Gouldner calls the "norm of reciprocity."[11] For the course of a lunch hour, gift giving has established a social relationship. It does so in all human societies under all sorts of circumstances.

The most celebrated instance of gift giving is the "Kula ring" described by Bronislaw Malinowski in the Trobriand Islands of the South Pacific.[12] No one questions the central importance of gift giving in many simple societies, but gift giving also plays a notable role in the modern world. For instance, in her study of a poor black community in the Midwest, Carol Stack found gift giving to be at the heart of the economic and social order. Because people had very little, they made what they had go further and last longer by continual redistribution. "These days," one of Stack's informants said, "you ain't got nothing to be really giving, only to your true friends, but most people trade. Trading is a part of everybody's life." Women, for instance, trade clothes and so gain greater variety in their wardrobes without additional cost. These transactions "create special bonds between friends. They initiate a social relationship and agreed upon reciprocal obligations."[13]

My impression is that women are more attuned to gift giving than are men in the American middle class as well as in the black lower class. Even affluent women exchange clothes for special occasions more than men do, exchange recipes, take responsibility for the handing down of children's clothes and toys, and remember to give birthday and anniversary cards and gifts. Men may be sometimes surprised when women react strongly to a social slight or signs of inhospitality but are less inclined to notice the care the same women take not to give social offense themselves but to maintain family and social ties, often through gifts and other exchanges.

The restudy of Middletown (Muncie, Indiana) examined Christmas gift giving and found that while men and women are both active in giving and receiving presents, women do most of the work attendant to this ritual:

The performance of the full-scale Christmas ritual is an enormous task performed, for the most part, by women. Women, as we have found, do most of the decorating, and most of the gift wrapping. They give more gifts in their own names than men do, and they purchase and wrap most of the gifts that are given jointly by couples or other male/female combinations. Christmas gift giving in nearly every household centers around a woman who is the chief performer of the ritual.[14]

In a study of what middle- and working-class families find important and meaningful about the material objects they possess, sociologist Eugene Rochberg-Halton found that objects received as gifts bulk large among people's most cherished possessions. Rochberg-Halton asked participants in his study which objects they especially cherished and how these objects were acquired. Forty percent of the objects mentioned had been received as gifts or had been inherited. This varied greatly across categories of goods. Forty-eight percent of the jewelry mentioned were acquired as gifts (and another 17 percent by inheritance), as were 40 percent of clocks (33 percent by inheritance), 44 percent of glassware (33 percent by inheritance), 47 percent of silverware (29 percent by inheritance), 83 percent of stuffed animals (6 percent by inheritance). In contrast, only 28 percent of visual art, 27 percent of appliances, 24 percent of clothing, 35 percent of vehicles, and 22 percent of candlesticks had been gifts. Sixty-five percent of house plants had come as gifts, often as cuttings from friends' plants, and so friendship came to be symbolized "through a bond of living matter." Gift objects are not "inanimate" but embody and personify the spirit of the giver.[15]

As Rochberg-Halton's data indicate, some objects are more suitable as gifts than others and, as Lévi-Strauss says, "precisely because of their nonutilitarian nature."[16] Many of the things people buy that are the most "useless" or superfluous or luxurious are things they buy as gifts for others. While advertising is often attacked for manipulating people into buying things they do not need, it is rarely noticed that many of the most un-needed purchases are used as gifts, in our society just as they are in primitive societies. One way to measure this practice is to examine the percentage of goods accounted for by Christmas season sales in any one year. If December sales were equal to any other month's sales, they would represent one-twelfth or 8.3 percent of annual sales. Anything more than 8.3 percent suggests that gift giving plays a role in sales. (With some categories of goods, other factors would matter: the sale of woolen mittens is likely to be higher in December than in July, quite apart from Christmas giving.)

As any retailer knows, December is the biggest month of the year for consumer sales. In 1980, according to the Department of Commerce, sales for December from all retail stores came to 10.5 percent of annual sales (the last quarter, October through December, accounted for 28.1 percent of sales). For department stores, the December figure is 15.8 percent (34.7 percent for the last quarter).[17] Thus, the very least one can say is that Christmas giving accounts for over 2 percent of annual retail sales. Of course, this underestimates the matter since the last weeks of November also include a substantial amount of Christmas buying. A better estimate of the actual role of Christmas giving in the economy may come from the restudy of Middletown which found that people spent 3.1 percent of individual income on 1978 Christmas gifts, 4 percent of family incomes when the average expenditures of married couples were pooled.[18]

If gift giving in general is important to the economy, luxury goods especially are objects of gift exchange. Macy's sells 25 percent of its annual supply of cosmetics in December.[19] Of flowers bought from FTD florists, 14 percent are bought in December. (Other months that have holidays at which time giving flowers is traditional are also high in sales: April, with Easter, has 10 percent of annual sales; May, with Mother's Day and school proms, has 14.6 percent. The next best month, with 8.8 percent of sales, is February, with Valentine's Day.)[20] December accounted for 12.4 percent of sporting goods sales in 1980.[21] During the Christmas season department stores sell more than 40 percent of their toys, 28 percent of their candy, 20 percent of tobacco and liquor, and 25 percent or more of cosmetics, drugs, toiletries, stationery, greeting cards, books, and art.[22] Men's stores do 16 percent of their business in December, liquor stores 11.6 percent.[23] It seems the less a product is "truly needed" the more likely it is to be bought, not for self-gratification, but as a gift. Candy sales are affected by another traditional occasion for "giving"—Halloween. Halloween sales account for $1.5 billion of the candy industry's $5.4 billion in annual sales.[24]

Christmas is a "festival of consumption"—but it is equally a festival of reunion, of restating and renewing ties of kinship and friendship. O. Henry's "Gift of the Magi" is the classic case. In this story, the two impoverished lovers sacrifice their dearest possessions to buy gifts for each other. The man sells his watch to buy a comb for his wife's lovely hair, and she cuts off her hair and sells it to buy a fob for her husband's cherished watch. The prevalence of gift giving suggests that people very often buy things not because they are materialistic but because they are social. What is unusual about our society is that we so often express our social attachments through newly purchased, newly manufactured (rather than ritually recycled or handcrafted) material goods.[25]

We have not forsaken traditional family values for material consumption; we consume materials very often to preserve families. It is more likely today than in the past for nuclear family members to be "dispersed over numerous households." With college attendance, particularly college attendance away from home growing rapidly since World War II, with the growth of single-person households, family life has not ended but has been territorially stretched and people consume both more durable goods (luggage) and more services like transportation and communication to hold this sort of family together.[26]

In a sense, people exploit advertising to make it do their bidding in establishing social ties. The exploitation is mutual; advertisers are well aware that people are as often gift givers as they are direct consumers, and they schedule their advertising accordingly. Because wristwatches are so often given as gifts, watch manufacturers concentrate their advertising in the Christmas season. Seiko, a watch company, spends 60 percent of its annual advertising budget in the last quarter of the year.[27] Health and beauty aid firms spend more than 60 percent of their ad budgets in the Christmas season.[28] Polaroid spends 50 percent of its media budget in the same period.[29] Overall, advertising is about as heavily weighted toward the final quarter as consumer spending is. Magazine ads for apparel and accessories, for instance, were 8.6

percent in December, 30.9 percent in the last quarter (compared to 14.2 percent in December and 32.5 percent in the last quarter for apparel sales in clothing stores). Total magazine advertising for beer, wine, and liquor was 15.4 percent in December, 36.2 percent in the last quarter (compared to liquor sales of 12.2 percent for December, 11.6 percent for liquor store sales).[30] Department stores, which in 1979 sold 16.7 percent of their goods in December, spent 12.5 percent of their budget for newspaper space in December, 9.2 percent of their store display budget, 13.8 percent of their radio and television advertising, or 12.2 percent overall in advertising and sales promotion.[31]

Manufacturers not only advertise more to take advantage of consumer gift giving but they shape the content of their advertising appeals accordingly. Shirley Polykoff, a celebrated copywriter, helped create the campaign for "Clairol Loving Care" hair rinse. She believed that appealing to women's vanity would not be enough. It was important to "reawaken . . . dissatisfactions" women feel about their gray hair. So she added to the print ad a photo of a smiling, middle-aged man, captioned: "Makes your husband feel younger too, just to look at you!" She comments in her autobiography: "You can see how this could practically turn the act of hair coloring into a selfless little something one did for one's loved ones."[32]

Advertising, then, can play off of the universal human practice of giving gifts to secure social relationships just as consumers can use advertising as a guide to what various goods mean, how much a good is a "status" good or a "luxury" product and, hence, suitable for gift giving. For gift-giving purposes, the quality of the good may be less important than cultural assumptions, partly shaped by advertising, about the product's status. The gift is a social statement, not a contribution to the recipient's material well-being. Advertising helps rank order the status of goods.

The role of advertising in helping to identify the "status" of a given good may be crucial not only for special gift-giving occasions or seasons but for specialized gift-giving social roles, the most important being that of housewife. Many purchases of "necessities" may be made because the purchaser sees them as gifts, statements of and reinforcements of social relationships.

Many housewives and the occasional househusband view shopping for food as a chore or a job at which they try to become more and more expert. People clip coupons, look for sales, buy seasonal produce, and use house or generic brands. But shopping and cooking are not tasks done on a contractual basis within the family. For many people, women especially, serving a meal is giving a gift. The wife and mother whose family does not eat her cooking is hurt not because money has been wasted but because love has been refused. She may identify certain meals as being especially gift-like, prepared with a cut of meat more expensive than usual; or butter instead of margarine; or the serving of a particularly favorite dish for her husband or child.

This extends beyond food shopping. For example, over 60 percent of men's underwear is bought by women.[33] In part, this is an expression of a traditional sexual division of labor and sexual stereotyping—men are not supposed to be interested in what they wear, while women are supposed to be responsible for household necessities. But there is a sexual element at play, too, an expression of intimacy in this "gift," and the purchase that could be just an act of maintaining minimally decent clothing becomes an act of enriching a social bond.

Do housewives, in fact, think of food shopping as part of gift giving, serving to sustain valued social relations? This is an empirical matter one could investigate. If they do, then an enormous portion of total consumption, for necessities as well as for luxury items, must be understood as preeminently social in nature, not individualistic or crudely materialistic or connected to trends toward narcissism.

There is some interview data to support this proposition. In the 1959 study *Workingman's Wife* by Lee Rainwater, Richard Coleman, and Gerald Handel, interviews with 420 working class housewives made it very clear that preparing meals was a task of demonstrating affection for or, at least, pleasing husbands. The woman's main consideration was not her own taste or her own convenience but "her husband's and her children's food fancies."[34] For the housewife, doing for others was (and is) a frequent and valued part of consuming. As Rainwater and colleagues concluded, "doing for others" is a major mode of behavior for working-class women. "It is the best way they know of relating to other people." They found working-class women especially indulgent in gifts for children but also in gift giving in general. "They do not draw a boundary line for their gift giving; they enjoy gift giving on any and all possible occasions and sometimes say that the money they have spent most pleasurably was 'whenever I've given people a gift and made them happy.' " Several times the authors quoted one woman as representative who, when asked what she would do with $1000 less income a year, responded: "I'd have to spend less money on the gifts I give to all the people I know. I'd just have to try to make my heart a little smaller."[35]

Most of the estimates of the role of gift giving in the economy that I have used here focus on Christmas gift giving, and as such underestimate the much wider role of gift giving throughout the year. British market research data discussed by J. Davis indicates that of all jewelry purchased annually in Britain, 50 percent is bought as gifts. For women's toilet preparations, 48 percent are bought as gifts, 70 percent for men's. Forty-five percent of clocks are given as gifts, 70 percent of watches, 59 percent of toasters, 20 percent of books, 20 percent of records, 27 percent of radios, and 90 percent of toys. In Britain, Davis estimates, 60 percent of beer and 30 percent of hard liquor are bought as gifts, reflecting the continuing power of the pub in British life. Comparable figures for American alcohol consumption would be much lower.[36]

I do not suggest that if a good is bought as a gift, that the materialism it expresses is necessarily benign. The social importance of Christmas giving in American society and the premium placed on costly gifts have social costs. Credit counseling centers see a lot of people in February and March each year as bills for Christmas giving become past due. At Christmas, people try to cement the social bonds that matter to them or, to speak of the pathological side of this activity, they try to use gifts to buy love or handle guilt. And they will go deeply into debt to do so.[37] Business knows this and is at liberty to take advantage of the sociality and generosity of consumers at critical junctures. Christmas is just one. People are also more "social" than "narcissistic" (though the elements are always intermixed) when buying for weddings, when arranging payment for funerals and cemetery upkeep, when sending son or daughter off to college, when shopping for a nursing home for one's parents. These are all situations where the social (and gift-giving) element in human relations overpowers self-regarding feelings in the course of a marketplace transaction. What I suggest, then, is that we should distinguish materialistic values—placing material above social or spiritual goals—from a materials-intensive way of life, which may use goods as means to other ends.

Not all groups in the population turn to the marketplace or the supermarket for gift buying. The most notable exception is children. Parents, as a class, rarely hand-make gifts for their children; they buy manufactured things. Children, in contrast, are more likely to make gifts for their parents than to buy them. This is especially true of young children who, as a class, have little disposable income but considerable disposable time. This makes them a rare group in a society where time is often in much shorter supply than money and where people pay a premium for convenience goods. All store-bought goods are, in a sense, convenience goods.

Social Membership and the Standard Package of Goods

Marx, a more complex and subtle critic of capitalism than is sometimes appreciated, notes an interesting irony in his *Economic and Philosophical Manuscripts.* The frightening invention of capitalism is not the creation of artificial or new needs. The terrible invention is the concept that there is such a thing as purely physical or biological need. Other social systems had treated human beings as social entities, not biological machines. These societies did not necessarily treat people equally or fairly but did take people to be social beings, spouses and in-laws in kinship systems, lords and vassals in political systems, and so forth. Only capitalism, according to Marx, conceived of human beings as raw material. And only capitalists dared calculate the minimum amount it would take to keep workers alive, healthy enough to work in factories and to reproduce in families a new generation of workers.[38]

For Marx, the destiny of the human being did not lie in the human tie to biology but in freedom from this bond. What made the human being a human being, as a species, was the ability to manipulate inorganic nature: to make, to work, to construct, to produce. "Admittedly," Marx observed, "animals also produce," but, he added, an animal "produces only under the dominion of immediate physical need, whilst man produces even when he is free from physical needs and only truly produces in freedom therefrom."[39] For Marx, who believed human beings to be human beings because of and through their labor, capitalism brought out the most of human creative capacities by universally extending industry. Its glory was to provide productive power for the creation of new needs and the exploitation of new human capacities.[40] The trouble with capitalism was that it exploited the proletarian many for the benefit of the capitalist few, that it did not return to workers the fair benefit for their labor, that it treated them not as human ends in themselves but as means to the end of production, that it built work-settings in which the worker was divorced from any meaningful relationship to the objects produced, and that instead of humanizing and fulfilling life it thereby contributed to the deadening of existence.

Of course, there are traditions of moral philosophy that hold that needs should be few, not many. Greek Cynics and Stoics promoted simplicity in life, and simplicity is part of many religious traditions in their monastic and ascetic ideals. The Puritan tradition has also stressed simplicity and plain-ness in living. And there is now a serious new attack on the view that an increase in needs or wants can be progressive: this is the ecological perspective. In the ecological perspective, all previous views in Western thought, including Marx's, have been deficient in viewing nature as "devoid of purpose" and in refusing to see the exploitation of nature to produce commodities as a process that, pushed beyond certain limits, could only create "discommodities." We now have a new necessity—to manage human needs and their satisfaction in a way that will maintain or restore a balance between human society and the natural environment.

And this new necessity may require limitations of the creation of new needs that can only be met by exploitation of nature.[41]

An evaluation of advertising and marketing today is obliged to think more critically than Marx did about the worth of "creating new needs," but it must also refrain from nostalgia for a golden era when people's needs were true and natural. People's needs have never been natural but always cultural, always social, always defined relative to the standards of their societies. This is the lesson of Smith and Marx, it is a truism of anthropology, and it has been reasserted in recent empirical work of sociologist Lee Rainwater. In interviews conducted in the early 1970s, Rainwater found people agreed about what goods and services a family should have as part of the "mainstream standard package" of consumption. People below the "mainstream standard package" felt themselves to be "making do" or "doing the best we can." People at the "mainstream standard package" level or above judged their positions as a function of the weight they attached to the mainstream and above-mainstream packages:

> Individuals will differ in the weights they apply to these levels. For those below the mainstream and for those at the mainstream with low mobility aspirations little weight will be attached to the above-mainstream consumption packages; for those oriented to higher status levels, higher weights will be attached to those packages. One would assume, however, that for all persons the weight attached to the mainstream budget is greater than that attached to the higher budgets—which is simply to say that the most important judgment people make about their standard of living is whether or not it is at least at the mainstream level for their society.[42]

Families select target standard packages. They want to consume more and better things, but not endlessly, not insatiably. They seek not social superiority, as a rule, but social *membership*. They want, as Rainwater puts it, "those attributes and resources that go into the construction of a virtual social identity for persons in their society."[43]

Again, human needs are social and relative. But Rainwater is making a second point: in American society and increasingly in other industrialized nations, social and relative human needs are defined in terms of level of income. Social membership and personal identity have come increasingly to be understood in monetary terms. As Rainwater writes, "When people are not protected from this inexorable dynamic of money economies by some local cultural enclave they cannot fail to define themselves most basically in terms of their access to all that money can buy."[44]

Notice that in Rainwater's discussion there is a shift from the individual person, the subject of interest to Smith and Marx, to the family unit. When Smith and Marx asserted that needs are social and relative, their notion of human needs was nonetheless highly individualistic. This is not an adequate understanding of what is going on. People do not define themselves as autonomous hulls in the water of life, accumulating the barnacles of material possessions. People see themselves as implicated in social systems, tied to other people through kinship, business, politics, affection, and shared experience. We are aware of instances when people sacrifice other people or their relationship with other people to acquire goods—the "miser" is the extreme type. But we also know that people will sacrifice goods to cement ties with other people. Gift giving and other forms of social exchange, as we have seen, are crucial processes in both primitive and modern societies. People universally find it necessary not only to possess but to share. Not only are people's individual needs defined socially, but their individual needs include a need for social connection which is sometimes expressed materially. Why people have increasingly defined social membership and personal identity in terms of income and the goods money buys is a question the next chapter will consider more carefully.

5

Historical Roots of Consumer Culture

IN AMERICAN SOCIETY, people often satisfy or believe they can satisfy their socially constituted needs and desires by buying mass produced, standardized, nationally advertised consumer products. This was not always the case nor is it today a universal phenomenon. Why should it be so prominent a characteristic of contemporary American culture?

One approach to that question is to seek out the historical roots of consumer culture, and that is the task for this chapter. A set of clues may be found in one of the most famous American novels, Theodore Dreiser's *Sister Carrie.* In 1900, Dreiser published this book about Caroline Meeber, a small-town Midwestern girl who goes to the big city, Chicago, to seek her fortune and her future. The first few pages of the novel quickly identify the new social world Carrie walks into and Dreiser saw growing up around him, a social world that gave rise to consumer culture.

The Meaning of Goods in an Urban and Mobile Society

It is notable that the protaganist of *Sister Carrie* is a woman seeking her fortune, not a man. This upends the conventions of Western myths and fairy tales and opens a new tradition that Sinclair Lewis continued in *Main Street* and any number of feminist novels of the past decade have extended. Carrie is eighteen years old, she intends to find her pot of gold and to have adventures, and if "romance" holds any privileged place in her scheme of things, that is at least not clear in the beginning.

A woman seeking a fortune is not parallel to a man seeking his. While Sister Carrie is looking for work and therefore is concerned to find a place in the production side of the economy, she is very sensitive, more so than a man is likely to be, to signs of status and person displayed in items of consumption. She notices every detail of the dress of the man on the train who speaks to her. Dreiser comments:

> A woman should some day write the complete philosophy of clothes. No matter how young, it is one of the things she wholly comprehends. There is an indescribably faint line in the matter of a man's apparel which somehow divides for her those who are worth glancing at and those who are not. Once an individual has passed this faint line on the way downward he will get no glance from her. There is another line at which the dress of a man will cause her to study her own. This line the individual at her elbow now marked for Carrie. She became conscious of an inequality. Her own plain blue dress, with its black cotton tape trimmings, now seemed to her shabby. She felt the worn state of her shoes.[1]

When a woman seeks her fortune, the group of independent, individualist, questing human beings has widened. It has also changed. Now success—and even the road to success—is not paved by work and career alone but by lifestyle and consumption.

It is notable that Carrie seeks her fortune, not by ship like Odysseus or raft like Huck Finn or foot like Tom Jones, but by train. Train travel, by the 1880s when the novel's action takes place, was a standard means of transportation, though only two generations old. Train travel differs from travel by foot or horse or wagon in a number of respects. It is, of course, faster. It is more comfortable. And it is socially distinctive. In train travel, one is a public person. One travels in the company of strangers where intimacy is a possibility—an opportunity or a danger—but where resources to avoid intimacy are also available. This made train travel unique as a form of transportation, but also made it a metaphor for the experience of the city dweller. If, as sociologists have argued, the modern world is a "world of strangers" and the city is a place of habitation where strangers are likely to meet, Carrie has become a city person from the moment she steps on the train.[2] And, indeed, she does meet a stranger, the sinister Charles Drouet.

Carrie arrives in Chicago and, after a night's sleep at her sister's, goes out looking for a job, walking through the wide streets and past the giant buildings. The scene, again, is a familiar one in literature, including nonfiction. Think of Benjamin Franklin, the young printer, walking alone through the streets of Philadelphia, looking for a job carrying two loaves of bread under his arm. By the end of the nineteenth century, it is an image of special importance. Dreiser himself delighted in walking through the streets of cities. As a newspaper reporter in the 1890s, he walked the streets both as vocation and as pastime:

> My favorite pastime when I was not out on an assignment or otherwise busy, was to walk the streets and view the lives and activities of others, not thinking so much how I might advantage myself and my affairs as how, for some, the lightning of chance was always striking in somewhere and disrupting plans, leaving destruction and death in its wake, for others luck or fortune.[3]

The scene of Carrie in the streets, then, is a forceful reminder that she is alone, anonymous, fresh and hopeful but nonetheless a reed in the gale of the city, unidentified, unsupported.

Carrie seeks a job at several department stores and Dreiser feels called upon to insert a small historical and sociological essay on department stores. Carrie is attracted to them because she has seen their ads in the *Daily News,* a Chicago paper she read in her hometown in Wisconsin. She walks into a department store and it is as if she has walked into fairyland:

> Carrie passed along the busy aisles, much affected by the remarkable display of trinkets, dress goods, stationery, and jewelry. Each separate counter was a show place of dazzling interest and attraction. She could not help feeling the claim of each trinket and valuable upon her personally, and yet she did not stop. There was nothing there which she could not have used—nothing which she did not long to own.[4]

The department store, like the city street, like the railroad coach or compartment, was a new kind of public place. It changed the entire act and art of shopping. One did not simply enter a shop and ask the storekeeper to go to his shelves or backroom for an item. In the department store, things were displayed, and the shopper had a range of things to observe. In Chicago in the 1890s, department stores were called "monsters," "inventions of the devil," "vultures," and "producers of crime, sorrow, and disgrace." These epithets were hurled not by communists or anarchists but by the North Side Businessmen's Association. Republicans in the state legislature introduced a law that would require a $20 license for any retail store carrying one line of merchandise, with the fee doubling for each additional line of goods. If a department store carried ten lines of merchandise, the fee would be $10,240. The measure did not pass but this legislative effort suggests the degree of business anxiety over the department stores.[5]

The department stores first, but then other retailers, began to change their business practices. *Speed* of sale became a factor it had never been before and the idea of "stock-turn" or, as we say today, turnover, became important. By the early 1900s, even dry goods and clothing stores in Emporia, Kansas, which had traditionally received carloads of goods twice a year, "began to get goods monthly in smaller packages; quick sales, quick turnovers in these stores were making more profits."[6] Customers became relatively more anonymous. They were less part of a buyer-seller relationship, more part of an audience for a spectacle of sales. With goods made visible before them, "eye-catching" appeal became a more vital attribute of a product, and merchandising for the retailer began to be less a matter of knowing the stock and more a matter of presenting it well.

Indeed, department stores made themselves great stages. The clerks acted as friendly, but elegant, hosts. People thought of the stores as social centers and dressed up to go shopping. Department stores displayed original paintings of new artists and claimed to do so better than museums. Department store owner John Wanamaker said: "In museums, most everything looks like junk even when it isn't because there is no care or thought in the display. If women would wear their fine clothes like galleries wear their pictures, they'd be laughed at."[7]

Daniel Boorstin has argued that the department stores democratized luxury by putting expensive goods on display before any customer who cared to peruse them.[8] It was not that simple. The department stores carried very high-priced goods and would sometimes provide an appropriately elegant, and forbidding, setting for them. Macy's introduced a ladies' waiting room in 1891 which, according to Macy's ads, was "the most luxurious and beautiful department devoted to the comfort of ladies to be found in a mercantile establishment in the city. The style of decoration is Louis XV and no expense has been spared in the adornment and furnishing of this room."[9] Luxury was not democratized so much as made markedly more visible, more public, and more often articulate—through advertising—than it had been before. The department stores did less to provide equality in consumption than to encourage a democracy of aspirations and desire. They contributed to the democratization of envy.

Carrie Meeber walked, but department stores could succeed at the end of the nineteenth century because at that time American cities became "riding" rather than "walking" habitations. Until the mid-nineteenth century, Eastern cities huddled close to their waterfronts. Travel was on foot or, if one was very wealthy, by carriage. In the 1820s hackney coaches began to appear. These were followed by the horse-drawn omnibuses that carried as many as forty people cheaply, comfortably, and quickly enough for persons of middling wealth to live beyond the walking distance of their employment and become omnibus commuters. One traveler in the 1850s marveled at New York's Broadway omnibus that brought together rich and poor, "men, women and children, in silks and rags—brokers and bankers, tinkers and tailors, laborers and lawyers."[10] But only later, when extensive intraurban rail lines developed and then cable lines and electric surface lines and then, by the turn of the century, elevated trains and subways, was a wider metropolitan area made available to large numbers of people at relatively little cost. This easy access to transportation changed the spatial possibilities of daily life. People did not any longer have to live within walking distance of their place of work; suburbs developed and the middle class especially began to move out and to become commuters to work. People did not have to shop in their own neighborhoods any more. They could take the train to some other part of town or to "downtown" to do their shopping. Thanks to newspaper advertising, they could learn what goods were available at what prices in all parts of the city if there were stores that sought a city-wide clientele for their wares.

The department stores were just such stores and they were crucial to subsidizing the growth of urban newspapers. In the 1880s, the ratio of editorial matter to advertising in daily metropolitan newspapers changed from about 70–30 to 50–50 or lower. Advertising revenue represented 44 percent of total newspaper income in 1880, 55 percent by 1900.[11] Of the expanding use of advertising in the late nineteenth century, the most important by far was department store advertising. Charles Russell, a New York reporter and editor, remarked that at the end of the nineteenth century the newspaper became "an appendage of the department store."[12] In Robert and Helen Lynd's survey of Muncie, Indiana, newspapers of 1890, 23 percent of all advertising in the papers was department store advertising.[13] Department store ads were important not only in size but in style. Wanamaker's, for instance, sought self-consciously to "journalize" advertising, to make ads more newsy, informationally accurate and up-to-date with copy changing daily.[14]

Carrie Meeber, at home in a small Wisconsin town, was one person, but alone in Chicago was someone else. If she was attracted to the goods in the department stores, her attraction was closely connected to her new and uncertain social position.

Where people live and die in the same small community, the people they associate with as adults are the same people they grew up with as children. When they look around for affirmation of their identity, when they seek, as Erik Erikson puts it, a sense of continuity in their own lives, the evidence is all around them.[15] People derive a sense of self as the self is reflected back in the opinions of other people. When "significant others" remain much the same throughout one's life, identity has a clear foundation. Indeed, it may never become problematic. Further, when a person's status in the community is established by birth or family, the consequences of one's own achievements or failures are not so far reaching. The ne'er-do-well son of the aristocrat is still an aristocrat. The peasant's son who learns to read and write and study the Bible is still a peasant and defers to the aristocrat. Status is no more problematic than identity.

No community was ever quite like the ideal I describe but many communities were more like it than almost any community has been since the industrial and democratic revolutions produced a highly mobile, urban, class society in which social mobility became a real possibility and a powerful ideology. Geographic and social mobility in modern society are especially potent forces for personal disruption. As Peter Berger and Thomas Luckmann have argued, mobility has severe psychological consequences.[16] Relations weaken with the people who socialized the mobile individual. The norms, rules, attitudes, and behaviors that to the child seemed natural, seem foreign to the adult who has moved away. What was internalized is now seen as external, arbitrary, even alien. The individual is separated from the past. This often is a great but wrenching liberation. One's roots are left behind and individuals thus become more and more dependent on people immediately around them to reaffirm their identities. Identity becomes less tightly connected to one's family of origin, more closely connected to one's associates, whoever they may be.

In contemporary society, geographic or social mobility does not just happen, people *expect* it to happen, so the family exercises a different kind of control than it once did. The family provides a socialization process for its children that anticipates their mobility. Children learn to pay attention not just to their parents but to their peer group and to the mass media. Their parents may encourage them to separate themselves from the family, to be independent. The battle in middle-class American households, when there is a battle, is not whether or not the child can go out with friends for the evening but *how long* the child will be allowed to stay out. From the parents' point of view, this is a struggle to retain authority but it is not intended to keep the child from friends. What the parents want the child to learn is that they must fight the battle, but the parents fully expect and intend to ultimately win a war only by losing each fight. The family remains crucial, but more and more, a common culture, that includes advertising and the mass media, plays its part. Berger and Luckmann argue that young people are encouraged to acquire "a prefabricated identity, advertised, marketed, and guaranteed by the identity-producing agencies."[17] This is too harsh. If the commercial and national forces for "prefabrication" through persuasion have grown, the local forces toward standard personalities through coercive religion, education, and family have weakened. This is worth remembering before condemning too quickly the new patterns of socialization.

Take, for instance, the evidence the Lynds' *Middletown* study provides on "anticipatory socialization." The Lynds found that Muncie, Indiana, mothers of the 1890s generation valued "strict obedience" and "loyalty to the church" as the most important attitudes to instill in their children. Working-class mothers of the 1920s also found these to be the most important social values but "business-class" mothers of the 1920s thought "independence" to be just as important as obedience and more important than loyalty to the church. They also cited "frankness" as being very important. In their new emphasis on independence and frankness, these mothers knew and planned for the fact that their children's world would differ from their own. They encouraged children to confront the new world and to be independent because their families could not teach them all they would need to know. At the same time, the parents feared the children would be lost to them unless frankness was also encouraged.[18]

With a more mobile society and, to some extent, a more open social fabric, realms in which choice rarely figured become open to individual decision making. Most important decisions—who to marry, what career to enter, what religion to adhere to—become matters of selection. As the early 1900s brought improved systems of transportation and communication and a vastly improved system for the distribution of goods to rural parts of the country, consumer "lifestyle" and individual expression and identity-formation through lifestyle became more widely available. William Leiss has ably argued that a society of high-intensity consumption is not so much one in which new needs are manufactured and foisted upon consumers as one in which citizens lose a secure understanding of what their needs are and to what extent commodities can satisfy them. Needs become "ambiguous" as individual choices multiply."[19]

The mass media help escort people into the wider world of choice, broadening horizons, blurring provincial demarcations. On the one hand, the media enlarge people's sense of their own and the world's possibilities; on the other hand, the media lead people to constantly compare themselves to others or to images of others. As Daniel Bell has suggested, "Mass consumption meant the acceptance, in the crucial area of lifestyle, of the idea of social change and personal transformation."[20] But as well, it left people in flux, in uncertainty, full of anxiety about social standing and meaning, vulnerable to the turns of fashion more than playful with them, just as Carrie Meeber walking down Van Buren Street in Chicago was vulnerable to the social forces around her.

In this world, external signs hold great importance and people leap at anything that can be used to signify. As anthropologist Claude Lévi-Strauss suggested of primitive totems, and as Mary Douglas has more recently suggested of commercial commodities, they are "good to think."[21] In other words, they are symbols that people use as maps for charting a complex and uncertain world. People in the new mobile, urban world of the late nineteenth century required new symbol systems. They needed to locate and identify themselves and they sought what they believed would prove "good to think." People could, and did, recreate villages in cities and reestablish location rooted in family and neighborhood. At the same time, they could not ignore the presence of a wider world: the mass media would not let them be long insensitive to it. Most people needed to connect themselves to the wider world, the socially and geographically mobile, most of all.

There were various ways to find identity and placement in the larger world. Income was especially convenient because it provided a *ranked* identification, because it was subject to transformation, and because it tended to be a good, though by no means perfect, index of a variety of socially meaningful traits, including political power and social standing. It had the disadvantage of being, by itself, invisible. Increasingly, however, an index for income was visible and available in the status and quality ranking of consumer goods. Material goods became "visible symbols of inner worth" in worlds where few other symbols had permanence or continuity. As Berger and Luckmann put it, where there is high mobility "conspicuous patterns of consumption take the place of continuous interpersonal contacts within an individual's biography. . . . Material objects rather than human beings must be called upon to testify to the individual's worth."[22] Consumer goods begin to be an index and a language that place a person in society and relate the person in symbolically significant ways to the national culture.

During the nineteenth century, more and more goods manufactured in factories rather than in homes poured onto the market. More and more necessities of life were bought outside the home and outside the neighborhood, too. An excellent example is clothing. In 1790, 80 percent of all clothing was made in the home for family use. A century later, for men and boys, 90 percent was made outside the home.[23] As for women's clothing, while much was still made at home, it was made on a store-bought sewing machine according to patterns purchased from women's magazine companies like Butterick's. As late as 1910, newspaper advertisements for yard goods outnumbered those for ready-made dresses in the newspapers of Muncie, Indiana, but by the 1920s Middletown, too, responded primarily to ads for ready mades.[24]

The availability of store-bought, ready-made clothing helped extend and democratize fashion. While clothing or ornament is used universally to mark sex, age, and status, "fashion" is primarily a Western and modern phenomenon, at least on a mass scale.

Fashion differs from dress in that it is not a traditional expression of social place but a rapidly changing statement of social aspiration. It emerged, as Ann Hollander writes, "as a form of presumption—the desire to imitate and resemble something better, more free, more beautiful and shining, which one could not actually aspire to be."[25] The early emergence of fashion was limited by the number of people able and willing to be fashionable and by the supply of fashionable things. In the nineteenth century, more people could participate in fashion as the development of machine-manufactured clothing made up-to-date goods more widely available. Fashion set a person in social space, linked to and differentiated from social groups. It also located a person in social time—in relation to others, being avant garde or *au courant* or behind-the-times, and in relation to one's own past, offering an index and symbol of the distance one had traveled from past experience and a readiness, or lack of readiness, to encounter something new.[26]

Fashion in dress, better than any other example of consumption, is a material, externalized symbol system that connects people to social worlds and individualizes them in those worlds. For more and more people in the late nineteenth century and after, clothing came to be expressive and signifying. But so, too, did other material objects. Where buying replaced making, then looking replaced doing as a key social action, reading signs replaced following orders as a crucial modern skill. Shorthands for expression and signification became more and more desirable and useful to urbanites; manufacturers exploited the desires of people for social location and identity with the production of "brand name" goods. Brand name goods *appeared* at the end of the nineteenth century for a number of reasons; they were *accepted* for the reasons discussed here. In a mobile society, commercial products with familiar names provide people with some sense of identity and continuity in their lives. And in a society with a high concern for social mobility, material possessions of known and ranked standing provide statements of social status and may provide entry into desired social worlds.

But it will not do to hang everything on this "identity" argument by itself. It explains too much, I think, and therefore too little. It is exactly the kind of argument by sociologists that rightly raises the hackles of historians. It is notoriously difficult to make such an argument historically specific. People have used a growing number of manufactured consumer goods for some time, beginning at least in the eighteenth century. Compared to the world of today, Carrie Meeber's notion of material variety looks anemic and the proliferation of brand names at the turn of the century paltry. At what point can it be said that people actively construct their identities from material things? If this is in some measure always true, when does it become predominantly true? And to what extent does it remain, even today, a rather modest truth, with people's surest sense of self and deepest foundation of social standing derived from family and occupation, not lifestyle?

That is one problem; there is another. People do not necessarily find whatever they may seek in the way of status and identity from consumer goods. Indeed as Marcus Felson has suggested, consumption today may do more to mask social standing than to express it. From the point of view of society, consumer lifestyles may confuse social ranking; from the point of view of the aspiring individual, however, this very confusion may serve personal ends.[27]

The growing importance of standard, identifiable products and brands may be conceived in a manner less dependent on psychological assumptions about identity. Some brand names, like "Yves St. Laurent," offer identity and status, but others, like McDonald's or Coca-Cola or Kentucky Fried Chicken, do not. Their promise is not identity but familiarity and reliability of product. Where consumers do not make their own goods and do not buy at neighborhood stores where they know and are known to the merchant, brand names become a form of consumer protection. The brand-name good, as economist George Akerlof argues, is "an institution which counteracts the effects of quality uncertainty. . . ."[28] Brand-name goods and other standard products such as the "convenience foods" that it is fashionable to complain about have this quality. Frozen concentrate rather than fresh orange juice has this advantage, as a waitress explained to writer John McPhee in his fruitless search for a Florida restaurant that served fresh orange juice: "Fresh is either too sour or too watery or too something. Frozen is the same every day. People want to know what they're getting."[29] A survey of five hundred housewives found that purchasing a major brand or a brand previously used is taken to be a better means of reducing risk in a purchasing situation than government reports or word-of-mouth information.[30] The housewives are not seeking status or identity when they opt for the brand name; they are minimizing risk to their families. In the late nineteenth century, they were doing the same thing. The world was changing so that available products were less often local and known and local retailers were more often large institutions serving a wider public than before. Further, the consumers themselves were less often local and known. Geographic mobility was high and immigration was at a peak. There was plenty of incentive, then, for shoppers to seek the guarantee of predictability that brand names would provide.

In Sister Carrie's world of the 1880s, all this was just beginning. Carrie Meeber was dazzled by goods, not by brand names. But in another generation, Sinclair Lewis's George Babbitt would be proud of his brand names. They connected his life in Zenith, Ohio, to the high and mighty of America. "These standard advertised wares—toothpastes, socks, tires, cameras, instantaneous hot-water heaters—were his symbols and proofs of excellence; at first the signs, then the substitutes, for joy and passion and wisdom."[31] For historian Daniel Boorstin, the goods of mass consumption are not to be denounced so glibly. He refers to the relations people establish with one another through the insignia of mass consumption, through the sharing of Pierre Cardin shirts or Harley-Davidson motorcycles as "consumption communities." This is a tendentious phrase; it incorporates into a slogan the very question that needs to be addressed about a consumer society: *is* there any community of consumption? And if there is, what kind of community is it? Does the sharing of goods—not the sitting down at table and breaking bread together but the impersonal sharing, the fact that John Smith from Buffalo and Jill Jones from Santa Barbara both wear Jordache jeans—does that establish a sense of community between them?

The answer is no, it does not establish any kind of community a person could put much stock in. Boorstin here is ideologue more than analyst. But may not Sinclair Lewis be an ideologue in the other direction? Is there not something to the sharing of things and the names for things that helps build a culture—at least a world of shared meanings if not shared ideals and relationships? Goods themselves are not (only) the enemies of culture and not (only) the debasement of culture and not (only) something foisted unwillingly upon defenseless consumers. Goods are constituents of culture and the sharing of their names is a part of what it means to partake of culture.

Culture, anthropologist Mary Douglas asserts, *is* the sharing of names—and this includes the sharing of names of material objects. When she looks at consumer goods in modern society, Douglas sees not a bundle of utilities, as the economist would, nor even a bundle of social ties, as I have been suggesting, but a bundle of symbols, elements in cultural classification schemes. For Douglas then, when people buy goods, they are not just trying to satisfy "needs" in a narrow sense but are trying "to construct an intelligible universe" with the goods they choose. She says:

> Enjoyment of physical consumption is only a part of the service yielded by goods; the other part is the enjoyment of sharing names. . . . the anthropological argument insists that by far the greater part of utility is yielded . . . in sharing names that have been learned and graded. This is culture.[32]

Surely there is something to this. A personal name is sometimes called a "handle" in American slang and this is a revealing term. Through the name, we handle or come in contact with and touch and hold people and things. Think of expatriates or travelers. Americans who travel abroad and meet fellow Americans do not typically reach out to each other by discussing the Declaration of Independence or the spirit of free enterprise. They talk about peanut butter and playfully compare the merits of Peter Pan and Skippy and Jif, or they discuss chocolate chip cookies, Frye boots, a 1957 Chevy, what they would give for a real milkshake, whether they have been on Woodward Avenue in Detroit or Melrose in Los Angeles, or to the Broome Street bar in Soho in New York. They take pleasure in the very saying of these names and in the familiarity the words establish.

But what kind of society is ours that produces the particular system of naming we have? What is special about a system in which words like "Chevy," "polyester," and "Holiday Inn" take on importance? Who does the naming in our society, who has the power of words, and how is that power used? Douglas's position, by itself, does not get to these issues. Her views provide no room for politics and no standards for judging the place of goods in society. For her, it seems, people make good cultural use of goods in any society at any time, and the number or kind of goods they use is beyond comment.[33]

The concepts of "identity" and "culture" and the changing needs of people in a mobile society do not suffice to explain the shift to a consumer society in the period 1850 to 1930. Nor do they explain "materialist" values. As Neil Harris points out, a consumer society is not the same thing as a materialist society; nineteenth-century Americans were regarded by most observers, including the trenchant Tocqueville, as archetypal materialists, even in 1830. But materialism was connected at that date to both consumption *and* production. People still made things at home and satisfied material longings that way. This became less true by the end of the nineteenth century. Industrialization displaced home industry and, in a rather short span of years, people found themselves unable "to match, in precision, variety, attractiveness, and especially cost, the provision of objects produced by American manufacturers, from clothing and furniture to food and drink." The changing nature and significance of consumption, then, grew not from autonomous changes in the life of the citizen or the family but from the intersection of such changes with the emergence of large-scale consumer goods industries. I turn, then, to a consideration of changes on the production side of the economy.[34]

Consumer Goods and the Production Side of the Economy

Whether it was Brandreth's Vegetable Universal Pills or Radam's Microbe Killer or Lydia Pinkham's Compound, nineteenth-century newspapers were covered with patent medicine advertising. The Lynds found that 25 percent of all advertising in the Middletown papers of 1890 was patent medicine advertising, slightly ahead of department store advertising.[35] When *Press and Printer* of Boston tabulated advertisers who made regular use of advertising, they found that 425 of the 2,583 enterprises counted sold medicines and drugstore items, more than double the next leading category.[36] It is hard to exaggerate the importance of patent medicines in the history of advertising. "The backbone of the typical advertising agency's business in the nineteenth century was patent medicine, and the Ayer firm was no exception to this rule," writes Ralph Hower, N. W. Ayer's historian. Patent medicine advertising made up a quarter of Ayer's total advertising volume in its first decade, the 1870s. It was "the mainstay of every agency of importance at the time." Some agencies even became part owners of the patent medicine companies—Rowell, Lord and Thomas of Chicago, and Pettengill and Company of Boston. Ayer did the same thing less deliberately, gaining an interest in exchange for unpaid bills.[37]

Ads for patent medicines intended two things. First, they sought to establish a clear, memorable *identification* for their product. This was more important than the particular "promise" about what the medicine would do. It was most important to establish a name people could remember, feel comfortable with, and believe to represent an important or well-established firm. The identification would often be with something exotic as in Hayne's Arabian Balsam, Hoofland's Greek Oil, Osgood's Indian Cholagogue, or Jayne's Spanish Alterative. Things remote, ancient, mystical were often used, relying where possible on established folk beliefs. Dr. Lin's Chinese Blood Pills suggested longevity. Turkish Wafers—for men only—suggested the romance and sex of veils and harems and hookahs.

Most patent medicine advertising was repetitious and dull. Many ads, all identical, would be placed in the same issue of the same newspaper. Dr. Donald Kennedy's Medical Discovery and Dr. T. Felix Gourard's complexion cure did not change copy during more than forty years of advertising. There was great weight placed on establishing and maintaining product identification, by the continuity and repetition of a name or trademarked image. Regarding the latter, James Harvey Young writes:

> The trade-mark, indeed, was a fixed star in a universe of flux. The ownership of medicines might change again and again, and so might the formula. The diseases for which medicines were advertised might vary over time, and sometimes even names were altered. Trade-marks, however, protected first by common law and then by federal statute, endured forever.[38]

Secondary to product identification was product *identity*. By identification, I mean simply the association of a name or picture with a given product. Product identity, by contrast, associates the product with its function and, to some extent, with its intended market. So, for instance, some of the patent medicines promised to be especially potent for women's illnesses or for common colds or for general nervousness or depression or for baldness or for sexual disorders. But most often, it appears, the patent medicines were relatively weak in product identity. This has to do with the products themselves: they were not standardized, they were not reliable, and they did not do the things they claimed. Not surprisingly, their claims changed from time to time. Further, although the medicine ads invoked medical authority or testimonials from ministers or scientific terminology and Latin names, the advertisers were well aware that they faced a skeptical public. Some ads tried to make use of the skepticism. In booklets advertising his Microbe Killer, William Radam attacked other patent medicines. Gullible people, he explained, would buy these worthless products because "the public likes to be humbugged." He went on: "People should not be led away by every charlatan who jumps up before them and talks; but as long as the world lasts there will probably be fools in it, and fools are a godsend to rogues."[39] Similarly, the manufacturers of Vin Mariani used as advertising a pamphlet mailed to physicians entitled, "The Effrontery of Proprietary Medicine Advertisers." The competition among medicines, carried out largely through advertising, was severe, and it has been estimated that less than 2 percent of remedies launched in New York had even modest success.[40]

In the mid nineteenth century, patent medicines were the most prominent advertised product. In the 1870s and 1880s, department store advertising came to match that of patent medicines. But, in retrospect, the development on the production and distribution side of the economy most important in creating an advertising-oriented consumer culture was the emergence of advertising for nationally branded goods. This was spawned by a relatively small group of new, technologically and organizationally innovative manufacturers. Nearly all of the first national advertisers were enterprises that used new continuous-process machinery to produce low-priced, packaged consumer goods. The massive increase in output made possible by the new machinery led manufacturers to build large marketing and purchasing networks and to engage in widespread advertising. These enterprises included many that remain to this day the leading advertisers in the country: Procter & Gamble, Colgate-Palmolive, H. J. Heinz, Borden, Eastman Kodak, Quaker Oats, Pillsbury, Campbell Soups, Carnation, Libby McNeil & Libby, and American Tobacco. They produced cigarettes, soap, canned foods, breakfast cereals, matches, and photographic film and equipment. These are, with a partial exception of photographic equipment, exclusively "experience" goods. Thus they are products whose advertising is likely to include very little direct information and is likely to focus on the reputability of the manufacturer. Probably the single largest newspaper advertiser in the 1890s was a firm of this sort, Royal Baking Powder.[41]

The Quaker Oats Co. may be taken as an example. Oats were raised in quantity in the late nineteenth century, especially in Iowa, Ohio, and Illinois. Ferdinand Schumacher, a German immigrant, was the first to develop a branded oat product for human consumption. When he began milling in Ravenna, Ohio, he used the same techniques millers had used since the fifteenth century. He believed his oatmeal to be a cheap and healthy substitute for the American breakfast that immigrants regarded as excessive. At first, then, his products circulated among German-American communities. But oatmeal and oat mush began to grow more popular and Schumacher soon had competitors. The competitors, too, operated on ancient milling techniques until Schumacher's innovation in 1875, a machine to convert hulled kernels into a coarse meal. About the same time, George Cormack at Rockford, Illinois, devised labor-saving systems for moving grain in and out of the mill. In 1877 Asmus J. Ehrrichsen, an employee of Schumacher's, developed the steel-cut process. Instead of crushing the grain through millstones, the hulled oats were cut into meal by fine knife blades, providing a uniform, flaky meal. A year later, Schumacher used porcelain rollers to manufacture rolled oats and converted his whole production to rolled oats which flaked rather than crushed grains.

In the meantime, one of Schumacher's competitors, Henry Parsons Crowell, was quickly adopting all the latest innovations. His mill, also at Ravenna, by 1882 became "the first in the world to maintain under one roof operations to grade, clean, hull, cut, package, and ship oatmeal to interstate markets in a continuous process that in some aspects anticipated the modern assembly line."[42] Crowell called his product "Quaker Oats." The development of highly efficient "continuous-process" methods was the first critical step in establishing a capacity for national advertising of cereals. The new technology expanded the industrial capacity of firms so that increasing production at little increased cost was no longer difficult. The main problem for the cereal manufacturers and others like them was "to move their goods quickly enough or to advertise them effectively enough to keep their high-volume production facilities operating steadily."[43]

Henry Crowell registered the trademark of a "figure of a man in Quaker garb" in 1877, the first registered trademark for a breakfast cereal. Crowell—and then Schumacher, too, when they joined forces with Robert Stuart of Cedar Rapids, Iowa, to create the American Cereal Company—pioneered in packaging, promotion, and advertising. Crowell introduced a folding carton for Quaker oats packaging, a method that had been patented only ten years before. Because the unfolded package lay flat, it could be easily printed on and so the Crowell carton displayed the Quaker emblem in four-color printing with recipes printed on the package. This was the beginning of the end of selling cereal to the retailers in bulk (although in health foods stores, the old methods of retailing have been revived).[44]

In 1886, for the first time, as the historian of Quaker Oats reports, a housewife could read a sales message on a food package: "We would call your special attention to the purity, rapidity of preparation, and the fact that they did not sacrifice sweetness and flavor for the sake of rapid cooking." This was followed by several recipes. It is curious that the message refers to the Quaker Oats company as "they" rather than "we." While the packaging was part of a continuous-process production, the company's copywriters clearly saw the package as something put around the product itself rather than as an integral part of the product and its identity.

The emphasis in advertising for nationally branded products, as for patent medicines, was more on identification than on identity. The advertising profession of the day "seemed to equate quality with quantity" and valued the ubiquity of a product name and trademark above all else.[45] For Quaker Oats, making the Quaker symbol well known was the all-important task. Claims for the specific merits of Quaker oats varied and types of appeals changed. Ads at different times connected Quaker products to "love, pride, cosmetic satisfactions, sex, marriage, good health, cleanliness, safety, labor saving, and status seeking."[46] But the Quaker Oats symbol was permanent and visible everywhere, on billboards, streetcars, newspapers, calendars, magazines, blotters, cookbooks, Sunday church bulletins, metal signs on rural fences, company-sponsored cooking schools, free samples given away house-to-house, booths at county fairs and expositions.

Quaker Oats did not limit itself to advertising as a tool, nor did the other early national advertisers. Advertising was but one aspect of a national marketing effort. According to historian Alfred Chandler, it was by no means the most important feature. More crucial than advertising was the development of national and sometimes global organizations of managers, buyers, and salesmen that the early mass marketing firms created. The new technology of continuous-process production made possible a new social invention—not advertising but the organization chart, a regular hierarchy of responsibility, an administrative structure responsible for marketing as well as the production of the manufactured good. In Chandler's view, the key innovation that made mass marketing possible was not advertising but corporate organization.

What happened with cereal happened with other products I have mentioned, too, and in the same era, between 1880 and 1900. These industries did not gradually drive out competitors to become slowly concentrated—they were oligopolistic almost from the beginning. Once established, it was very difficult for competitors to break into the market. Why? Chandler's answer is:

> The most imposing barrier to entry in these industries was the organization the pioneers had built to market and distribute their newly mass-produced products. A competitor who acquired the technology had to create a national and often global organization of managers, buyers, and salesmen if he was to get the business away from the one or two enterprises that already stood astride the major marketing channels.[47]

While advertising may be today a "barrier to entry" into markets, it was not a barrier in the late nineteenth century.[48] What was a barrier was the extensive marketing organization and the long-term ties between executives and managers and jobbers and retailers that constituted the human side of the organization. That was not easy for newcomers to duplicate. However, if advertising was not guaranteed market power in relation to competitors, it was certainly a form of market power in relation to retailers. Manufacturer advertising gives a firm direct communication to consumers and a way of forcing retailers into distributing their product without making price concessions to the retailer.[49]

By the turn of the century, advertising had become an important element in the American economy. Some of the reasons for the rise of advertising can be understood as "market driven": advertising provided information about what goods were available for sale in a society that no longer consisted of face-to-face economic relations. Some of the early informational advertising and the department store advertising was market driven, in this sense. So, too, was the development of warehouse catalog advertising, such as that of Sears and Roebuck. But some of the development of advertising is better thought of as "producer driven": for firms where technology had solved production problems, advertising arose as part of a marketing effort to sell goods whose supply could be increased easily at little additional production cost. In the case of the patent medicines, advertising was the main marketing tool. For nationally advertised, branded products that arose in continuous-process production industries after 1880, advertising was one important element in a marketing mix that included direct salesmanship, packaging, and the establishment of hierarchical, national marketing organizations.

The distinction between market-driven and producer-driven advertising bears on the controversy over whether advertising creates or simply responds to felt needs. To the extent that advertising arose in response to social and economic changes in a mobile market society, it is difficult to see it as an original or prime cause of consumer culture. To the extent, however, that technological developments in industrial manufacturing precipitated growing investment in distribution and sales and advertising, advertising can be seen as a somewhat independent, not solely reactive, force in American society. I do not think the historical record resolves the debate about advertising's role in creating "needs," but I do think it reveals some of the complexity of the issue and makes it hard for anyone to leap with unqualified certainty to one side ("advertising just responds to social trends") or the other ("advertising is the creator of consumer culture").

The Media and the Agencies as Promoters of Promotion

Having considered, at least briefly, social changes that altered people's desires for goods and susceptibility to advertising and changes in manufacturing that led to markedly greater incentives for businesses to seek national distribution and the advertising that accompanies it, I have addressed the largest factors in the late nineteenth century that paved the way to a goods-intensive consumer culture. But a long footnote needs to be added on additional forces that institutionalized advertising itself as an element in the consumer complex. Advertising is a relationship between a producer (or distributor) who advertises, an agency that creates the ad, a medium that carries the ad, and an audience of consumers to whom the ad is directed. I have thus far considered market-driven forces that enabled the rise of advertising (changes in the lives of the people who represent the market for consumer goods) and producer-driven forces (changes in the technology of industry and the social organization of retailing). There were also changes in the mass media and the emergence of advertising agencies—together these can be taken as "self-generating" sources of advertising. The media live off advertising revenue and the advertising agencies' reason for existence is advertising. The presence of these institutions in the economy has been a force for the growth of advertising.

The first advertising agents were more the servants of the newspapers than of the firms that bought advertising space. Volney B. Palmer (1799–1864) is generally regarded as the first agent, having begun his business in Philadelphia in 1841. He was an agent for newspaper publishers around the country with authority to make contracts with advertisers on behalf of the publishers. Soon thereafter, the typical agent became a true middleman, a space jobber who sold newspaper space to advertisers and then bought the space to fill his orders. This was typical of agents in the 1850s.

As the agency system developed, agents moved from space jobbing to "space wholesaling." The leading agent of the 1860s and 1870s, George Rowell, initiated the practice of buying newspaper space in advance, in large lots, and reselling it in smaller lots to advertisers. In 1867, Carlton and Smith (and later J. Walter Thompson) began the "advertising concession agency" in which the agent made annual contracts with newspapers he served, taking over "most of the risk and management of the *entire* advertising space in the papers."[50] Competition among agents was based in part on the assurances of the agents to advertisers regarding circulation figures of the papers they represented. Rowell began in 1869 to publish a directory of newspaper circulation figures; as this directory became established, it was more and more difficult for newspapers to continue their decades-old habit of lying about circulation.

Nonetheless, the advertising agency remained for some time an institution of very limited scope. It bought and sold space. It did not produce ads. But its activities, however limited, provided businesses a real service, thanks to the growth of national markets and the developments in transportation and communication that made that growth possible. Merchants did not know much about the media for advertising outside their own town or region. Agents emerged to exploit business's ignorance of institutions that had become relevant for commercial success. The advertising agency's growth parallels the rise of credit agencies, which appeared about the same time. Both rated the worth of out-of-town businesses: the credit agency judged businesses one might sell or extend credit to, the advertising agency judged the value of newspapers as media for advertising. Both tried to standardize rating systems, the credit agency trying to make reliable judgments about net worth and the advertising agency trying to establish newspaper circulations reliably.[51]

This is not to say that businesses all quickly recognized that advertising agencies would be useful—or that advertising itself would be useful to them. From 1840 to 1870, according to advertising historian Ralph Hower, "the agency's chief service . . . was to promote the general use of advertising." In the 1870s and after, agencies actively propagandized for the idea of advertising. In 1876 N. W. Ayer & Son began publishing *The Advertiser's Guide,* a quarterly magazine with reprinted newspaper articles, jokes, and short news items "together with material urging the advantages of advertising." In 1886 Ayer developed its motto, "Keeping Everlastingly At It Brings Success," meant not so much to encourage its own employees as to remind businessmen of the advantages of advertising regularly.[52]

The first promotional work of the agencies, then, was to sell the idea of advertising to business. At N. W. Ayer and other agencies, this work continued into the twentieth century, indeed, to this day. Ayer's first efforts to be more than a space broker—to write copy, obtain illustrations, and plan whole campaigns—were designed as ways to promote the idea of advertising to Ayer's own potential clients. Between 1900 and 1910, Ayer advertised its own services in *Profitable Advertising* and *The Bill Poster* and for years thereafter in *Printer's Ink.* Between 1919 and 1932 Ayer regularly placed full-page ads in *Saturday Evening Post* and *Literary Digest,* speaking in general terms of the philosophy of advertising at Ayer.

The advertising agency began to shift from an institution serving the media to an agency serving the advertiser when George Rowell developed the "open contract" system in 1875. Rowell announced:

> One thing we clearly perceived . . . , that advertising agencies succeeded best when studying the interests of advertisers not newspapers. . . . We have fully decided to announce as a rule for our future guidance (but which we have followed pretty closely for the past three years) that we will not hereafter be a party to any competition for advertising contracts.[53]

N. W. Ayer followed suit, taking Rowell's scheme a step further to a full "open contract" in which an advertiser agreed to an exclusive arrangement with an agent for a period of time. There would not be competition for the advertiser's business on each occasion for advertising. The agent would learn over time the best way to handle a given advertiser's account. The contract would be "open," meaning that specifications for where to buy advertising space would be flexible, the advertiser making final decisions.[54]

Only after this change did advertising art and copy become part of the responsibility of the agency. Between 1880 and 1900, agencies began to write copy for their clients. As the volume of advertising increased, skill in writing copy became more important. Buying more space or using heavier type or larger type sizes was not enough, and agencies that could offer services in writing more persuasive advertisements gained a competitive edge. As early as 1880, N. W. Ayer announced to businessmen that they had skills in the composition and illustration of newspaper ads. Only in 1900, though, did Ayer establish a separate Copy Department. The first systematically trained copywriting staff began at Lord and Thomas (later to become Foote, Cone & Belding) in 1904 under the guidance of Albert Lasker and John E. Kennedy.[55]

As agencies became established, they became an independent

force promoting the idea of advertising, and so did their trade journals and trade associations. The early years of *Printer's Ink*, begun in 1888 as a promotional tool for George P. Rowell's agency, were dominated by its efforts at "interpreting and justifying the work of the general advertising agent to advertisers and potential advertisers." While the boosterism receded somewhat in the early twentieth century, *Printer's Ink* in the 1890s was full of homilies like "Advertising is the steam propeller of business success" and "United they stand, divided they fall—business and advertising."[56] When advertising clubs began to appear, they, too, became boosters for the idea of advertising in the business world. The first, the Sphinx Club, was organized in New York in 1896. A national association of clubs, the Associated Advertising Clubs of America, held its first meeting in 1905 and by 1916 had more than fifteen thousand members. *Printer's Ink* held in 1915 that the chief value of this club movement was "the education of businessmen generally to the importance of advertising as a business force."[57] The advertising agencies, however successful they may have been in stimulating the growth of advertising in general, were surely successful in promoting the use of agencies by businesses. In examining directories of advertisers, historian Daniel Pope found that 20 percent of firms listed as advertisers in New York in 1901 used advertising agencies, but that this increased to 35 percent in 1911. In Boston, similarly, the figure jumped from 20 percent in 1901 to nearly 50 percent in 1911.[58]

The media, too, increasingly dependent on advertising revenue, actively promoted the use of advertising. The media try to convince businesses that it pays to advertise and that, in particular, it pays to advertise in one specific medium. Today, the pages of advertising trade journals are full of advertisements from radio stations, television stations and networks, magazines, and newspapers. Each extols its own ability to attract the largest consumer audience or the most affluent consumer audience or the largest audience per dollar spent on advertising. While the media today are particularly competitive, this is not a new development. The *San Diego Union*, for instance, in the 1890s, took pains to inform prospective and current advertisers that advertising was worthwhile. The front page "ears" in 1891 often included messages to advertisers. From June 18 to June 25, 1891, for example, the left-hand ears read: "The Brainiest Advertisers in this enterprising city use the daily and weekly Union right along. They wouldn't stay if it didn't pay them." If that was not encouragement enough, the right-hand ear said: "It pays to Advertise. In the Spring. In the Summer. In the Fall. In the Winter."

The advertising agencies, meanwhile, were growing not only larger and more important but more self-important. Agencies, especially the larger agencies with national advertisers as clients, sought to gain "professional" standing for advertising men. Thus they eagerly supported a move toward "scientific" advertising by sponsoring market research and by welcoming the language and literature of psychology into advertising work. Old-timers like George Rowell were not friendly to psychology, but others seemed to be obsessed with discovering what "human nature" is. American ad men were particularly taken with the work of Walter Dill Scott at Northwestern, an academic who became the earliest guru of scientific advertising.[59]

The psychology that entered market research and advertising was eclectic. Behaviorists, Freudians, and a host of others co-existed. One of the most eminent psychologists of his day, John Watson, when forced from his position at Johns Hopkins, left the academic world for a job at J. Walter Thompson where he quickly rose to a position as vice-president. Watson is representative of psychologists in market research in his fundamental assumption that all people are alike. As he wrote in 1935, "As a psychologist, I decry the fact that we are all trained so much alike—that there is so little individuality in the world. But, as an advertising man, I rejoice; my bread and butter depends on it."[60] But the first development of significance in market research was not to see the common elements in human nature but to see the obvious differences; especially to recognize that there are two sexes and that women, not men, are the primary consumers in American culture. "The proper study of mankind is MAN," said one ad in *Printer's Ink*, ". . . but the proper study of markets is WOMAN."[61] It was a cliché among advertisers by the 1920s that women are the "purchasing agents" of their families; the trade journals cited the figure that 85 percent of all consumer spending is done by women.

Even shaving cream and safety razors were advertised to wives. The view of the man as hapless, a bumbler—a figure who reappeared in comic strips like "Blondie" or television sitcoms like "Ozzie and Harriet," was well known in ads in the 1920s:

> What does a man know about complexion, the skin? Nothing. He rips and hacks away at his face and then washes it with strong soap, sprinkles on a little powder, and believes he is a beauty parlor wizard.
>
> You, the woman of the family, understand what the care of the skin means. You realize that a good lotion is invaluable. Protect that foolish husband of yours against himself; start that college-boy son of yours in the right path—put a bottle of Facefriend in the bathroom closet and see that they use it after shaving. They know no better—help them.[62]

Or, again:

> Jim always buys the same old ties, doesn't he? Year after year . . . dark blue with white dots is a standby. Men are unbelievably primitive in such matters. Here are ties, modern in pattern and stylish in fabric. Go to the nearest haberdashery and say: "I desire to select some neckties for my husband" (Sweetheart, Son or Father, or Brother). Dig Jim out of the dark-blue-and-white-dot habit. Make him stylish whether he wants to be or not. Help him in his utter helplessness.[63]

If the difference between men and women came to be seen as important, so did the difference between the affluent and people of moderate means. In Britain, advertising literature between the wars "strongly emphasized that the low-paid were able to buy only a limited range of products."[64] In the United States, this was also clear. The advertiser understood the difference between "quality" and "mass" audiences, as Walter Lippmann observed in 1922 in *Public Opinion:*

> . . . in respect to most commodities sold by advertising, the customers are neither the small class of the very rich nor the very poor. They are the people with enough surplus over bare necessities to exercise discretion in their buying. The paper, therefore, which goes into the homes of the fairly prosperous is by and large the one which offers most to the advertiser. It may also go into the homes of the poor, but except for

certain lines of goods, an analytical advertising agent does not rate that circulation as a great asset.[65]

While the language of psychology, in the 1920s and again in the 1950s, attracted the greatest interest and controversy in advertising, sophistication about basic sociological variables like class and gender has had a more pronounced impact on advertising practice.

The advertising agencies by the 1920s were becoming institutions of considerable resources and confidence. But advertising agents were not only men of confidence; they were confidence men. Their livelihood depended on selling to business the idea that advertising was an effective marketing tool. It would be naive to read their sales pitches to the business community as honest accounts of the power of advertising. Yet this is what Stuart Ewen has done in *Captains of Consciousness,* probably the best-known book among nonspecialists on the origins of American advertising. For Ewen, advertising is "a cultural apparatus aimed at defusing and neutralizing potential unrest."[66] It was part of a political attack on organized labor in the early decades of this century. What scientific management was to the workplace, advertising was to the cultural realm, an effort at control of the workers. Business sought to "invest the laborer with a financial power and a psychic desire to consume." Through advertising, classes engaged in production—and in politics—became masses, preoccupied with consumption and the passive enactment of corporate-manufactured dreams.[67]

Abstractly, Ewen's account makes sense—a view that sees the system of corporate capitalism as a highly rational and self-conscious juggernaut. Historically, however, it is without foundation. There are three problems with the construction of the argument. First, the evidence is, as I have suggested, inappropriate to the conclusions. Almost all the businessmen Ewen cites are not "captains of industry" showing their self-conscious understanding of the capitalist system but corporals of advertising and marketing, trying to make their case to the business world in terms they think will most delight it.[68]

Second, it does not make sense to imagine that capitalists who wanted to keep down "the workers" would try to do so by placing ads for consumer goods in magazines with an affluent, middle-class readership. Yet advertising was strongly directed toward the middle class and most of Ewen's examples of advertisements come from *Saturday Evening Post* and *Ladies Home Journal* and other magazines whose readership was affluent. And female. Capitalists may not all be mental giants but it seems unlikely that they would try to hold down working-class, largely male, rebellion by writing toothpaste and deodorant ads to a middle-class, largely female, readership.

Third, research reported after publication of Ewen's work suggests that despite growing affluence in the 1920s, the working class did not share very much in the prosperity. It is probable that the workers could not afford very many of the widely advertised goods. One's psychological hunches can then work either way—either this would lead the workers to work harder to be able, one day, to join in middle class prosperity, or it would lead to frustration that might trigger political activity.[69]

Ewen recognizes, near the end of his book, that advertising in the 1920s was not *successful* in changing the habits of the working class, in part because the workers did not have money to consume and in part because advertising tended to be directed toward the affluent. He then restates his thesis more modestly, holding that business in the 1920s created in advertising a "model of social control."[70] That is a more cautious position, but it still assumes a self-consciousness in the business community that I do not believe can be demonstrated. That advertising is a form of social control can scarcely be denied, but that it was a calculated, classwide effort at social control is very doubtful. The development of advertising did not happen accidentally but nor was it a self-conscious business scheme to turn workers into consumers.

The problem of advertising is more complex. Twentieth-century advertising and twentieth-century consumer culture have roots in the changing nature of the market in the late nineteenth century which developed along with changes in modes of transportation and communication, urban growth, and a cultural climate for and social fact of social and geographic mobility. In addition, changes in the manufacturing processes in various industries and the capacity to increase output without substantial increases in product costs encouraged a new emphasis in business on marketing and distribution; the growing independent influence on business of the media and advertising agencies also stimulated the development of advertising.

The social transformation that gave rise to advertising not only made mass-produced and advertised products more important to people but altered the criteria for consumption, the qualities in goods deemed desirable. The growth of a consumer society has been a qualitative as well as a quantitative change. I have now sketched in the general context for this position; the next chapter offers a case study to identify more precisely what it means.

6

The Emergence of New Consumer Patterns: A Case Study of the Cigarette

THE UNITED STATES became the first consumer society beginning in the late nineteenth century with the growth of the department store and the rise of national advertising.

And the United States became the first consumer society in the 1920s with the development of installment buying, the mass marketing of the automobile, and the creation of common national tastes through the movies and radio.

And the United States became the first consumer society in the 1950s with the rapid rise in real family income, the suburbanization of the population and the establishment of new social norms of home ownership and two-car ownership, and the emergence of television as a powerful new advertising medium.

And—the United States never was the first consumer society because England became a consumer society in the eighteenth century. Most of the major industries of early industrialization were consumer goods industries and a wave of "fashion" spread from the aristocracy to the middle class in everything from clothing to crockery to books and clocks.[1]

Not all of these positions can be right, though good arguments can be made for any of them. Carving a conceptual category—"consumer society"—out of the flux of history is to some degree an arbitrary task. There has not been an overnight revolution in the habits or views of Americans (or the British, for that matter) regarding material goods. For instance, a traditional Christian belief in the virtue of thrift still influences American thought and feeling, even though some observers see its death presaged in the expansion of consumer credit in the 1920s, others see it as having been killed off by the "me" generation of the 1970s, and others observe that it has been under heavy fire since the 1700s when traditional views of "luxury" were overturned in economic thought.[2] There is no single point in history before which we were all nature's children, after which we became the sons and daughters of commerce.

I will not go any further in attempting to date the birth of an American consumer culture. Instead, I want to say something about the character of that culture and the nature of modern consumption, visible by the 1920s if not earlier. I want to explore what I shall call the democratization of goods and the emergence of "convenience" as a desirable product characteristic. Convenience is a desired attribute of goods primarily in socially democratic and relatively affluent societies. I will develop this point through a case study of the growing popularity of the cigarette in the 1920s and, in doing so, will make a second point: that major consumer changes are rarely wrought by advertising. Advertising followed rather than led the spread of cigarette usage and it was the convenience and democracy of the cigarette, coupled with specific, new opportunities for its use, that brought the cigarette into American life.

The Democratization of Goods

Everywhere in the 1920s, it seems, there was discussion of the "fast pace" of modern life, a quickened heartbeat to the whole social order. Historian James Truslow Adams, among others, wrote of the quickening "tempo":

> Whether any more "events" are happening in the universe now than in earlier times would lead us into unfathomable bogs of metaphysics, but for our purpose it is enough to grant that more events are happening to each man of which he is conscious. In other words, a resident of New York to-day is getting more sensations and of a more varied sort than the Neanderthal or early man of several hundreds of thousands of years ago. Owing to this number and variety of sensations and his constantly shifting environment, modern man is also called upon to make a far greater number of adjustments to the universe than was his remote relative in the caves and forests of Germany or Java. It is the number of these sensations and adjustments in a given time that makes the tempo of life. As the number and variety of sensations increase, the time which we have for reacting to and digesting them becomes less, as it does also for adjusting ourselves to our environment when that alters at an advancing rate. The rhythm of our life becomes quicker, the wave lengths, to borrow a physical concept, of that kind of force which is our mental life grows shorter.[3]

By the 1920s, lives could be led not only in different ways, depending on class and ethnicity and region, but at different *paces*. There was a new sense of the scarcity of time, accelerated by the increasingly large array of choices available to people. There was more choice, or the sense of more choice, in part because the newspapers, movies, and radio brought to people a strong sense of other social worlds, other possibilities. The advances in mass production methods made goods and luxuries unheard of a generation before potentially available to large numbers of people. In the supermarket there were more product categories, and within these more brands to choose from. Brands proliferated. One study of small-town Midwestern consumers found 101 different brands among 210 purchased pianos and equally impressive numbers of brands of cars, radios, phonographs, and washing machines.[4]

At the same time, there was a democratization of goods. As Daniel Boorstin has observed, products that once held some kind of uniqueness by being available only at certain times of the year or only in certain parts of the country were increasingly available year-round and throughout the country, thanks to canning, refrigerated railroad cars, and other technological and social developments.[5] Not only the means of production but the modes of consumption became "continuous process." Extending Boorstin's observation, products are democratized in three other ways.

First, they become more standard as they come to be produced for a mass audience. They are easier to handle, easier to "do it yourself" without great skill on the part of the user; both a mediocre cook and a great cook make equally good cakes from a cake mix. Both an adept smoker and a novice smoker can get about the same satisfaction from a cigarette, but this is much less so with a pipe or cigar. Both a French chef and an ordinary citizen can order an acceptable meal at McDonald's without a faux pas, but this is not true at Maxim's. Standard products and standard situations for shopping make it easier for the unskilled consumer to avoid embarrassment and to become equal to the adept consumer.[6]

Second, products become not only more standard but milder and easier to use. They become convenient. I will try to suggest in this chapter that convenience is a democratic quality. Convenience is an attribute that has as much to do with the social uses and social meaning of a product as with its engineering. The more convenient a good, the more it is equally available for the use of men and women, adults and children, the hardy and the dainty, the veteran and the novice.

Third, there is democratization when goods are consumed in increasingly public ways. This happened in many respects in the

1920s, as the *Middletown* study suggests.[7] Lunch became a meal consumed away from home, in the presence of nonfamily members. For the middle class, the spare time of adolescents increasingly became time away from home, in cars and at the movies. A decline in the dependence on domestic servants was coupled with increasing reliance on a national market for consumer goods for washing, cooking, and cleaning chores. There was a growth in business luncheons, club memberships, and other voluntary associations for both men and women, providing more extrafamilial public occasions. Media—notably the women's magazines—quickly became consumption tutors, taking over for mother and grandmother—and for good reason. Mother and grandmother could adequately advise so long as the young person's sphere of movement did not extend far beyond the family circle. With changes in employment, mobility (brought on by the automobile), and exposure to a wider world by way of movies and other mass media, mother and grandmother were no longer quite so relevant. Public, rather than private, standards of consumption became more salient. People increasingly saw their own consumption pattern in comparison to a wide group of other people. And one could see not only people of "one's own sort" but could peek at the consumption pattern of very different people. The social order, as the Lynds put it, began to shift from a set of plateaus to a single slope and so there was both a democratization of vision and, as I have already suggested, a democratization of envy.[8]

Another change underlies all of these. Products become more democratic when people become more equal. Manufacturers can try to expand the market for a product whose use has traditionally been limited to one sex, class, race, region, or age group when the relevant social distinction changes its character or loses its force. In the 1920s, this happened as women gained ground toward social and civic equality. Their movement into new social roles made them more than ordinarily susceptible to the siren call of the marketers. Women were newly *public* people and needed, more than before, social currencies acceptable in the public world defined by men. The cigarette was one such social coin and a particularly convenient one: cheap, visible, an identifying mark, both easily flaunted and easily hidden, a topic of talk, a token of comradeship and, to boot, a comfort in anxious moments.

The spread of cigarette smoking, particularly among women, was one of the most visible signs of change in consumption practices in the 1920s, and one that has been cited frequently as evidence of the new powers of advertising and marketing. Between 1918 and 1940, American consumption grew from 1.70 to 5.16 pounds of cigarette tobacco per adult.[9] During the same period, advertising budgets of the tobacco companies bulged, movies pictured elegant men and women smoking, and public relations stunts promoted cigarettes.

Some contemporary observers concluded that advertising *caused* the increase in cigarette smoking among women. For instance, in 1930, Clarence True Wilson, board secretary of the Methodist Episcopal Church, declared: "If the advertising directed to women ceased, it is probable that within five years the smoking woman would be the rare exception."[10] Scholars in recent years have accepted a similar view. Erik Barnouw, for instance, holds that advertising was responsible for bringing women into the cigarette market.[11]

This conclusion is difficult to sustain for a number of reasons, the most obvious of which is that tens of thousands of women began smoking cigarettes in the 1920s *before* a single advertisement was directed toward them. It is more accurate to observe that cigarette smoking among women led tobacco companies to advertise toward the female market than to suggest that advertising created the market in the first place. The mass media played a role in spreading the cigarette habit among women, but it was primarily the information conveyed in news stories, not the persuasion attempted in advertisements, that helped in the first instance to legitimate smoking among women in the 1920s.

The power of the mass media in influencing taste and consumption patterns must be seen in context. If advertising and news helped legitimate smoking among women, what began the social trend in the first place? To answer that, I will consider the sociology of consumption more broadly, examining the variety of factors that underlie changes in consumption patterns.[12]

But the question of women smoking cigarettes is only half of the puzzle of tobacco consumption in the 1920s. There is a second key issue. If it was a cultural revolution for women, who had never smoked at all in large numbers, to turn to cigarettes, it was also a revolution for men, who had smoked cigars and pipes, to turn to the "feminine" cigarette. At the beginning of the twentieth century cigarettes were banned in the U.S. Navy at the same time that the cigar was widely accepted. The cigarette was regarded as "a debasement of manhood."[13] The *New York Times* in 1925 made note of the growth of smoking among women but felt that the importance of this trend "has been greatly overestimated. . . . The women smokers probably do not account for more than a billion of the 72,000,000,000 cigarettes we use up."[14] Industry sources estimated that women smoked as much as 12 or 14 percent of all cigarettes by 1930, an important quantity but still a small proportion of the total.[15]

Men were switching to cigarettes at a rapid rate. Cigarette tobacco outsold pipe tobacco for the first time in 1919; it passed cigars in 1921 and it outsold chewing tobacco for the first time in 1922.[16] A measure of the relative importance of cigarette smoking for men and women comes from "The Fortune Survey" in 1935. The survey separated men from women and people over forty from those under forty and reported what percentage of each group smoked cigarettes:[17]

	Men	*Women*
Under 40	65.5	26.2
Over 40	39.7	9.3

Clearly, many more men than women smoked cigarettes, and younger people were more likely than older people to have adopted the cigarette habit.

While cigarette consumption grew enormously during the years between the wars, total tobacco consumption remained stable. In 1918 the total tobacco consumption (cigarettes, cigars, pipe tobacco, chewing tobacco, and snuff) was exactly the same as it would be twenty-two years later in 1940—9.12 pounds per adult. The rise of cigarette smoking was accompanied by the *fall* in other tobacco uses. Not only did women begin to smoke, but men changed their smoking preference in droves. What accounts for the movement of men to cigarettes? This is the second puzzle.

The Public Legitimation of Cigarettes for Women

For all practical purposes, the story of cigarettes begins in 1881, when James Bonsack patented a cigarette-making machine that manufactured up to forty times what the best skilled workers could produce by hand. Within a decade, the cost of producing a cigarette was reduced to one-sixth of what it had been. When James Buchanan Duke turned exclusively to machine production in 1885, he quickly saturated the American market. Production was no longer a problem; the only task was to sell.[18]

Cigarette smoking grew steadily from 1880 on. By 1890, the use of cigarette tobacco ran even with that of snuff. This state continued into the 1890s, but cigarette use declined in the period 1900–1905 and only equaled snuff again in 1911. It did not reach the level of consumption of any other tobacco form until the early 1920s, when it passed pipe tobacco, cigars, and chewing tobacco. By 1935 cigarettes represented more than half of all tobacco consumption.[19]

The cigarette is distinguished from other tobaccos by its mildness. After the 1870s, cigarette tobacco was flue- rather than fire-cured. The barns where tobacco is dried and cured are heated with flues running through them rather than with open wood or charcoal fires, making the tobacco milder. It produces a slightly acid rather than alkaline smoke. In alkaline form, nicotine can be absorbed through the linings of the mouth and nose without inhaling, as with chewing tobacco, pipe tobacco, and snuff. All of these forms permit a gradual intake of nicotine without inhaling. Flue-cured tobacco, in contrast, must be inhaled if nicotine is to be absorbed because only in the lungs will the acid smoke be converted to alkaline. The result is a smoke not only mild but more addictive than other tobaccos.[20]

Cigarette tobacco after World War I became milder than that which was available before the war. Just before the war, blended tobaccos had come into use, replacing some of the stronger Turkish tobaccos. When the war interrupted trade and cheaper Turkish brands lost out completely, the newer, mild cigarettes came to dominate the market.[21] After the war, import and revenue duties were high, Turkish tobacco production declined sharply, and American cigarette production grew quickly, from thirty billion cigarettes in 1917 to sixty billion in 1923.[22]

This change to a milder cigarette, it is reasonable to assume, reduced the cost of "trial" of new smokers; that is, because the cigarette was milder, the discomfort for trying it was reduced and the chances of being initially disgusted by it and not taking up the habit as a result, minimized.

If the war helped provide a more palatable cigarette, it also provided many young men and women with their first smoking experience. The tobacco industry was fond of quoting General "Black Jack" Pershing: "You ask me what we need to win this war. I answer tobacco as much as bullets." Boxcars from the tobacco states moved toward the seaports with signs painted on their sides, "Roll Your Own Into Berlin," "The Makings for U.S., the Leavings for the Kaiser," "America's Best for America's Bravest," and "When Our Boys Light Up the Huns Will Light Out."[23] Following the lead of the French and the British, American military leadership recommended that soldiers receive tobacco rations in addition to food and drink rations. When the War Department approved this suggestion, "a wave of joy swept through the American army," according to the *New York Times.* Rations were issued at .4 ounces of tobacco per day with one hundred cigarette papers for every four ounces or, alternatively, four ready-made cigarettes per day, or .4 ounces of chewing tobacco per day. Not only military authorities but volunteer groups supplied soldiers with tobacco. The Y.M.C.A. and the Red Cross lifted their opposition to smoking during the war and sent cigarettes to the soldiers overseas.[24]

No promotional scheme could have matched a war for spreading the cigarette habit, connecting it emotionally with relief and comradeship in the most trying of circumstances, associating a feminized product with the ultimately masculine endeavor. Its use in wartime was favored over other tobacco because of its convenience: one did not have to carry along a pipe nor did it take the time and attention of a cigar. It could be picked up and put down or stubbed out quickly. (The war stimulated other conveniences, too. For instance, the Gillette Company sold the War Department 3.5 million razors and 32 million blades and this strongly encouraged the relatively new habit of self-shaving.)[25]

Women as well as men took up the smoking habit during the war:

> Women war-workers took up the habit abroad, and women at home in their men's jobs and new-found independence did likewise. Within the next three or four years cigarette smoking became the universal fashion, at least in cities, and children born since the war take smoking mothers for granted.[26]

This contemporary observation is clearly an exaggeration, but there is no reason to doubt that some women who had never smoked learned that the physical threshold to smoking was lowered by the mild tobacco and that the social threshold was lowered when laboring in a war industry.[27]

While observers of the social scene in the 1920s most often pointed to the war or to the changing status of women as reasons for the growth of cigarette smoking, tobacco manufacturers themselves explained the trend by citing the large-scale manufacture of mild, blended tobacco.[28] In fact, all of these elements played a part; it would be hard to know which one contributed most decisively.

While the cigarette was mild, resistance to it was not, especially with regard to women smokers. Throughout the 1920s, controversy over women smoking was a salient news item. This was notably so in reports on smoking in colleges and on public transportation.

Take the case of women's colleges, which the *New York Times* covered closely. The *Times* reported as early as 1921 that the University of Chicago banned smoking among women students.[29] By 1925 such stories were front page news. Women who were allowed to smoke at home felt their liberties were infringed upon at school. The Vassar College students' council, in response to agitation over a rule prohibiting smoking, polled students on whether they smoked away from school, whether their parents approved of their smoking, and what school regulations for smoking should be adopted. A week later the results were in and the *Times* provided front-page coverage: 433 Vassar girls liked cigarettes; 524 did not smoke; about 400 sets of parents disapproved of their daughters' smoking; 302 approved according to the daughters; 278 students voted to continue the smoking prohibition; 539 favored more lenient rules. A month later the students nonetheless banned smoking on the grounds that "smoking is not yet established as a social convention acceptable to all groups throughout the country."[30]

The *Times* in 1925 also reported on smoking at Radcliffe and at Smith.[31] It was front page news that M.I.T. permitted women to smoke at dances, while Goucher College prohibited students from smoking both on campus and in public places in Baltimore.[32] A study at Bryn Mawr showed that less than half of Bryn Mawr women smoked, but the Self-Government Association petitioned the college president to set aside a smoking room in each dormitory. President Marion Edwards Park consented, saying that a change in attitude toward smoking by women had come about and that it was natural for this change to be reflected among college students. She repealed the 1897 ban on smoking. The *Times* editorially endorsed the Bryn Mawr decision, though in condescending tones, hoping that by allowing cigarettes in certain places, "what once was a feat of defiance becomes rather a bore. . . ."[33]

These accounts reinforce the conclusion of historian Paula Fass that "smoking was perhaps the one most potent symbol of young woman's testing of the elbow room provided by her new sense of freedom and equality."[34] Fass shows that, while the *Times* may have approved the Bryn Mawr decision, many other opinion leaders were shocked. The president of Kansas State Teachers College said that "nothing has occurred in higher education that has so shocked our sense of social decency as the action at Bryn Mawr," and many other college presidents and deans agreed. But however shocked the authorities were, the Bryn Mawr decision was a recognition of the social fact that by 1925 large numbers of college women smoked cigarettes. One-third of the women at Ohio State said that they smoked at least occasionally; a student leader at Rhode Island State in 1924 claimed that "practically all the girls smoke." The student newspaper at the University of Illinois covered the smoking issue often in 1924 and made it clear that enlightened student opinion felt it perfectly acceptable for women to smoke.[35]

By the end of the twenties, there was still opposition to women smoking on campus. At their 1929 conventions, sororities Pi Beta Phi and Alpha Gamma Delta voted to ban smoking in chapter houses.[36] But more and more, colleges were coming to accept smoking among women students. Goucher, which just a few years before had banned smoking, reversed itself in 1929. Acting President Hans Froelicher said, "This practice has become so general that public opinion in the student body demanded the change in the rule to bring it within the law, for fear that disregard for this law would breed disrespect for all laws enacted under the student government."[37]

The campus was not the only locus of social conflict and comment over women smoking. A second center of conflict was public transport. News coverage in the *New York Times* dates to 1921 when a news item noted that the Canadian Pacific Railroad had installed smoking compartments for women in its cars.[38] A reporter in 1923 took a seat in the smoker between New York and Philadelphia and noted that many of the forty men, but none of the ten women in the car were smoking. An hour out of the station one woman lit up. "There was a general straightening of backs and turning of heads. The fat man opposite the woman dropped his paper and frankly stared." The reporter concluded that it was still socially unacceptable for women to smoke in public: "It is being done, because railroads are opening their smoking cars to women, but it is not being done comfortably."[39] Pullman Company bulletins by 1923 were announcing that if women's smoking could not be curbed, women's smoking compartments would have to be installed.[40] In 1925 the Chicago, Milwaukee, and St. Paul Railroad added a women's smoker to its Chicago-Seattle run. The Detroit streetcar system ruled that women could smoke on the streetcars, a development the *New York Times* bemoaned in an editorial. Women were allowed in the smoking room of the White Star Liner *Homeric,* despite men's complaints dating back several years that women occupied seats in the smoking rooms. The Erie Railroad decided to allow smoking in the dining car because women requested it.[41]

Part of the reason for agitation by women for smoking inside is that smoking outside was still unacceptable. It was a shock for the people of Dayton, Tennessee, to see women smoking openly in the street as visitors streamed in for the Scopes "monkey" trial in 1925.[42] As late as 1937 a market research firm found that 95 percent of male smokers smoked in the street but only 28 percent of them believed it right for women to do likewise.[43] That women smoking outside was an issue is suggested by this 1928 report:

> A few years ago an enterprising taxi driver did a thriving business in the Wall Street district during the noon hour by driving around women who wanted to smoke a cigarette or two before returning to their offices. None of the women rode any considerable distance. But the taxi driver had a continued run of passengers.
>
> The taxi was about the only place these women could smoke with any sense of freedom. In the restaurants they would have felt conspicuous. In the offices it was quite out of the question. An unwritten law said that women must not smoke in business houses. Today there is hardly any place except the street where a woman cannot smoke with equanimity.[44]

Women were conspicuous as smokers because people were not used to seeing women smoke. But they were conspicuous also because, wary of smoking outdoors where they feared disapproval, they smoked inside in places where men had never smoked—railroad diners, retail stores, and art galleries. Frances Perkins took out after women smokers in an essay in the *New Republic,* "Can They Smoke Like Gentlemen?" She noted that

President Nielson of Smith College had announced that smoking would be restricted to two fireproof rooms after several dormitory fires were caused by cigarettes. He said, "The trouble is, my dear young ladies, you do not smoke like gentlemen." Perkins wholeheartedly agreed, complaining of women who smoke in restaurants all through their dinners and in railway dining cars; men, she observed, always politely retire to the smoking car. In years of gallery going, she added, she had never seen a man smoke at an art exhibition. "It remained for a couple of plain middle-aged women to mess up the floor and haze up the air, successfully obscuring the exquisite colors of Georgia O'Keefe at a recent showing." Her main concern was that women smoked in retail stores, including the major department stores. In men's clothing shops, hardware stores, or florist shops, she wrote, there was, by custom, no smoking. But in stores frequented by women, the prevalence of smoking was a serious fire hazard.[45]

The colleges' establishment of smoking rooms in dormitories and creation of liberal smoking regulations and the streetcars', railroads', and shipping lines' provisions for women smokers helped legitimate the cigarette for women. Further, these changes were covered prominently in the press and this surely gave support to the spread of the cigarette habit among women. In times past, smoking had been associated only with scandalous women but now one could read in the newspaper that prominent, young, wealthy women smoked. In 1925 an inspection report on the New York Women's Workhouse in New York showed that smoking was very common among the inmates, but it refused to recommend that smoking be prohibited on the grounds that "if a recent canvass of Vassar College showed nearly 50 percent of the girls to the manor born smoking, this is not surprising in a women's workhouse."[46] It is possible, of course, that New York is a special case or that the *New York Times* is an unrepresentative source, although the data from the Midwest colleges lend support. The South and West to this day differ from the East and Midwest in patterns of tobacco use. Still, I think this evidence is a good basis for the presumption that women in large numbers were smoking cigarettes by the mid-1920s.

Cigarette Advertising and the Meaning of Smoking to Women

Meanwhile, cigarette manufacturers were cautious in appealing directly to women. Curtis Wessel, editor of the *United States Tobacco Journal,* wrote in 1924 that "all responsible tobacco opinion" found the habit of women smoking so "novel" that "it would not be in good taste for tobacco men as parties in interest to stir a particle toward or against a condition with whose beginnings they had nothing to do and whose end, if any, no one can foresee."[47]

When advertisers did begin to address women directly, they did so cautiously. The first notable cigarette ad directed toward women was a Chesterfield ad in 1926 showing a romantic couple at night, the man smoking, the woman sitting next to him, with the caption, "Blow Some My Way."[48] Most ads for cigarettes, even ads with an audience of women in mind, showed only men smoking. The *New Yorker* in 1926 printed a full page ad for Miltiades Egyptian cigarettes that featured a drawing captioned, "After Theatre," with a man and a woman in evening dress. The man is smoking and says to the woman, "Somehow or other Shakespeare's heroines seem more feminine in modern garb and smoking cigarettes. . . ." He advises her to exercise care in choosing a cigarette—but she, as usual, is not shown smoking.[49] A Camel cigarette ad in *Time* in 1926 shows two men lighting up, two women looking on.[50] An ad in *Time* for Fatima Turkish Cigarettes claims, "It's What the Younger Crowd Thinks About It!" and shows a man and a woman waterskiing, but only the man smoking.[51] A Camel cigarette ad in *The Outlook* in 1927 shows two men and a woman at a nightclub, both men smoking and the woman not smoking.[52]

In 1928 and 1929, R. J. Reynolds ran a series of back cover full-color ads in *Time* for Camel cigarettes. Some of these continued to show men smoking, women looking on. But some made it clear that women smoke Camels too, although the ads do not always go so far as to show women smoking. In one ad, "Don't Be Selfish," an elegantly dressed man offers a cigarette to his fashionable woman companion.[53] In another, a woman is shown in a classy shop, buying a box of Camels which the clerk is carefully wrapping. The caption says, "Camels, of course. The more you demand of a cigarette, the quicker you come to Camels."[54] Another ad, "Well Bred," dares to show two women smoking at the track. The copy compares horses and women in its praise of "breeding" and "a capacity for selection."[55]

I examined the *New York Times,* the *San Diego Union,* and *Time* magazine and found no ads picturing women smoking or obviously appealing to women as smokers before the late 1920s. (I examined four weeks of each year for *Time* from 1923 through 1935 and two weeks for each newspaper for the years 1918, 1921, 1924, 1927, 1930, and 1933.) In the late twenties, appeals to women appear and in a few years become very direct. American Tobacco's campaign for Lucky Strike was the most notable, emphasizing in testimonial ads featuring women that Luckies were not harsh to the throat. One ad in the *New York Times* in 1927 showed opera star Ernestine Schumann-Heink recommending Lucky Strike as soothing to the throat; another pictured actress Florence Reed also recommending the cigarette that offered "no throat irritation."[56] Beginning in 1928, American Tobacco advertised Lucky Strike as a good alternative to eating candy. Their famous slogan, aimed at the female consumer, was "Reach for a Lucky instead of a sweet." Chocolate manufacturers feared that women were doing exactly what the tobacco makers urged and the complaints of confectioners made news.[57]

The confectioners were not alone in opposing cigarettes. There was a strong anti-cigarette movement that enrolled Henry Ford and several notable academics and public health leaders, among others. It was especially influential among women's groups. The national Women's Christian Temperance Union (W.C.T.U.) was active in opposing the use of cigarettes among women and children. Their 1921 annual report noted that Iowa's anti-cigarette law had been weakened, North Dakota's had been strengthened, Oregon had instituted a law against smoking where foods are exposed for sale, and Minnesota was working on a similar law. The Union's Anti-Narcotics Department resolved to campaign for strict enforcement of laws forbidding the sale of tobacco to minors, to increase its efforts against misleading advertising, and to attack the increasing habit of smoking among women.[58]

By 1927, the Anti-Narcotics Department reported that chapters had sponsored 6,699 anti-smoking programs that year, nineteen state poster contests, and the distribution of 580,223 pages of anti-smoking literature. In essay contests, over 27,000 anti-smoking essays had been submitted. In Portland, Oregon, the W.C.T.U. successfully protested the decision of the leading department store to show a female mannequin in the window holding a cigarette. The women convinced the store to have the mannequin hold a rose. In campaigns, the nature of which the reports of the W.C.T.U. does not specify, members crushed 219,560 cigarette stubs and 39,713 cigar stubs.[59] The Mt. Vernon, New York, chapter urged that women's smoking be confined to private places.[60] Despite W.C.T.U. agitation, the Atlantic City School Board refused to bar women who smoke from teaching in the public schools.[61] The W.C.T.U. helped lobby for laws prohibiting smoking in places where food was displayed for sale, and by 1927 twenty-one states had such laws. But some legislation was going the other way. In 1927 Kansas legalized cigarette sales, repealing a twenty-year-old statute, though retaining a prohibition on all cigarette advertising and cigarette sales to minors.[62]

When cigarette advertising to women became more prominent, there was a backlash—just as the tobacco companies had feared. Bills to restrict cigarette advertising were introduced in the legislatures in states including Illinois, Michigan, and Idaho. Efforts sprang up around the country to protest an American Tobacco billboard that featured a "girl of tender years actually smoking cigarettes." The National Education Association passed a resolution at its annual meeting in 1930 condemning "the fraudulent advertising of certain manufacturers in their efforts to foster cigarette-smoking." It urged schools to select for school libraries periodicals that did not carry tobacco advertising.[63] Both the Cleveland Boy Scouts Council and the Sioux Falls, South Dakota, City Commission objected to billboards that pictured women smoking.[64] Protest reached the floor of the U.S. Senate in 1929 when Senator Smoot rose to say: "Not since the days when public opinion rose in its might and smote the dangerous drug traffic, not since the days when the vendor of harmful nostrums was swept from our streets, has this country witnessed such an orgy of buncombe, quackery and downright falsehood and fraud as now marks the current campaign promoted by certain cigarette manufacturers to create a vast woman and child market for the use of their product."[65] Advertising, it appears, precipitated criticism of tobacco companies and, a least for a time, intensified public opposition to women smoking.

Why did women take to cigarettes in the 1920s? I have approached the question indirectly. I have not presented the extensive literature on why people take up smoking, what kind of satisfaction they get from it, why they tend to begin as teenagers, and so on.[66] Those questions examine the psychology of the individual smoker and ask why someone would deviate from a healthful norm to take up smoking. My interest, in contrast, is to understand how the norm itself changed, how smoking became socially acceptable.

What did smoking mean for women? In Sinclair Lewis's *Babbitt,* published in 1922, there are several mentions of women smoking, and this in the decidedly uncosmopolitan town of Zenith, Ohio. George Babbitt's teenage son Ted, fighting with his girl friend Veronica, exclaims: "It's disgusting of you to smoke cigarettes. . . ." Babbitt's wife does not touch tobacco, but Babbitt himself has an affair with Tanis Judique who, to his surprise, is a smoker:

> "Do give me a cigarette. Would you think poor Tanis was dreadfully naughty if she smoked?"
>
> "Lord, no, I like it!"
>
> He had often and weightily pondered flappers smoking in Zenith restaurants, but he knew only one woman who smoked—Mrs. Sam Doppelbrau, his flighty neighbor. He ceremoniously lighted Tanis's cigarette, looked for a place to deposit the burnt match, and dropped it into his pocket.
>
> "I'm sure you want a cigar, you poor man!" she crooned.
>
> "Do you mind one?"
>
> "Oh, no. I love the smell of a good cigar; so nice and—so nice and like a man."[67]

For men, cigarettes meant refinement—a feminine sensibility. Had there been a Marlboro man in 1922, he would have smoked a cigar. For women, on the other hand, cigarettes suggested some naughtiness, some sexual openness, an allegiance to and association with younger, stylish women. Of course, it depended where one was coming from. For Shirley Polykoff's mother, a Ukrainian immigrant, smoking meant American-ness. She wanted to become American as quickly and fully as possible and so "she was one of the first ladies in her tenement to smoke a cigarette."[68] In a 1922 piece of magazine fiction, "Women Cigarette Fiends," Mr. and Mrs. John Smith, affluent Middle Westerners, visit their daughter at a fashionable finishing school in New York. Mrs. Smith, active in the Anti-Tobacco League, refuses to eat in the hotel dining rooms where women smoked openly. To her horror, she learns that her daughter has become expert in smoking and that there are even smoking rooms set aside for the girls at the school.[69] Again, the cigarette is connected to the young, the cosmopolitan, and the naughty.

Smoking a cigarette was a social symbol of considerable power in the 1920s. Women used cigarettes to mark themselves as separate from the past, different from past women. In all human societies, there are markings that distinguish people in their social identity—men are different from women, children from adolescents, adolescents from adults. These are physical differences, of course, but they are also social stations, always reinforced and restated culturally by clothing or other body markings and differentiated, socially mandated forms of behavior. In modern societies, people mark themselves not only in social space but in social time. Through goods, they indicate their relationship to one another and also accent their relationship to the spirit of the times. They display their modernity or their resistance to modernity. They mark their allegiance to groups that embrace social change or to groups that hold to tradition. In the 1920s, cigarettes came to be a personal and social marker for "the new woman," a sign of divorce from the past and inclusion in the group of the new, young, and liberated.[70]

This was the cultural theme that public relations agent Edward Bernays tried to capitalize on when, in 1929, working for American Tobacco's Lucky Strike brand, he organized a contingent of women in New York's Easter Parade. Each woman smoked a Lucky and the cigarettes were touted as "torches of liberty." Bernays takes credit for having significantly promoted smoking among women by this feat, but his self-congratulatory claim cannot be taken at face value. As we have seen, women by 1929 were smoking in public (though not in the street) in large numbers and advertisers were appealing openly to the female market. If Bernays was not especially perceptive in seeing that cigarettes represented independence to women, he was nonetheless commercially correct to pick up on the theme.[71]

Symbols may not only confirm members of an emergent social group in a new identity but, at the same time, may be likened to a prism in concentrating light on a subject, generating heat and even fire. The cigarette was such a symbol in the 1920s, a focus of anxiety and antagonism toward the "new woman" and the changing sex roles she embodied. Cigarette advertising provided a way to legitimate and naturalize women's smoking. It was a weapon in the fight among tobacco companies for market share, of course, but it was, like most advertising, conservative, venturing to challenge established ways in the population only when evidence of new market patterns was in plain view.[72] Despite the importance of the commercial interests involved in spreading the use of cigarettes among women, the change that occurred was a cultural one. It was made possible by changes in the cigarette product itself, by World War I's transformation of social habits, and by a new class of women who sponsored the cigarette in its political and social battles. In the 1920s, a cigarette in the hands of a woman meant a change in the language of social interaction. Such changes may be vigorously contested. They were at that time, just as they have been more recently when "Ms" and "he or she" entered the spoken language and came to be used, at least in some circles, naturally. That advertising has played a role since the late 1920s in promoting smoking among women should not blind us to the fact that this change in consumption patterns, like many others, has roots deep in cultural change and political conflict that advertising often responds to but rarely creates.

Men Move to Cigarettes: The Culture of Convenience

The question of why large numbers of men switched from cigars and pipes and chewing tobacco to cigarettes is still unresolved. There may be a clue, again, in *Babbitt.* George Babbitt thought himself "of a breeding altogether more esthetic and sensitive than Thompson's." How did he know? "He was a college graduate, he played golf, he often smoked cigarettes instead of cigars, and when he went to Chicago he took a room with a private bath."[73] Something similar is reflected in the story of Mr. and Mrs. John Smith visiting their daughter in New York. Mr. Smith, a regular cigar smoker, switches to cigarettes on arrival in the big city: ". . . in New York, like many men of his kind, he smoked cigarettes, a transition of taste charged to the metropolitan life."[74] Is the cigarette more suitable than other forms of tobacco for metropolitan life?

Certainly people *believed* the cigarette to be an urbane and "citified" smoke. It somehow captured better than other forms of tobacco the pace of urban life. As a *New York Times* editorial suggested in 1925: "Short, snappy, easily attempted, easily completed or just as easily discarded before completion—the cigarette is the symbol of a machine age in which the ultimate cogs and wheels and levers are human nerves."[75]

The convenience of the cigarette distinguishes it from all other forms of smoking tobacco and contemporaries of the twenties acknowledged this. Cigarettes required much less time and attention than other forms of tobacco use. A news story in the *Washington Evening Star* of December 8, 1922, reported that a man took both hands off the steering wheel of his automobile to light a cigar. The car hit a tree and the man's companion hurtled through the windshield. She sued for $20,000 and was awarded $1,500. The lesson seems clear: the accident would not have happened if the man had been smoking a cigarette. Even chewing tobacco required more attention than the cigarette. Woodrow Wilson, speaking on the rural migration to the cities, complained that "it is impossible for people to think in big cities." Jokingly, he added, "Whatever else may be said of the habit of chewing tobacco, this much must be admitted in its favor, that it makes men think because they must stop between words to spit."[76]

Cigarettes are quicker and easier to use than any other kind of smoking. They fit more easily into brief moments of relaxation, they are more readily used while working or otherwise engaged, and they are more easily managed without the use of one's hands.[77] They are also more "standard" and hence more reliable products. The quality of the smoke is more or less guaranteed, and there is nothing the smoker can do to alter it. With a pipe, the quality of the smoke is more dependent on the skill and patience of the smoker and, to a lesser extent, this is true of cigars as well. The cigarette is the standardized, reliable, quick and easy smoke. It is the McDonald's of the tobacco trade, the fast food of smoking. And all of this made the cigarette the preferred smoke for people aiming for a streamlined, cultural modernity, involved in the fast pace of city life, spending more time in automobiles, and feeling free to experiment with a product that departed from conventional norms of masculinity.

If there is good reason to believe that cigarettes grew in popularity because they were more convenient, there is more of a problem to determine why in the twentieth century "convenience" should have been a desirable quality in a tobacco—or in other products. Is tobacco historian Richard Tennant right to suggest that the cigarette has a "natural adaptability" to the rhythms of urban life?[78] Was the *New York Times* right to suggest that the cigarette was especially suited to a machine age when the "nervousness" of the worker is heightened?[79]

It is tempting to believe that "convenience" has always been a desirable quality. Yet convenience becomes especially desirable only when "time" becomes an objectified and precious commodity itself. Only when people come to conceive their lives as involving the "spending" of time do they come to care about the "saving" of time by the use of convenience goods.

This position has been worked out theoretically by several economists. Gary Becker has argued that there is an incentive to economize on time if the relative cost of time increases. This happens as, in increasingly affluent societies, real income for work per hour has increased. The time then spent "not working" is relatively more expensive in terms of income lost by not working. Thus people measure, monitor, and value their time spent not working more carefully than in the past. Under these conditions, the cost of goods relative to the cost of time decreases. People who are increasingly affluent can more easily afford a quickly cooked steak than a cheaper but more time-consuming stew. The result is the familiar American wastefulness of goods and preoccupation with time: ". . . the tendency to be economical about time and lavish about goods may be no paradox, but in part simply a reaction to a difference in relative costs."[80]

Staffan Burenstam Linder has written a provocative analysis of "the increasing scarcity of time" in the affluent middle class. Some societies, he writes, have a time surplus: "Productivity is so low that a certain proportion of time yields nothing whatsoever."[81] This is the case in very poor societies. Wealthier societies are "time affluence cultures" where people place greater importance on time but are not governed by the clock. And then there are "time famine" cultures, like the American, where time budgeting is crucial and the clock or watch is omnipresent.

In time-famine cultures, rational behavior may *appear* irrational. For instance, when time is short, "impulse buying" may be the most rational shopping strategy. It is more rational to make an occasional mistake than to spend precious time collecting information to make a better judgment. Advertising, too, takes on greater importance—and greater value for the consumer—in a time-scarce society. Advertising may provide "quasi information for people who lack the time to acquire the genuine insights."[82] Advertisers simultaneously close the information gap by providing information and exploit the information gap that remains by using noninformational persuasion. Linder argues:

> . . . as soon as one lacks complete information, one is also exposed to the possibility of being influenced by advertising. One actually *wants* to be influenced by advertising to get an instant feeling that one has a perfectly good reason to buy this or that commodity, the true properties

of which one knows dismally little about. Only unintelligent buyers acquire complete information.[83]

In a time-scarce society, efforts to conserve time may take the form of an increasingly extravagant use of consumer goods. And these goods will be used more intensively in a variety of ways. One can, for instance, buy more expensive goods and use them for the same amount of time as one used less expensive goods. Or one can use a number of different goods simultaneously—as the unhappy man tried to do while lighting his cigar in his automobile. Or one may try "successive consumption," as Linder calls it, using each commodity for a shorter time. This is the strategy that the cigarette makes available to the tobacco user, the ballpoint pen to the writer, and the disposable diaper to the parent.

The recognition that consumers buy time with money has improved economic theory, and it sheds some light on the demand for a "convenience" tobacco in the 1920s. Even so, this revised economic analysis remains conceptually stingy as an account of the empirical world—the rise of cigarette smoking in particular and the premium put on convenience goods in general. In the case of cigarettes, an analysis of the Becker or Linder sort offers no explanation for why women started smoking and thus added a new time-consuming activity to their time-scarce lives. If many of the women who began smoking had been teenagers or college girls, not part of the job market nor motivated in any profound way by concern for time budgeting, the economic explanation would not be wrong but simply not relevant.

But even for the men who switched to cigarettes, the economic analysis is insufficient. First, men did not choose cigarettes *directly* to save time. What may have happened is that men entered into activities that limited the amount of time they could afford for smoking. They were now, for instance, driving automobiles, riding in closed buses or subways, working in buildings in which they traveled in elevators, and working in rooms without good air circulation. These situations led them to find cigarettes relatively more appealing, cigars and pipes and chewing tobacco relatively less appealing than before. Cigarettes became the more convenient form of tobacco use.

But notice that "convenient" does not mean simply "less time consuming." A "convenient" good is not necessarily the same thing as a "labor-saving" good. "Convenience" means *suitability* and there are more determinants of suitability than are dreamed of by economists. One determinant, for instance, is degree of offensiveness. If we are to learn anything from the advertisements for tobacco in the 1920s and 1930s, it is that they stress the "mildness" of cigarettes. Cigarette ads directed toward women frequently stressed that cigarettes did not "irritate" the throat. Cigarettes also did not irritate other people as much as alternative forms of tobacco use. By the early 1930s, ads in the dying cigar industry nearly all stressed the mildness of their products.[84]

What *is* mildness? Whatever it is, it relates directly neither to time nor to income. People seek in their consumer decisions not only to maximize their income and their available time. They have other goals, too. One goal is "connection" or "circulation." In a small or closed society, this desire visibly arises in people's delight in gossiping. In larger societies, characterized by extensive and readily available systems of transportation and communication, people develop strong desires to be "in touch" because they are at so great a risk of losing touch. People not only want to be valued in their own circles but want to be available to enter new social groups. People seek ways to increase their mobility or social circulation. They will take a variety of avenues toward this end. Not only will they seek income, not only will they seek to conserve time, but they will also make decisions to minimize the risks of social isolation.

Among other things, this need has implications for convenience goods. Goods are "convenient" not only because they are labor saving or time saving but because they are nonrepellent. Some goods "put off" people more than others. In the quest for social circulation, such goods—like cigars—are to be avoided. If there is a producer's interest in mild goods to appeal to the widest possible audience, there is also a consumer's interest in developing a taste for mild goods because they do not offend. When, for other reasons, people have made choices (to drive in cars, to work in closed quarters) that increase the offensiveness of old habits, there will be a market for new tricks.

Women are the key consumers in American society with respect to the desire for social circulation. Women are supposed to be the sexual magnets, pulling men to them; the social glue, buying the gifts and cards and making the telephone calls that hold family and friends together; and the cultural antennae, ears to the wind for news of what will make the family or its children fit in and get ahead. The cigarette is an unusual case of a product by which women asserted *themselves* collectively and advanced the social circulation of their gender as a whole; the cigarette served as a symbol of women's renewed demand for equality.

The rise of the cigarette in the 1920s, then, can be seen as a case study in the democratization of goods, a complex interplay of changing social structure, cultural innovation, and commercial opportunity. This is not an isolated case. I suspect, for instance, that the democratization of goods—and a reaction to it—may help account for the stunning popularity of designer jeans in the late 1970s. People spend less money, as a percentage of their income, on clothing today than they did ten years ago. A low-budget family spent 11.6 percent of its budget on clothing and personal care in 1970, 9.0 percent in 1980; an intermediate-budget family's clothing allocation dropped from 10.7 percent to 7.6 percent; and a high-budget family dropped from 10.7 percent to 7.4 percent.[85] The stunning fact of designer jeans was not that the jeans were expensive beyond all reason but that people could "get away with" wearing them in semiformal situations and posh surroundings. The important trend of dress in the 1970s was toward informality. Consequently, today men no longer wear hats at all, ties are no longer required, dress slacks are not de rigueur, women need not wear dresses or skirts on "dress" occasions. This does not mean one can wear just anything. But it is much easier to dress acceptably with a limited wardrobe than it once was. For people who do not know by training or instinct what it is to dress well, "brand name" goods are themselves a democratization. People took to designer jeans as a reaction against Levis, a revolt against dressing down, and yet, they did not return to previous standards of dressing up. Designer jeans grew popular, they were imitated in cheaper versions, and fashion was democratized again.

How Consumer Patterns Change

Marketers seek to present their products, and especially their new products, as distinctive, having some features or providing some benefits to consumers that other available products cannot equal. Occasionally their efforts at product differentiation rest on the "image" that advertising conveys rather than any material attribute of the product itself—Marlboro as a "real man's" cigarette is one of the most famous examples.

But Marlboro cigarettes were not a distinctive new product and Marlboro efforts at differentiation gained a share of the cigarette market very successfully without reorganizing that market in any notable way. In contrast, when a genuinely novel product enters the market, it sometimes has the power to establish a new criterion of evaluation. The first commercially successful "non-aspirin pain reliever" increased the salience of stomach irritation (that aspirin sometimes contributes to) as a criterion for evaluating pain relievers. The first commercially successful home computer set new standards of what a home business machine could do and so led consumers, on their way to the store to buy a new electric typewriter, to stop in their tracks and wonder what "capabilities" they really wanted.

A new criterion for consumer choice need not be created by private firms. The EPA's auto emission requirements established new criteria of evaluating cars in the early 1970s.[86] With visible new criteria that American car manufacturers clearly did not meet, there was plenty of free publicity for foreign companies like Honda that *did* meet the tests. The greatest power a company can have would be to establish a new criterion of judgment; it happens rarely. More often, the trick is to be ready when a new criterion comes along.

What are the forces that establish new criteria of judgment of products? Almost any of the cultural, social, political, economic, or technological forces one might imagine could play a role. Nor can it be doubted that sometimes a new product itself will be stunning enough to upset the applecart of evaluation and establish a new criterion itself. A firm with the "first" product to enter a field can reap long-lasting advantages from having been first; the first product often is taken to be the "premier" product.

Not only may new products help set new standards of evaluation; old products may be re-evaluated in new times. People may not even know what criteria they use to evaluate products or what the conditions are that make for product success or failure. Big cars were sustained by taken-for-granteds like cheap oil and the absence of stylish American small cars. Chocolate bar sales were sustained by the baby boom. Men's hats were sustained by urban living, the no-car or one-car family, and certain traditional attitudes toward male grooming. There is an invisible infrastructure of consumer taste. Manufacturers frequently do not know what accounts for their success—until it is gone, if ever.

The more complex or far reaching a change in consumer behavior, the more involved are the infrastructural changes that permit and reinforce the new consumer activity. A monograph by Norman Moline on the introduction of the automobile to the small town of Oregon, Illinois, gives a good sense of this cultural pattern. The American automobil industry can be dated to about 1897 but only in 1903 did the first citizen of Oregon buy a car. That was big news and the local paper reported all automobile purchases for the next decade. By 1911 there were 275 cars in Ogle County and the Ogle County Auto Club was formed to lobby for better roads. Ads for cars first appeared in the Oregon paper in 1908—just three column inches that year, five column inches in 1909, but 1,131 by 1914 and 2,538 by 1915. Advertising was not the primary marketing tool. Door-to-door salesmen were very important; their task was to get a person into the car and let him drive it for himself. Also crucial was simply the fact that one's neighbors—particularly one's wealthy and respected neighbors—were buying.[87]

The visible and impressive novelty of the car was itself a form of promotion on the part of the car owners themselves, but it was by no means the only promotion that early car owners engaged in. There were races and parades sponsored by local motor clubs. There was also a fashion of automobile-related talk. A lumber ad of 1918 asked: "Are you a 1918 model? If you are a model husband, a 1918 model, you are equipped with all the modern improvements. Be a self-starter. We have made over many a one-cylinder, tin wheeze of a husband into an up-to-date, high power Super Six." Once car ownership began to spread, so did the infrastructural changes that made it a permanent part of the landscape—improved roads (the first paved rural roads in America were laid in 1909, thanks in large part to lobbying by bicyclists and auto drivers), traffic lights (installed in Oregon's five main intersections in 1918), and painted lines for angled parking (1923). Heated garages were built for central auto storage since cars could be driven in Oregon only from April through December; not until 1924 was there any provision made for snow clearance but the cars did not, in any event, drive well in the cold.[88]

Once the car as a cultural given was established, patterns of living appeared that took its availability for granted. Oregon car owners could live in one town and work in another; community organizations drew membership from more than one town and increased the frequency of their meetings; Oregon began to promote itself as a tourist center with an annual flower show and scout circus and other events that would draw out-of-towners; interscholastic athletic competition developed; Oregonians increasingly traveled to larger towns nearby, and out-of-town businesses began to be much more prominent in the advertising columns of the local paper.[89]

Any new consumer product that does not disappear quickly as just a fad or fashion is probably related to deep social currents. It relies on relatively lasting social changes for its success and, if it is as significant as the automobile or the cigarette, it may set up further social, legal, or cultural changes that reinforce its hold on the public. A marketer unattuned to social trends may stir an eddy in the stream of consumption but, to be a great success, will have to ride a wave already in formation.

Oddly enough, with all the market research that goes on, there is little systematic understanding of the nature of consumption, little or nothing in the way of agreed-upon views of what trends in social life affect consumption, little effort to grasp the quality of consumption on the level I have begun to discuss here. No one really knows why people drink less coffee than they used to, why cigars died out, why light and white liquors are doing better, why the hat industry folded. One can always say, after the fact, what qualities of a product made it a success, but no one seems to know enough to say in advance what product will be a sure winner. To the extent that anything is known, it is the simplest sort of knowledge—that working women will have different needs than nonworking women, that good quality at a low price is attractive to consumers, that there are fewer children and more elderly people than there used to be, and that people of different age groups and different social patterns have predictably different desires.

This cigarette case study has tried to reach a little deeper, to recognize the social roots of significant changes in consumption patterns and to characterize what a change in consumer activity might signify. It also has served as a reminder that advertising generally works to reinforce consumer trends rather than to initiate them. Critics of advertising in the 1920s and today have regarded the adoption of cigarette smoking by women as a clear-cut proof of the power of persuasive advertising to dramatically change consumer habits. It is not so; the matter turns out to be not so obvious at all.

As I have argued, this does not mean that advertising is impotent. There are social groups especially vulnerable to advertising's exhortations and all people occasionally find themselves in unusual social situations where they are susceptible to a sales pitch. Still, I do not think we will come to terms with American consumer habits and consumer values until we recognize advertisements as but one piece in a larger puzzle.

My discussion thus far has left aside one vital issue, in some respects the key issue. Whether advertising initiates consumer trends or only reinforces them, advertisements are a pervasive part of the American aural and visual environment. It is impossible to ignore their wider role in providing people a general education in goods, status, values, social roles, style, and art. What can be said about this more general and frequently more troubling influence of advertising? I will explore this problem in the next chapter.

7

Advertising as Capitalist Realism

ADVERTISING, as the early agency Lord and Thomas put it, is "salesmanship in print." It is just that simple, just that complex. Understanding advertising entails understanding the difference between personal and printed or broadcast communication; the differences entailed in the "decontextualization" of thought and feeling that systems of mass communication make possible. With the invention of writing in human history, anthropologist Jack Goody observes, "Speech is no longer tied to an occasion: it becomes timeless. Nor is it attached to a person; on paper, it becomes more abstract, more depersonalized."[1] For Goody, this opens the way to science, to the growth of criticism, and to a more tolerant attitude toward one's own frame of reference. But the same forces that enable people to see themselves as individuals independent of social and traditional contexts make people susceptible to the appeals of mass media, including advertising. This is an openness or susceptibility qualitatively different from the householder's vulnerability to the direct sales pitch. Among other things, it connects the consumer not only to an item for sale and a person selling it but to an invisible, yet present, audience of others attuned to the same item for sale and the same symbols used to promote it. The advertisement, like the sales talk, links a seller to a buyer. Unlike the sales talk, it connects the buyer to an assemblage of buyers through words and pictures available to all of them and tailored to no one of them. Advertising is part of the establishment and reflection of a common symbolic culture.

Advertising, whether or not it sells cars or chocolate, surrounds us and enters into us, so that when we speak we may speak in or with reference to the language of advertising and when we see we may see through schemata that advertising has made salient for us. Whether advertising is, as David Potter claimed, the distinctive institution of an affluent society,[2] or, as Mason Griff wrote, the "central institution of mass society,"[3] can at this point be legitimately doubted. At the same time, it is a distinctive and central *symbolic* structure. And, strictly as symbol, the power of advertising may be considerable. Advertising may shape our sense of values even under conditions where it does not greatly corrupt our buying habits. I want now to take up the position of the UNESCO MacBride Commission (and many others) that advertising "tends to promote attitudes and life-styles which extol acquisition and consumption at the expense of other values."[4]

The Concept of Capitalist Realism

When a person places a classified ad or when a department store announces a January white sale, the intention is to sell goods. In the classifieds, this usually means a unique transaction—a particular house is for sale, a particular job is available, a particular used car is offered. When the given item is sold, the ad is discontinued. With the department store, the situation is less individualized. The store wants to attract customers not only to the linens department but to the store in general and not only in January but always. Still, the ad does relatively little to attract customers except to announce what goods it has to sell at what price. This may be an effort to make a store-loyal customer as well as to sell the product. But the main task is to identify the product, plainly, and to announce its price, breathlessly.

National consumer goods advertising differs sharply from this model of advertising. The connection between ad and sale, so direct in classified ads, or between ad and customer contact, reasonably direct in the January white sale ad, is very remote in the national consumer-goods ad. It is indirect in both space and time. The commercial for Coca-Cola or Alka-Seltzer does not say how the customer can buy the advertised product; it does not typically announce a phone number to call or a place to shop. It takes for granted the consumer's shopping skills and it assumes the successful distribution of the product to retail stores. In time, it does not presume a quick response of customers to its efforts. It does not presume that the consumers it wants to reach will see any given showing of the ad or, seeing it, quickly respond by buying. It is a general reminder or reinforcer, not an urgent appeal to go out and buy. What the ad says or pictures, then, is obliged to be relatively placeless and relatively timeless. National consumer-goods advertising is highly abstracted and self-contained. Where particular places are shown, they are generally flattened —a car, for instance, displayed in front of the Capitol building in Washington, does not connect the car to a particular place but to a familiar image of a place, photographed from the most familiar head-on spot. What is shown is more recognizable as a postcard than as physical space. A 1980 VW ad airbrushed out the statue of Ulysses S. Grant when it shot an ad in front of the Capitol because "only a small piece of it was sticking above the car. It looked confusing, so we took it out."[5] Particular times are almost never identified in magazine and television advertising, though timeless occasions are—the birthday party, the New Year's party, the weekend.

Similarly, the people pictured in magazine ads or television commercials are abstract people. This is not to say they are fictive characters. In a play or television series, actors generally portray particular people with particular names who, in the fictive universe they occupy, exist in a set of relations with other fictional characters and have a range of meanings within that world. An advertisement is not like this, it does not construct a fully fictive world. The actor or model does not play a particular person but a social type or a demographic category. A television actress, for instance, will be asked to audition for commercials that call for a "twenty-six to thirty-five-year-old P&G housewife." She is not supposed to represent a twenty-six-year-old or a thirty-year-old or a thirty-five-year-old but a "twenty-six–thirty-five-year-old" housewife, the sort likely to buy Procter & Gamble products. The age range from twenty-six to thirty-five corresponds not so much to a physical type as to a presumed social type with predictable consumer patterns. It is a demographic grouping used for market research. An actress seeking a role in a television commercial is expected to have two wardrobes ready for auditions—standard and "upscale." She is to represent either the middle-American housewife or the affluent American housewife, but never a particular person.[6]

There are apparent exceptions to this rule of abstractness but they themselves are instructive. Think, for instance, of the Polaroid camera commercials (of about 1977–82) in which James Garner apparently speaks as James Garner. But does he? After all, he is not really married to Mariette Hartley, the actress who plays his wife in the commercial. They are playing a couple (indeed, they are playing a couple playing). Some kind of fiction is being created. It is a fiction that rests for success on viewers knowing a lot about James Garner. But the television audience knows little or nothing about James Garner, the person. Garner does not play himself, the person, nor does he play a particular fictive character. Instead, he plays what I would call the generalized James Garner role, the type for which James Garner is always cast—handsome, gentle, bumbling, endearing, a combination of Bret Maverick from "Maverick" and Jim Rockford from "The Rockford Files."

Similarly, Robert Young did not play himself in the Sanka coffee ads where he identified himself as Robert Young. He played the generalized Robert Young character, a combination of his role as Jim Anderson in the television series "Father Knows Best" and his title role in "Marcus Welby, M.D.," quintessentially cheerful, moderate, mature, and full of good sense.[7] Even in many straightforward testimonial ads, the person played is not the actor or athlete as a human being but the actor or athlete flattened into a celebrity, a person, in Daniel Boorstin's nice phrase, "known for his well-knownness."[8]

Television stars who do commercials, ostensibly in their own names, invariably present their television personalities, not their own. When American Express sought to emphasize that their traveler's checks offered travelers security, they "looked for a spokesman perceived by the public as an authority on crime." Thus the choice of Karl Malden; not because he is Karl Malden, but because he once was Lt. Mike Stone in "The Streets of San Francisco." Similarly, Bill Cosby was used in Jello Pudding commercials because he had established himself in so many programs for children and was in a position to remind mothers that children like Jello.[9]

The task of the television personalities in commercials is to *appear,* suggesting and pulling back into well-established characters. The viewing audience will do the rest. Thus, established fictional characters may be as successful as well-known personalities. Old Lonely, the Maytag repairman, has done commercials for two decades and so has Mr. Whipple for Charmin; Madge the Manicurist (for Palmolive dishwashing liquid), Speedy Alka-Seltzer, and the Hamm's beer bear have been on and off the air for a generation. For the unknown actor, doing a television commercial presents an odd challenge. It is a kind of anti-acting. As one actress, Linda Stratton, put it: "You have to pull back into yourself, rather than project like on the stage. It's an entirely different technique that must be learned."[10]

This flat, abstract world of the advertisement is part of a deliberate effort to connect specific products in people's imaginations with certain demographic groupings or needs or occasions. Sometimes, in an effort not to exclude any potential customers from identifying with the product, advertisers choose not to show *any* people in their ads. For a generation from the 1930s into the 1950s, Guinness stout did not show people drinking in their ads: "This policy of non-identification was deliberate. It was argued that if Guinness was a drink for everyone, to identify it with a particular section of the market would be to limit its appeal."[11] In other cases, market research or good hunches or common sense identifies the specific population group most likely to consume the advertised product in quantity. Then an abstract representation of that group will be pictured in the ad.

Thus, abstraction is essential to the aesthetic and intention of contemporary national consumer-goods advertising. It does not represent reality nor does it build a fully fictive world. It exists, instead, on its own plane of reality, a plane I will call capitalist realism. By this term, I mean to label a set of aesthetic conventions, but I mean also to link them to the political economy whose values they celebrate and promote.

This is a different intention from that of Erving Goffman who notes some of the same features of advertisements and refers to them as "commercial realism."[12] For Goffman, commercial realism is "the standard transformation employed in contemporary ads," the particular kind of public portraiture advertising uses. Goffman suggests that commercial realism differs in two respects from the way people present themselves in actual life. In real life, according to Goffman, human activity is highly ritualized. People act out and live in social ideals, presenting to the world stereotyped pictures of themselves. In advertising, this is even more true; advertising is "hyper-ritualization." Second, advertising is *edited.* In both life and advertising, people present social ideals. But, in life, people are "stuck with a considerable amount of dull footage." People cannot edit their behavior enough to provide a purely ritualized social ideal. In commercial realism, editing is thorough and the social ideal is thereby portrayed as completely as possible.[13] Goffman's position is helpful but it is limited to characterizing the conventions of commercial art rather than trying also to link them to their cultural role in advanced capitalist societies. Of course, that may not be a task one can ultimately master, but I think it is worth attempting.

I can make what I mean by capitalist realism more clear by comparing it to socialist realism, the term from which, obviously, I have derived it. Socialist realism is official, state-sanctioned and state-governed art as practiced in the Soviet Union. As the First Soviet Writers' Congress defined it in 1934, socialist realism is an art obliged to present a "correct historically concrete representation of reality in its revolutionary development" and to do so in a form that will educate "the working masses in the spirit of socialism."[14] In practice, this means that artists and writers must meet certain aesthetic and moral demands. In theory, these demands are all in the service of a kind of realism. Socialist realist art must be faithful to life—but in certain prescribed ways:

1. Art should picture reality in simplified and typified ways so that it communicates effectively to the masses.
2. Art should picture life, but not as it is so much as life as it should become, life worth emulating.
3. Art should picture reality not in its individuality but only as it reveals larger social significance.
4. Art should picture reality as progress toward the future and so represent social struggles positively. It should carry an air of optimism.
5. Art should focus on contemporary life, creating pleasing images of new social phenomena, revealing and endorsing new features of society and thus aiding the masses in assimilating them.[15]

Without getting into a study of Soviet art, it should be apparent that the parallels are strong between what socialist realism is designed to do and what advertising in capitalist society intends to do, at least, national advertising for consumer goods. One could easily say that advertising tries to present a "correct historically concrete representation of reality in its capitalist development." What I will suggest in the next few pages is that American advertising, like socialist realist art, simplifies and typifies. It does not claim to picture reality as it is but reality as it should be—life and lives worth emulating. It is always photography or drama or discourse with a message—rarely picturing individuals, it shows people only as incarnations of larger social categories. It always assumes that there is progress. It is thoroughly optimistic, providing for any troubles that it identifies a solution in a particular product or style of life. It focuses, of course, on the new, and if it shows some signs of respect for tradition, this is only to help in the assimilation of some new commercial creation.

I do not want to suggest that magazine and television advertisements are always "realistic" in any conventional sense. Often commercials seek realism, but sometimes the aesthetic mode is surrealism, especially in ads for products, like perfume, closely connected in the culture to dream, fantasy, and desire. Sometimes the ad is in the mode of comedy or farce. The Federal Express television commercials with a Federal Express employee talking at a superhumanly rapid clip offer an example of this sort. Television commercials may picture ordinary citizens playing themselves—a self-consciously realistic style, or they may have well-known actors in consumer roles, or they may have little-known actors playing consumers, or they may do without actors altogether and use animation. Most of these forms are well enough established to generate parodies of them in other commercials. Not all of these forms employ the usual conventions of dramatic realism, but all of them tend toward the kind of abstractness I have outlined. They are set out of time and out of space. In most cases, real or surreal, sentimental or comic, straight or camp, they present simplified social scenes that show the world "as it should be," they picture people as representatives of larger social categories, and they seek an accommodation with whatever is new or newly marketable.

At present, efforts at a kind of realism or even super-realism dominate the making of advertisements, even in ads that are not, in dramatic form, realistic. For instance, there is a vogue for actors who do not look like actors. Karl Malden (for American Express Co.) and Robert Morley (for British Airways) are actors with character rather than beauty, "real-people actors." Robert Meury, copy chief at Backer & Spielvogel says, "We've been using celebrities in our Miller Lite spots from the start. But never just any celebrity—and never just any context. We make sure our stars are guys you'd enjoy having a beer with. And the locations we film in are always real bars. We even let our celebrities have a hand in the copy—the more involvement the better. After all, it isn't a performance we're after; we just want our spots to feel *real.*" Joe Sedelmaier, one of the most successful and original directors of commercials, on location in Los Angeles to cast a commercial for the Del Taco fast food chain, complained, "It is impossible to cast in L.A. Everyone looks plastic."[16] The whole American Express campaign, "Don't leave home without it," plays with the idea of celebrity, featuring famous people who are not *visually* well known. This inverts the conventions of celebrity advertising and induces the viewer to participate in the ad as in a guessing game.

The choice of "real" actors and real settings is matched by a move toward graininess rather than slickness in the film itself. There is also a move toward a kind of "documentary" style in television commercials that major advertisers, including Xerox Corp., Miles Laboratories Inc. (Alka-Seltzer), The Stroh Brewery Co., and General Motors Corp., favor. This "open camera" approach relies less on storyboard preparation of a commercial, more on what may happen spontaneously when the film is rolling. In 1983 Whitehall Laboratories (Anacin) initiated a kind of super- or hyper-realism in its television advertising.[17]

Of course, "real" is a cultural construct. The makers of commercials do not want what is real but what will seem real on film. Artificial rain is better than "God's rain" because it shows up better on film or tape. Seeking sites for the filming of the "Reach Out and Touch Someone" commercials, N. W. Ayer's staff sought not just actual homes but homes that would look real. By that, they meant homes that would look *stereotypical,* homes that would be consistent with a type they sought to picture as representative. Nothing in the commercial should distract the viewer. Nothing should lead the audience to criticize, to say, "That doesn't look real." So each piece of furniture had to be consistent with the overall image of the house even if, in fact, few houses are like the one depicted. In commercial production, there is a passionate, obsessive attention to making every detail look "right."[18]

If anything, advertising looks more real than it should. As Barbara Rosenblum writes in her study of professional photography, advertising photography uses "crisp focus" to create "a dense and busily detailed surface. Light is used in conjunction with focus to create a hypertactile effect. Things look real; in fact, almost too real." The surface is "overaccented," she says, and this "keeps the viewer's interest up front, in the foreground or middleground."[19] The rich, cinematic, often crowded detail in magazine ads and television commercials is most unlike the simple, bold wall posters of China or the Soviet Union and very unlike America's own social realist art of the thirties. The aesthetic sensibility is very different. The emotional intensity is very different, too; socialist realism is emotionally overextended, tugging toward inspiration, while capitalist realism is either cool, relishing understatement because it relies on common understanding with its audience, or sentimental, appealing openly to basic human feelings it is certain are already in place. There is no drawing out or up. The effort is to do with art what a former Foote, Cone & Belding creative chief urged his employees to do in writing copy for the consumer: "Talk to him in a way that gets him nodding in agreement before you try to sell him something."[20] The similarity between advertising and socialist realism is that both forms subordinate everything to a message that romanticizes the present or the potential of the present. If the visual aesthetic of socialist realism is designed to dignify the simplicity of human labor in the service of the state, the aesthetic of capitalist realism—without a masterplan of purposes—glorifies the pleasures and freedoms of consumer choice in defense of the virtues of private life and material ambitions.

Is Advertising State Art?

Advertising is not an official, state art.[21] There is no rulebook from an ad writers' congress. The government provides no positive guidance for advertising. It does provide some limitations on what advertisers may say. The Federal Trade Commission regulates advertising, avowedly in the interest of promoting full and fair information in the marketplace. The courts have some authority over advertising, too, though the tendency in recent decisions has been to deny it, extending First Amendment protection to "commercial speech." The government registers and protects patents and trademarks and thus encourages new product innovation and, by extension, the advertising that accompanies it. The government provides direct and indirect subsidies of advertising, not least of all by being a major advertiser itself in military recruiting and other areas.[22] What is official about advertising, if anything, is not that it is to a limited degree government regulated or government subsidized but that the government tacitly gives approval and support, along with the rest of society, to *unofficial* expression.

It would be playing with words to speak of advertising as "official" art. But to do so offers some interesting clarification. For instance, in the conflict over the 1980 Moscow Olympics in the wake of the Soviet invasion of Afghanistan, commentators of all political stripes deplored the fact that the Soviets intended to use the Olympics for "propaganda" purposes, to promote the communist way of life. Of course, Moscow intended exactly that. But how different is this from the way Americans used the 1980 Winter Olympics in Lake Placid? What is the sum of advertising for Minolta Corp., General Foods Corp. (Maxwell House), Texas Instruments Inc., Levi Strauss & Co., and the American Broadcasting Company if not efforts to advance the "American" or "capitalist" way of life?[23]

But only occasionally do advertisements invoke a sense of the nation as a whole, as in Olympics sponsorship or in a slogan like, "America is turning Seven-Up." Only occasionally do commercials make direct reference to American political ideals—Franklin Roosevelt brought the New Deal, John Kennedy the New Frontier, and Procter & Gamble brings to menstruating women "New Freedom." Reference to the nation as a whole is probably more common in American advertising than in European advertising. A British advertising executive, David Bernstein, has observed that American ads talk more about "America" than British ads speak of "Britain." In slogans like, "America shops for values at Sears" or "Helping insure the American way of life," advertising directly assimilates to its marketing goal the promotion of patriotic sentiment.[24] Still, most ads do not explicitly draw attention to the American polity but focus on homely toothpastes, cat foods, laundry detergents, and canned beers. If these ads are not strictly "official," can it be said nonetheless that they are advertisements for "capitalism" or the "American way of life"?

Taken collectively, these ads do articulate some of the operative values of American capitalism. As Soviet art idealizes the producer, American art idealizes the consumer; their tractor in the fields is matched by our home entertainment center in the den. Our advertising is clearly different from the univocal, centrally organized, and tightly controlled Soviet propaganda efforts. But it, too, is socially sanctioned and omnipresent. To engage in an elaborate analysis of advertising content is not my intention here. It seems clear enough that advertisements often point to middle-class material comfort as an enviable condition. It is also clear that advertisements reproduce and even sometimes exaggerate long-standing social inequalities. Black people are still largely invisible in advertising. Women are depicted as subordinate to men, childlike in both their charm and their dependence. All ideals and values are called into the service of and subordinated to the purchase of goods and the attainment of a materially satisfying style of life.[25]

One study nicely reveals a larger theme. Brigitte Jordan and Kathleen Bryant examined five hundred magazine advertisements in which couples were pictured. They drew their samples from popular magazines, women's magazines, men's magazines, and general circulation periodicals. They found, as one would expect, that the couples are almost always portrayed as happy, often happy in their intimacy. Couples are shown having fun, being affectionate, expressing sexuality, or demonstrating commitment to each other. There are no old, poor, sick, or unattractive couples in the ads. However the couples are pictured, they are invariably attentive to each other. As Jordan and Bryant argue, couples in life often are doing different things, even when they are together; there is regularly "mutual inattentiveness in the company of each other." Not so, in advertising. The authors found only six ads out of five hundred in which the couples were not shown in "explicit mutual reference."[26]

This suggests, again, that typification and idealization are the modes by which advertisements are produced. There is no intention of capturing life as it "really" is, but there is every intention of portraying social ideals, representing as normative those relatively rare moments of special-ness, bliss, or dreamlike satisfaction. What kind of satisfaction is pictured may vary widely—it may be sexual, it may be familial, it may be the expression of social values like the long-term commitment of a husband and wife to each other. It may be the values of male friendship at a bar or on a fishing trip, the intimacy of parent and child relations expressed in a telephone call or in a mother-daughter conversation that revolves around a commercial product. One Coca-Cola commercial I saw screened at a convention of advertisers showed a boy running in a field. It cut to the farmyard where two attractive people, obviously mother and father, were standing by the barn. They open the barn doors and the camera goes back to the boy running faster. Back to the barn, a pony is brought out. The happy faces of the parents—sharing, by the way, a Coke. The boy, surprise and joy on his face, coming closer. The parents, smiling at each other, drinking a Coke, perhaps tears in their eyes. The boy, joyous, hugging the pony. The proud parents. The boy, looking lovingly at his Mom and Dad. The parents, looking at each other. At the boy. And that was all. It was beautifully done. It brought the hint of tears to my own eyes and it evoked great enthusiasm in the auditorium. The advertisement does not so much invent social values or ideals of its own as it borrows, usurps, or exploits what advertisers take to be prevailing social values. It then reminds us of beautiful moments in our own lives or it pictures magical moments we would like to experience.

There is little one would want to call "capitalist" in these moments. Indeed, if capitalism is a system promoting private ownership, these ads are oddly anticapitalist or noncapitalist, honoring traditions of social solidarity like family, kinship, and friendship that at least in principle are in conflict with the logic of the market. What is capitalist is that these values are put to work to sell goods, invoked in the service of the marketplace. And what is also distinctively capitalist is that the satisfactions portrayed are invariably private, even if they are familial or social; they do not invoke public or collective values. They offer a public portraiture of ideals and values consistent with the promotion of a social order in which people are encouraged to think of themselves and their private worlds. Think of how hollow public service announcements generally sound. They, too, invoke values that matter to people. But they do not have the all-important frame that encompasses product advertising; they do not end in a sales pitch. Advertisements normally are complete only if there is, explicitly or implicitly, a call to the viewer or reader to take a small, do-able action well within his or her experience. The public service announcements ask for a sacrifice or gift, if they ask for anything. People are capable of sacrifice and of giving, but the television announcement that asks for sacrifice seems incongruous.[27]

The Functions of a Pervasive Art Form

If advertising is not an official or state art, it is nonetheless clearly *art.* The development of painting, photography, and prints in the fine arts has been intimately intertwined with the development of commercial art for a century. While few American writers have joined Malcolm Cowley in exclaiming that literature "should borrow a little punch and confidence from American business,"[28] artists and photographers from Toulouse-Lautrec on have frequently done commercial art or been influenced by it. The difference between fashion photography and photography as art is subtle, if it exists at all, and certainly the techniques and innovations in fashion photography influence photography as fine art as often as the other way around. In recent years, television commercial techniques have influenced film and commercial directors have become makers of feature films.[29]

Needless to say, most advertising is dull and conventional, as creative workers in the business are the first to point out. But there is no question that advertising shapes aesthetic tastes, and at least occasionally educates the eye in ways serious artists can applaud. Critics quick to attack the "desires" advertising promotes are apt not to notice, or having noticed, to reject, the visual tastes advertising shapes. One can gaze, as literary historian Leo Spitzer observed, "with disinterested enjoyment" at an advertisement whose claims for its product do not seem the least bit credible. Advertising "may offer a fulfillment of the *aesthetic* desires of modern humanity."[30] In a study of children's attitudes toward television commercials, Thomas Robertson and John Rossiter found a sharp decline in the extent to which children trust commercials, from first grade to third grade to fifth. But when asked if they *liked* commercials, the decline was less severe.[31] Even cultivated and critical adults, if honest, will acknowledge very often a certain "liking" or aesthetic appeal in ads they may in other respects find offensive.

It is important to acknowledge, then, that advertising is art—and is often more successful aesthetically than commercially. (In a 1981 survey of what television commercials people find the "most outstanding," a third of the people who selected Kodak ads praised James Garner and Mariette Hartley for their roles. In fact, Garner and Hartley appeared in Polaroid commercials—aesthetically successful without leaving as strong a commercial impression as the sponsor might have wished.)[32] We collect it. Old candy and coffee tins, old Coke signs, old tourist brochures, these are our antiques, our collected unconscious. But if advertising is art, the question remains: What does art do? What does art that is intended to do something do? What does art do, especially art as pervasive and penetrating as advertising in the contemporary United States?

As obvious as this question seems to be, its formulation is not yet satisfactory. Does advertising turn people into consumers? Does it create needs and desires? Or does it rest for its minimal plausibility on exactly the world its critics (and some of its proponents) claim it is creating? Take, for instance, James Duesenberry's theory of consumer behavior, which he derives from the simple assumptions that (1) people see goods around them superior to what they own and (2) that people believe high-quality goods are desirable and important. Surely advertising reinforces the belief that high-quality goods are desirable and important and surely it leads people to see representations of superior goods around them but it does not seem reasonable to imagine that advertising had much to do with creating these conditions in the first place. Duesenberry takes the belief in the worth of superior goods to lie deep in American culture:

In a fundamental sense the basic source of the drive toward higher consumption is to be found in the character of our culture. A rising standard of living is one of the major goals of our society. Much of our public policy is directed toward this end. Societies are compared with one another on the basis of the size of their incomes. In the individual sphere people do not expect to live as their parents did, but more comfortably and conveniently. The consumption pattern of the moment is conceived of not as part of a way of life, but only as a temporary adjustment to circumstances. We expect to take the first available chance to change the pattern.[33]

That sounds like a world advertising would love to create, if it could. But it also sounds like the world Tocqueville described in 1830, well before advertising was much more than long gray lists of patent medicine notices in the newspapers. It sounds as much like a world likely to invent modern advertising as a world that modern advertising would like to invent.

Then what does advertising do?

Advertising might be said to lead people to a belief in something. Advertising may make people believe they are inadequate without Product X and that Product X will satisfactorily manage their inadequacies. More likely, it may remind them of inadequacies they have already felt and may lead them, once at least, to try a new product that just might help, even though they are well aware that it probably will not. Alternatively, advertising may lead people to believe generally in the efficacy of manufactured consumer goods for handling all sorts of ills, medical or social or political, even if a given ad fails to persuade that a given product is efficacious. There is the question of belief in a small sense—do people put faith in the explicit claims of advertisements, change their attitudes toward advertised goods, and go out and buy them? And there is the question of belief in a larger sense—do the assumptions and attitudes implicit in advertising become the assumptions and attitudes of the people surrounded by ads, whether or not they actually buy the advertised goods?

Social critics have argued that the greatest danger of advertising may be that it creates belief in the larger sense. It has been common coin of advertising critics that advertising is a kind of religion. This goes back at least to James Rorty who wrote of the religious power of advertising, holding that "advertising . . . becomes a body of doctrine."[34] Ann Douglas has written that advertising is "the only faith of a secularized consumer society."[35] In more measured tones, Leo Spitzer relates advertising to the "preaching mentality" in Protestantism and says that advertising "has taken over the role of the teacher of morals." The advertiser, "like the preacher" must constantly remind the backslider of "his real advantage" and "must 'create the demand' for the better."[36]

Others have observed that many leading advertisers were the children of ministers or grew up in strict, religious households.[37] The trouble with these remarks, and others like them, is that they fail to establish what kind of belief, if any, people actually have in advertisements. And they fail to observe that advertising is quintessentially part of the profane, not the sacred, world. Marghanita Laski has observed of British television that neither religious programs nor royal occasions are interrupted or closely juxtaposed to commercial messages. This is true, though to a lesser degree, with American television—the more sacred the subject, the less the profanity of advertising is allowed to intrude. If it does intrude, the advertiser takes special pains to provide unusually dignified and restrained commercials. If the advertiser fails to make such an adjustment, as in the commercial sponsorship of a docudrama on the Holocaust in 1980, public outrage follows.[38]

So I am not persuaded by the "advertising is religion" metaphor, on the face of it. But the problem with seeing advertising as religion goes still deeper: advertising may be more powerful the *less* people believe in it, the less it is an acknowledged creed. This idea can be formulated in several ways. Northrop Frye has argued that advertisements, like other propaganda, "stun and demoralize the critical consciousness with statements too absurd or extreme to be dealt with seriously by it." Advertisements thus wrest from people "not necessarily acceptance, but dependence on their versions of reality." Frye continues:

> Advertising implies an economy which has some independence from the political structure, and as long as this independence exists, advertising can be taken as a kind of ironic game. Like other forms of irony, it

says what it does not wholly mean, but nobody is obliged to believe its statements literally. Hence it creates an illusion of detachment and mental superiority even when one is obeying its exhortations.[39]

Literary critics have been more sensitive than social scientists to the possibility that communications do not mean what they say —and that this may be the very center of their power. There has rarely been room for the study of irony in social science but irony is a key element in literary studies. Leo Spitzer, like Frye, observes that ads do not ask to be taken literally. In a Sunkist oranges ad he analyzed, he found that the ad "transports the listener into a world of Arcadian beauty, but with no insistence that this world really exists." The ad pictures "an Arcady of material prosperity," but Spitzer holds that the spectator "is equipped with his own criteria, and subtracts automatically from the pictures of felicity and luxury which smile at him from the billboards."[40]

According to Spitzer, people are detached in relation to advertising. They feel detached, disillusioned, and forcibly reminded of the tension between life as it is lived and life as it is pictured. This is a characteristic attitude toward precious or baroque art. In this attitude, no condemnation of the excess of the art is necessary because one is so firmly anchored in the matter-of-fact reality that contradicts it.

For Spitzer, people are genuinely detached in relation to advertising. They view it from an aesthetic distance. For Frye, in contrast, people have only "an illusion of detachment." For Frye, it is precisely the belief people have that they *are* detached that makes the power of advertising all the more insidious. Advertising may create attitudes and inclinations even when it does not inspire belief; it succeeds in creating attitudes because it does not make the mistake of *asking* for belief.

This corresponds to the argument of a leading market researcher, Herbert Krugman, of General Electric Co. research. He holds that the special power of television advertising is that the ads interest us so little, not that they appeal to us so much. Television engages the audience in "low-involvement learning." Krugman's argument is that the evidence in psychology on the learning and memorization of nonsense syllables or other trivial items is very much like the results in market research on the recall of television commercials. He draws from this the suggestion that the two kinds of learning may be psychologically the same, a "learning without involvement." In such learning, people are not "persuaded" of something. Nor do their attitudes change. But there is a kind of "sleeper" effect. While viewers are not persuaded, they do alter the structure of their perceptions about a product, shifting "the relative salience of attributes" in the advertised brand. Nothing follows from this until the consumer arrives at the supermarket, ready to make a purchase. Here, at the behavioral level, the real change occurs:

> . . . the purchase situation is the catalyst that reassembles or brings out all the potentials for shifts in salience that have accumulated up to that point. The product or package is then suddenly seen in a new, "somehow different" light although nothing verbalizable may have changed *up to that point.*[41]

Consumers in front of the television screen are relatively unwary. They take ads to be trivial or transparent or both. What Krugman suggests is that precisely this attitude enables the ad to be successful. Were consumers convinced of the importance of ads, they would bring into play an array of "perceptual defenses" as they do in situations of persuasion regarding important matters.

Any understanding of advertising in American culture must come to grips with the ironic game it plays with us and we play with it. If there are signs that Americans bow to the gods of advertising, there are equally indications that people find the gods ridiculous. It is part of the popular culture that advertisements are silly. Taking potshots at commercials has been a mainstay of *Mad* magazine and of stand-up comedians for decades. When Lonesome Rhodes meets Marsha Coulihan, station manager for a country radio station, in Budd Schulberg's story, "Your Arkansas Traveler," he says to her: "You must be a mighty smart little gal to be handlin' this here raddio station all by yourself." She replies: "My good man, I am able to read without laughing out loud any commercial that is placed before me. I am able to pick out a group of records and point to the guy in the control room each time I want him to play one. And that is how you run a rural radio station."[42]

If advertising is the faith of a secular society, it is a faith that inspires remarkably little professed devotion. If it is a body of doctrine, it is odd that so few followers would affirm the doctrine to be true, let alone inspired. Christopher Lasch has seen this problem. He argues that the trouble with the mass media is not that they purvey untruths but that "the rise of mass media makes the categories of truth and falsehood irrelevant to an evaluation of their influence. Truth has given way to credibility, facts to statements that sound authoritative without conveying any authoritative information."[43] But this analysis will not do for the problem of advertising. People are not confused about the importance of truth and falsity in their daily lives. It is just that they do not regularly apply judgments of truth to advertisements. Their relationship to advertisements is not a matter of evidence, truth, belief, or even credibility.

Then what is it? Whether Krugman's formulation is right or wrong, his view at least leads us to ask more pointedly what kind of belief or nonbelief people have in relation to advertising. Again, this is in some sense a question about religion. The form of the question of whether or not people believe advertising messages is like the question of whether or not people believe in and are affected by religious teachings. On the latter question, anthropologist Melford Spiro has distinguished five levels at which people may "learn" an ideology:

1. Most weakly, they may *learn about* an ideological concept.
2. They may learn about and *understand* the concept.
3. They may *believe* the concept to be true or right.
4. The concept may become salient to them and inform their "behavioral environment"—that is, they may not only believe the concept but organize their lives contingent on that belief.
5. They may internalize the belief so that it is not only cognitively salient but motivationally important. It not only guides but instigates action.[44]

Tests of the effectiveness of advertising are most often tests of "recall"; ads are judged by the market researchers to be "effective" if they have established Level 1 belief, learning about a concept. Advertisers, of course, are more interested in Levels 4 and 5, although their ability to measure success at these levels is modest. Most theories of advertising assume that the stages of belief are successive, that consumers must go through Level 1 before Level 2, Level 2 before Level 3, and so on. What Krugman argues and what Northrop Frye can be taken to be saying, is that one can reach Level 4 without ever passing through Level 3. The voices of advertising may inform a person's "behavioral environment" without inspiring belief at any time or at any fundamental level. The stages are not sequential. One is independent from the next.

"What characterizes the so-called advanced societies," Roland Barthes wrote, "is that they today consume images and no longer, like those of the past, beliefs; they are therefore more liberal, less fanatical, but also more 'false' (less 'authentic') . . ."[45] Barthes is right about the present but very likely exaggerates the break from the past. A few years ago I saw a wonderful exhibit at the Museum of Traditional and Popular Arts in Paris, dealing with religion in rural France in the nineteenth century. The exhibit demonstrated that religious imagery was omnipresent in the French countryside. There were paintings, crucifixes, saints, and Bible verses adorning the most humble objects—plates, spoons, cabinets, religious articles of all sorts, especially holiday objects, lithographs for the living room wall, greeting cards, illustrated books, board games for children, pillowcases, marriage contracts, painted furniture for children, paper dolls, carved and painted signs for religious processions, and so forth. Of course, the largest architectural monuments in most towns were the churches, presiding over life crises and the visual landscape alike. And, as French historian Georges Duby has argued, the grandeur of church architecture was intended as a form of "visual propaganda."[46]

None of this necessarily made the ordinary French peasant a believing Christian. There were pagan rites in nineteenth-century rural France, as there are still today. Nor, I expect, did this mass-mediated reinforcement of Christian culture make the peasant ignore the venality of the church as an institution or the sins of its local representatives.

Still, the Church self-consciously used imagery to uplift its followers and potential followers, and there was no comparable suffusion of the countryside by other systems of ideas, ideals, dreams, and images. When one thought of salvation or, more modestly, searched for meanings for making sense of life, there was primarily the materials of the Church to work with. It has been said that languages do not differ in what they can express but in what they can express *easily*.[47] It is the same with pervasive or official art: it brings some images and expressions quickly to mind and makes others relatively unavailable. However blatant the content of the art, its consequences remain more subtle. Works of art, in general, anthropologist Clifford Geertz has written, do not in the first instance "celebrate social structure or forward useful doctrine. They materialize a way of experiencing; bring a particular cast of mind into the world of objects, where men can look at it."[48] Art, he says, does not create the material culture nor serve as a primary force shaping experience. The experience is already there. The art is a commentary on it. The public does not require the experience it already has but a statement or reflection on it: "What it needs is an object rich enough to see it in; rich enough, even, to, in seeing it, deepen it."[49]

Capitalist realist art, like socialist realism, more often flattens than deepens experience. Here I judge the art and not the way of life it promotes. Jack Kerouac may deepen our experience of the road and the automobile, but the advertising agencies for General Motors and Ford typically flatten and thin our experience of the same objects. This need not be so. The AT&T "Reach Out and Touch Someone" commercials for long-distance telephone calling sentimentalize an experience that genuinely has or can have a sentimental element. If these ads do not deepen the experience they at least articulate it in satisfying ways.

There is another side to the coin: if an ad successfully romanticizes a moment, it provides a model of sentiment that one's own more varied and complicated experience cannot live up to. Most of our phone calls, even with loved ones, are boring or routine. When art romanticizes the exotic or the exalted, it does not call our own experience into question, but when it begins to take everyday life as the subject of its idealization, it creates for the audience a new relationship to art. The audience can judge the art against its own experience and can thereby know that the art idealizes and falsifies. At the same time, the art enchants and tantalizes the audience with the possibility that it is *not* false. If it can play on this ambiguity, art becomes less an imitation of life and turns life into a disappointing approximation of art.

The issue is not that advertising art materializes or "images" certain *experiences* but, as Geertz says, a *way of experiencing.* The concern with advertising is that this way of experiencing—a consumer way of life—does not do justice to the best that the human being has to offer and, indeed, entraps people in exploitative and self-defeating activity. But what can it really mean to say that art materializes a way of experience? What does that *do?* Why should a social system *care* to materialize its way of experiencing? The individual artists, writers, and actors who put the ads together do not feel this need. They frequently have a hard time taking their work seriously or finding it expressive of anything at all they care about.

Think of a smaller social system, a two-person social system, a marriage. Imagine it to be a good marriage, where love is expressed daily in a vast array of shared experiences, shared dreams, shared tasks and moments. In this ideal marriage, the couple continually make and remake their love. Then why, in this marriage, would anything be amiss if the two people did not say to each other, "I love you"? Why, in a relationship of such obviously enacted love, should it seem necessary to say out loud, "I love you"?

Because, I think, making the present audible and making the implicit explicit is necessary to engage and renew a whole train of commitments, responsibilities, and possibilities. "I love you" does not create what is not present. Nor does it seal what is present. But it must be spoken and respoken. It is necessary speech because people need to see in pictures or hear in words even what they already know as deeply as they know anything, *especially* what they know as deeply as they know anything. Words are actions.

This is also true in large social systems. Advertising is capitalism's way of saying "I love you" to itself.

The analogy, of course, is not perfect and I do not mean to jump from marriage to market with unqualified abandon. But in social systems writ large—and not just capitalism but all social systems—there are efforts both individual and collective to turn experience into words, pictures, and doctrines. Once created, these manifestations have consequences. They become molds for thought and feeling, if one takes a deterministic metaphor, or they become "equipment for living" if one prefers a more voluntaristic model or—to borrow from Max Weber and choose a metaphor somewhere in the middle, they serve as switchmen on the tracks of history. In the case of advertising, people do not necessarily "believe" in the values that advertisements present. Nor need they believe for a market economy to survive and prosper. People need simply get used to, or get used to not getting used to, the institutional structures that govern their lives. Advertising does not make people believe in capitalist institutions or even in consumer values, but so long as alternative articulations of values are relatively hard to locate in the culture, capitalist realist art will have some power.

Of course, alternative values *are* available in American culture. In some artistic, intellectual, and ethnic enclaves, one can encounter premises and principles that directly challenge capitalism and the expansion of the market to all phases of life. In contrast, the mainstream news and entertainment media operate within a relatively circumscribed range of values. But even in this narrower discourse, there is often criticism of consumer values or of the excesses of a consumer society. I came upon attacks on materialism, suburbia, conformity, and advertising in the 1950s as a student in social studies classes in a public junior high school and high school. Only a few years ago, people spoke contemptuously of the "me generation" and President Jimmy Carter diagnosed a national "crisis of confidence," opining that "we've discovered that owning things and consuming things does not satisfy our longing for meaning."[50] Recent lampooning of "Preppies" and "Yuppies" (young, upwardly-mobile professionals) betrays anxiety about, if also accommodation to, consumption as a way of life. So I do not suggest that advertisements have a monopoly in the symbolic marketplace. Still, no other cultural form is as accessible to children; no other form confronts visitors and immigrants to our society (and migrants from one part of society to another) so forcefully; and probably only professional sports surpasses advertising as a source of visual and verbal clichés, aphorisms, and proverbs. Advertising has a special cultural power.

The pictures of life that ads parade before consumers are familiar, scenes of life as in some sense we know it or would like to know it. Advertisements pick up and represent values already in the culture. But these values, however deep or widespread, are not the only ones people have or aspire to, and the pervasiveness of advertising makes us forget this. Advertising picks up some of the things that people hold dear and re-presents them to people as *all* of what they value, assuring them that the sponsor is the patron of common ideals. That is what capitalist realist art, like other pervasive symbolic systems, does. Recall again that languages differ not in what they can express but in what they can express *easily*. This is also true in the languages of art, ideology, and propaganda. It is the kind of small difference that makes a world of difference and helps construct and maintain different worlds.

8

An Evaluation of Advertising

ADVERTISING was barely a speck on the screen of American culture when Alexis de Tocqueville visited America in 1830 and observed "a kind of decent materialism" emerging. Restrained as it was, Tocqueville assured his readers that it "will not corrupt souls" but he worried that it would "soften and imperceptibly loosen the springs of action."[1] By 1900, with advertising established as a business institution of modest but growing proportion, concern about the materialism of the modern world had achieved great intensity. Max Weber expressed the passion well in the final pages of *The Protestant Ethic and the Spirit of Capitalism,* an essay focusing on Europe but strongly influenced by his recent trip to America. Weber wrote that "material goods have gained an increasing and finally an inexorable power over the lives of men as at no previous period in history." For him, material goods that had served the early Puritan as a sign of grace had come to be not sign but final substance, the goal that personal striving sought to attain. A world of spirit was losing out to a world of matter and the human project seemed encased in the leaden-ness of things.[2]

That is still the indictment a consumer culture must face. Advertising and marketing, as part of the cultural complex of materialism, are codefendants. The indictment is strengthened by ecological concern that human *life,* as well as human spirit, is threatened by the headlong rush to produce and to consume.

The defenders of marketing and advertising seek a separate trial. Perhaps, they admit, there are things wrong with a consumer culture, but advertising is not responsible for them. Marketing, they say, merely identifies and responds to human needs and does not—cannot—create the motivations that propel the race of consumption. They are appalled that critics imagine they have such overwhelming powers. They easily brush off criticism that attributes to advertising untold magical influence, extraordinary psychological sophistication, or primary responsibility for creating a consumer culture. They show that they work to reach people already predisposed to the product they are selling, that their appeals stress solid product information as often as they engage in emotional manipulation, and that the consumer is so fickle and the world so complex that their best-laid plans go astray as often as not.

All of this is true. But it is a much less sturdy defense of marketing than it appears. The pseudopopulist rhetoric of "discovering needs" and giving the public what it says it wants is misleading on at least four counts.

First, marketers do not actually seek to discover what consumers "want" but what consumers want *from among commercially viable choices.* One can hardly blame marketers for this, but because of it, one cannot accept the rhetoric of "we have the consumer always in mind." Marketers keep the consumer in mind only to the degree that the consumer defines his or her own prospects in terms agreeable to marketers. Thus consumers are not asked if they would prefer public television to advertising-supported television or public transportation to private automobiles or government-supported health care to private physicians.

Developers survey consumers to find out what kind of housing project they prefer, but they do not ask if a public park would be more desirable.

Nor do they ask consumers if they prefer long-term consumer benefits to short-term. Nor do they ask if consumers would like a role in corporate decision making, some representation of consumer interests on the boards of private firms. As marketers read people's preferences for particular products, they take everything else in society as settled—the legitimacy of a market economy, the good sense of devoting the nation's wealth to things that can be commercialized in the short-run, the justice of focusing commercial development on the needs of consumers with the majority of dollars rather than on the needs of the majority of consumers, and the rightness of leaving the task of identifying needs and desires in private hands not responsible to public oversight. In short, the consumers the marketers listen to are not persons, not citizens, but thin voices choosing from among a set of predetermined options. The "people" the marketers are concerned with are only those people or those parts of people that fit into the image of the consumer the marketer has created.

Second, marketers do not listen to all people equally. There is nothing democratic or populist about an approach that listens ten times as carefully to the person with $10,000 in discretionary income as to the person with $1,000. But that is what marketers do. The point is to make money, not to please people. The marketers keep their eyes on the main prize—pocketbooks, not persons. This yields an array of consumer choices top heavy in luxury, and it sometimes works directly to diminish the array of goods available to the person of modest means. For instance, in the competition for the affluent person's dollar, more and more extras become standard equipment on automobiles and other products, and the low-income consumer has no choice but to go deeper into debt to pay for the simplest model, now weighted with superfluous "standard" equipment. In Third World countries, national and multinational corporations provide a highly inappropriate array of products for local needs because they serve largely the very small affluent population in those nations. This is especially noticeable and dangerous in an area like that of health care: "Since middle-income and rich consumers represent the main market for modern drugs, pharmaceutical companies concentrate on furnishing remedies for middle-class ailments like general fatigue, headaches, and constipation rather than for low-income diseases like leprosy, filariasis, and tuberculosis."[3]

Third, marketers wrongly assume that since "good advertising kills a bad product," they can do little harm; people will only buy what they find satisfying. This works, as I have argued, only if people have enough information available to know what the range of possibilities is and how to purchase wisely. This is not true for many populations: poor people, children, Third World peoples, people entering new social roles, people with limited time or uncertain emotional stability for making decisions. Even with educated, middle-class adults, where the product sold is complex and where the normal adult is not able to make informed comparisons among products, advertising or other marketing practices can lead people to buy things that they do not need, things that will not "satisfy" their desires, and things that are not good for them. Financial institutions that advertise adjustable-rate mortgages have in some instances been guilty of an old-fashioned "bait and switch" tactic addressed to consumers smart enough not to fall for the practice when it concerns less complex products. The ads emphasize the below-market "teaser" interest rates and play down the true cost of the loan.[4] Life insurance is another case in point. Middle-class, educated people who want both some security and some savings buy whole life insurance when many of them would be better off buying cheaper term life insurance and investing the difference in an ordinary passbook savings account. People are unusually anxious about and ill informed about life insurance; tens of thousands have unwisely turned over their money to insurance companies.[5]

Finally, the marketing ideology mistakenly assumes that responding to discovered, felt needs among consumers is an innocuous activity—that "the people say they want it" is defense enough of a business practice. Obviously, a conscientious marketer would want to circumscribe such a view to say that some goods are harmful and should not be sold or promoted even if people want them. Drug pushers who claim they sell only to people who are already heavy users, are not likely to gain one's sympathy. Marketers and advertisers understand this and while they do not *collectively* take positions on the worth of products, they find ways to accommodate individual moral views. Thus many advertising agencies gracefully excuse employees from working on accounts such as those for cigarettes or liquor if their personal moral positions forbid it.

But responding to consumers' expressed desires is potentially harmful even when the product in question is within the bounds of acceptable usage. Even when advertising and other marketing practices respond to expressed desires, they surely reinforce those desires, give them life, embodiment, and provide them a permanence they might not otherwise attain. If there is an infrastructure of consumption—a set of social conditions that predispose one toward certain patterns of consuming, there is also a superstructure of consumption, a set of consuming images, that does its part, too, to make a given product normal, acceptable, convenient, manageable, and popular. There is no proof of this hypothesis and no way to specify the precise effects of promotional efforts. But that they play a role is as obvious as their provable demonstration is elusive.

Advertising not only promotes specific products but also fosters a consumer way of life. As I have insisted, there are many other factors that also promote consumerism, but this does not mean advertising's contribution can be overlooked.

However misconceived the arguments of advertising's critics, the defense of advertising has been obtuse and disturbingly indifferent to genuine concerns about the morality of marketing. There is plenty to be concerned about. If American materialism has often been decent and virtuous, as Tocqueville observed, it has not always been so, and the key institutions in the cultural complex of materialism are implicated in its failings. What degree of responsibility should one ascribe to advertising? It is not possible to say. But nor is it possible to think through the role of advertising in society without coming to some views about the rights and wrongs of the institution and stating them clearly. A few concluding remarks, then, in evaluation of the role of advertising in American society:

1. Advertising serves a useful informational function that will not and should not be abandoned. It helps people know about available consumer choices and helps them make more rational consumer judgments. This is especially true of price advertising and strongly informational advertising. Even when advertising is not very informative, it can be a modest form of consumer protection, providing consumers some knowledge of the availability of products and so making them less dependent on the local retailer.

2. Advertising probably has a socially democratizing influence but one with an ultimately inegalitarian outcome. It lets the people who are not in-the-know in the know. It helps people to recognize what external signs have currency and helps them know how to move in social circles they may not otherwise have access to or knowledge about. The distribution of consumer goods is much more egalitarian than the distribution of wealth in the form of stocks, bonds, and Swiss bank accounts.[6] This may lead people to imagine the world to be more genuinely egalitarian than it is. This may make people more acquiescent, accommodating them to a stratified society whose degree of inequality is protected by its relative invisibility.

3. The most offensive advertising tends to have the least informational content. It thus has the slightest defense as a legitimate feature of the economic system. However, it helps sustain the media. Until we devise some better way of supporting a relatively free and relatively varied media system, this is an incidental but important virtue of advertising. If advertising were more informative and espoused a more diverse set of values, it would support the media just as well. What is defended by this argument is advertising in the abstract, not the actual advertising we have. Further, advertising does not support the media in a way well designed to foster a healthy democracy. Advertising is skewed toward upscale audiences. Large circulation newspapers with working-class or general readerships have suffered as advertisers have shifted to television and specialized upscale print publications. Advertising supports the media but by no means in a way ideal for the democratic process.[7]

4. Some advertising promotes dangerous products or promotes potentially dangerous products to groups unlikely to be able to

use them wisely. Liquor advertising to the young or to the heavy drinker, if it is effective even in the slightest, is socially costly and morally questionable.[8] The advertising and marketing of infant formula in Third World countries where poverty and ignorance guarantee widespread abuse of the product is a grotesque case of the pursuit of profit gone berserk. It is the kind of savagery that people of some future generations may look back on as we look back to slavery, witch burning, or infanticide.

5. Nonprice advertising often promotes bad values, whether it effectively sells products or not. It peppers the airwaves with the insouciant promotion of values that, on a personal basis, few advertisers or copywriters or artists would affirm for themselves or their children. It speaks to people as no decent person would talk to a friend or neighbor or customer. An egregious instance in the past year is the advertising for home computers which, on negligible evidence of the importance of computers in children's educational development, encourages parents to believe they will be ruining their children's lives if they do not shell out a few thousand dollars now for a computer. This advertising, and too much other advertising, takes advantage of people's anxieties or fondly held hopes in order to make money. Whether it works or not, it is indecent.[9]

Advertising often incorporates key values of family, love, and friendship, but it all too often promotes values that our religious traditions, our schools, and our most respected counselors urge us to reject. Too much advertising winks at sexism or encourages it. Too much advertising encourages and legitimates self-indulgence while executives from the corporations that do the advertising self-righteously bemoan the decline of the work ethic in America.

6. Advertising could survive and sell goods without promoting values as bad as those it favors now. Some liquor companies promote "moderate drinking" in their ads. These ads provide information at the same time that they promote a product. Some cereal companies now provide information about balanced meals in their ads while still plugging their brand of cereal. This seems to me a step forward. Automobile ads that stressed the dangers of driving and the advantages of safety features would not be

taken amiss. Perhaps marketing departments and advertising agencies could even encourage auto manufacturers to install safety equipment that for decades they have resisted. It is certainly possible to harness the techniques of advertising for prosocial ends without making commercials anti-business. Advertising techniques in the Third World, for instance, have been employed not only to sell infant formula in a way that guarantees infant deaths but also to instruct people in boiling water and other practices that help preserve health and life.[10]

7. Advertising is but one factor among many in shaping consumer choice and human values. The question, ultimately, is not one of how people independently arrive at a set of desires. Desires are never independently arrived at, but are socially constructed. The important question is what social conditions will be most conducive to autonomous, rational choice. What is the sum of the influence of advertising, family, school, government policy, and the promotional efforts of private industries on personal values? How does a nation that assigns more independent decision-making authority to private enterprise than does any other developed country in the world shape desire and form or deform human preferences?

Although advertising is but one factor among many, there are serious objections to it that do not apply to some of the other forces in the formation of need and desire. Advertising comes from *outside* the community whereas parents and often (though not always) teachers are a part of a person's community. The objection to advertising is an objection to a "foreign power" and critics from both left and right object to advertising for much the same reason that critics from both ends of the political spectrum have supported local control of schooling. One's children are going to be influenced by forces outside the family—how can one hold those forces responsible? Can the outside forces be made answerable to the community? There are ways for a community to exercise some control over its school system or over government policy, but there is scarcely any effective way to regulate the messages that come into the community from the mass media, especially the broadcast media. Where one's exposure to advertising is relatively "voluntary" as it is with print advertising, objections to advertising as a "foreign power" are modest. But where exposure is largely unavoidable, as it is with billboards, radio and television, advertising is objectionable as an outside, literally unaccountable influence.

Advertisements are a ripe object for analysis. They are too vivid a body of evidence about what is base in American life to be overlooked. But I hope that critics of advertising will not misspend their energies by taking symbol for substance and believing that the analysis of advertising can substitute for an understanding of the economic, political, social and cultural forces that give rise to it and contribute to the social phenomena often attributed to it.

I hope that people who work in advertising will consider my suggestions for making their activities less "the single most value-destroying activity of a business civilization" in Robert Heilbroner's overblown but still troubling words.[11] Advertising can be, in some measure, an art that enhances human and humane values. Some individual advertising workers would fervently welcome any opportunity to make their craft one they could be proud of, not just aesthetically, but morally. But there is very little that professional associations in the business have done to make this possible. There are responsible voices in advertising, to be sure. The generally liberal, "good government" tone of *Advertising Age* is a case in point. But it seems to me that the professional associations in advertising have been more concerned to defend the worth of advertising than to worry about creating an activity they would not need to be so defensive about. Despite the existence of the Advertising Council, there is no tradition of *pro bono* work in advertising as there is in law; despite the National Advertising Review Board, there are no serious standards of condemnation for work that promotes products or values that advertising workers would not accept in their own homes. Nor is there a sense that all communication is an interaction and, potentially, an education. The range of educative possibilities in a page of print or a thirty-second spot is limited, but the opportunity, however small, remains—and remains largely untapped.

Having criticized the advertising industry, I should also say that there is not much that the universities, including the business schools, have done to make advertising better understood, let alone more responsible and responsive to other institutions of moral leadership. As for my own world of social science, I hope that more of my colleagues will take up the suggestions here and in other recent works for a new sociology of consumption. It is time for a study that will not be a reflexlike intellectual revulsion at the world of goods but an effort to understand what place material culture might hold in a good world.

NOTES

Introduction

1. Christy Marshall, "FCB Chief Raps TV Nets," *Advertising Age,* May 9, 1983, p. 2. Leo Bogart and Charles Lehman, "The Case of the 30-Second Commercial," *Journal of Advertising Research* 23 (February-March 1983): 11–18.

2. On the concept of the "mock reader" or the "implied audience" see Walker Gibson, "Authors, Speakers, Readers, and Mock Readers" in Jane P. Tompkins, *Reader-Response Criticism* (Baltimore: Johns Hopkins University Press, 1980), pp. 1–6. (The essay originally appeared in *College English,* February 1950, pp. 265–69.)

3. Fred Posner, "Advertising Efficiency: An Intensely Personal Matter" (New York: N. W. Ayer Inc., 1982).

4. Christopher Lasch, *The Culture of Narcissism* (New York: W. W. Norton, 1978), p. 72. Lasch's concern is with the consumer as a person who finds life's meaning in the purchase of economic goods and services. See also Otis Pease, who writes that the modern task of advertising is to convince the citizen "to conceive of himself primarily as a consumer of goods," in *The Responsibilities of American Advertising: Private Control and Public Influence, 1920–1940* (New Haven: Yale University Press, 1958), p. 1. Others are troubled by a "consumer orientation" that extends to nonmarket action and a "market mentality" as a style of personality that takes everything in life to be a matter of private choice, including even the choice of religious commitment. See, for instance, Thomas Luckmann, *The Invisible Religion* (New York: Macmillan, 1967), pp. 98–106 on the consumer orientation to the sacred cosmos and ultimate meanings.

5. James Coleman, *The Asymmetrical Society* (Syracuse: Syracuse University Press, 1982), p. 132.

6. Stuart Ewen, *Captains of Consciousness: Advertising and the Social Roots of the Consumer Culture* (New York: McGraw-Hill, 1976), p. 12.

7. John K. Galbraith, *The Affluent Society* (Boston: Houghton Mifflin, 1958).

8. See Ellen Willis, "Consumerism and Women," *Socialist Revolution* 1 (May–June 1970): 76–82.

9. Alexis de Tocqueville, *Democracy in America,* vol. 2. The term "decent" is from the new translation by George Lawrence, ed. J. P. Mayer (Garden City, N.Y.: Doubleday Anchor, 1969), p. 534 and the term "virtuous" is from the Henry Reeve translation, ed. Phillips Bradley (New York: Vintage Books, 1945), p. 141. The French term is "matérialisme honnête."

10. Daniel Bell, *The Cultural Contradictions of Capitalism* (New York: Basic Books, 1976), p. 68.

11. It does become comical in federal hearings. See, for instance, the account of marketing professor Michael Ray's testimony to the FTC in which he argued that television advertising for over-the-counter drugs *cannot possibly* mislead people because people get information from other sources as well as advertising and because people pay so little attention to television ads that they do not process their specific cognitive claims. Federal Trade Commission, *Advertising for Over-the-Counter Drugs* (Washington, D.C.: U.S. Government Printing Office, 1979), 68–72.

12. Sentry Insurance, *Consumerism at the Crossroads* (Stevens Point, Wis.: Sentry Insurance, 1977), report of a survey conducted by Louis Harris and Associates and the Marketing Science Institute. The *Newsweek* poll is reported in *Newsweek,* May 4, 1981, p. 51. See also Herbert Gans, *The Levittowners* (New York: Pantheon, 1967), pp. 190–93 and Herbert Gans, *The Urban Villagers* (New York: Free Press, 1962), p. 194 for middle-class and working-class skepticism of television advertising. There is very little ethnographic observation of the place of television in people's lives. Gans's observations are all the more valuable for their rarity. There are some very perceptive remarks about the role of television in everyday life from the citizens of Akenfield in Ronald Blythe's *Akenfield* (New York: Dell, 1969). See, for instance, the accounts of the Reverend Gethyn Owen and Francis Lambert, pp. 72–76, 129–37. Also useful is James Lull, "The Social Uses of Television," *Human Communication Research* 6 (Spring 1980): 197–209. An observational study of how people watch television advertising is Gary A. Steiner, "The People Look at Commercials," *Journal of Business* 39 (April 1966): 272–304.

13. Christopher Lasch, *The Culture of Narcissism* (New York: W. W. Norton, 1978), p. 73.

14. Paul Lazarsfeld, "Remarks on Administrative and Critical Communications Research," *Studies in Philosophy and Social Science* 9 (1941): 9–10.

Chapter 1

1. Jeremy Tunstall, *The Advertising Man in London Advertising Agencies* (London: Chapman and Hall, 1964), p. 16.

2. George P. Rowell, *Forty Years an Advertising Agent: 1865–1905* (New York: Printer's Ink, 1906), p. 30.

3. Personal interview, 1979, with creative writer. I interviewed twenty advertising workers at agencies in New York, Chicago, and San Diego. The largest number of interviews were at large, well-known firms in New York. I also picked up some first-hand knowledge by attending the *Advertising Age* "Advertising Week" meetings in Chicago in 1979 and an American Enterprise Institute conference of advertising practitioners and academics in Washington in 1980. In addition, I interviewed officials at the Federal Trade Commission.

4. Julian Simon, *Issues in the Economics of Advertising* (Urbana: University of Illinois Press, 1970), pp. 284–85.

5. There are other important economic effects of advertising that economists have studied. Whether advertising leads to higher or lower retail prices and whether or not advertising is a "barrier to entry" and hence a mainstay of monopoly power, are key issues. These and other major economic issues concerning advertising are reviewed in Mark Albion and Paul Farris, *The Advertising Controversy: Evidence on the Economic Effects of Advertising* (Boston: Auburn House, 1981).

6. See Steuart Henderson Britt, Stephen C. Adams, and Alan S. Miller, "How Many Advertising Exposures Per Day?" *Journal of Advertising Research* 12 (December 1972): 3–10.

7. David A. Aaker and John G. Myers, *Advertising Management* (Englewood Cliffs, N.J.: Prentice-Hall, 1975), p. 52.

8. A. J. San Augustine and W. F. Foley, "How Large Advertisers Set Budgets," *Journal of Advertising Research* 15 (October 1975): 11–16. Colin Gilligan, "How British Advertisers Set Budgets," *Journal of Advertising Research* 17 (February 1977): 47–49.

9. Aaker and Myers, *Advertising Management*, p. 78.

10. Richard Schmalensee, *The Economics of Advertising* (Amsterdam: North-Holland, 1972), p. 43.

11. Ibid., p. 85.

12. See David A. Aaker, James M. Carman, and Robert Jacobson, "Modeling Advertising-Sales Relationships Involving Feedback: A Time Series Analysis of Six Cereal Brands," *Journal of Market Research* 19 (February 1982): 116–25, a study which finds weak or nonexistent advertising/sales relationships in the products examined. See also Rebecca Colwell Quarles and Leo W. Jeffres, "Advertising and National Consumption: A Path Analytic Re-examination of the Galbraithian Argument," *Journal of Advertising Research* 12 (1983): 4–13, 33. Also relevant is Leo Bogart, "Is All This Advertising Necessary?" *Journal of Advertising Research* 18 (October 1978): 17–26. On the Anheuser-Busch studies, see Russell L. Ackoff and James R. Emshoff, "Advertising Research at Anheuser-Busch, Inc. (1963–68)" *Sloan Management Review* 16 (Winter 1975): 1–15. This and other related studies are reviewed in David A. Aaker and James M. Carman, "Are You Overadvertising? A Review of Advertising-Sales Studies," *Journal of Advertising Research* 22 (August 1982): 57–70.

13. Ronald S. Bond and David F. Lean, *Sales, Promotion, and Product Differentiation in Two Prescription Drug Markets* (Washington, D.C.: FTC, U.S. Government Printing Office, 1977), pp. 65–68.

14. In the Soviet Union, advertising and product differentiation appear to serve as consumer protection, enabling the consumer to identify shoddy goods and to complain about them. See Marshall I. Goldman, "Product Differentiation and Advertising: Some Lessons from the Soviet Experience," *Journal of Political Economy* 68 (August 1960): 346–57. See also M. Timothy O'Keefe and Kenneth G. Sheinkopf, "Advertising in the Soviet Union: Growth of a New Media Industry," *Journalism Quarterly* 53 (Spring 1976): 80–87. There is also advertising in China that is seen as propaganda and as a rational means to provide distributors and ultimate consumers with information about new products. See James Chu, "Advertising in China: Its Policy, Practice and Evolution," *Journalism Quarterly* 59 (Spring 1982): 40–45, 91.

15. Patent medicines have been notorious since the medicine shows of the eighteenth and nineteenth centuries. The life insurance notoriety is more recent. See FTC, Bureau of Consumer Protection, Bureau of Economics, *Life Insurance Cost Disclosure* (Washington, D.C.: U.S. Government Printing Office, 1979).

16. Mark Albion and Paul Farris, *The Advertising Controversy: Evidence on the Economic Effects of Advertising* (Boston: Auburn House, 1981) reviews the literature on the price/quality relationship. Another relevant study is Robert B. Archibald, Clyde A. Haul-

man, and Carlisle E. Moody, Jr., "Quality, Price, Advertising, and Published Quality Ratings," *Journal of Consumer Research* 9 (March 1983): 347–56, which found that after the publication of quality ratings of running shoes in *Runner's World,* advertising expenditures for running shoes in the three leading runners' magazines were greatest for the best shoes. Advertising levels indicated not only high-quality products but "good buys." Even before the ratings were published, there was a weak positive correlation between quality and level of advertising. Of course, the running shoe market is obviously a special one and it might be better to have tested running-shoe advertising in general publications rather than in publications for the most expert consumers.

17. Michael Waldholz, "How a 'Detail Man' Promotes New Drugs to Tennessee Doctors," *Wall Street Journal,* November 8, 1982, p. 1. One older estimate is that consumer-goods industries spent $2.50 on personal selling for every $1.00 spent on advertising, industrial-goods industries spent $5.00 on personal selling for every $1.00 on advertising. Edward L. Brink and William T. Kelley, *The Management of Promotion: Consumer Behavior and Demand Stimulation* (Englewood Cliffs: Prentice-Hall, 1963), p. 14.

18. Scott Miller, creative director at McCann-Erickson, quoted in Margo Miller, "Why Are Coke's Ad Men Smiling?" *Boston Globe,* March 22, 1980.

19. Fred L. Lemont, "Room at the Top in Promotion," *Advertising Age,* March 23, 1981, p. 61.

20. Thayer C. Taylor, "How Do Your Sales Costs Rate?" *Sales and Marketing Management* 129 (September 13, 1982): 59–64. The data come from Federal Trade Commission "Line of Business" studies for 1974, 1975, and 1976. See also "FTC Tells Lines-of-Business Data," *Advertising Age,* October 19, 1981, pp. 42–43. See also FTC, Bureau of Economics, *Statistical Report: Annual Line of Business Report, 1976* (Washington, D.C.: U.S. Government Printing Office, 1982).

21. John W. Wood, *The Instrument of Advertising* (London: Wood, Brigdale and Co., 1978), p. 4. Wood is chair of Wood, Brigdale, an advertising agency. Wood, Brigdale commissioned David Ives Associates to conduct the interviews with marketing professionals in blue chip British firms.

22. Jon Udell, "The Role of Price in Competitive Strategy," p. 319, in Bernard Taylor and Gordon Wills, *Pricing Strategy: Reconciling Customer Needs and Company Objectives* (Princeton: Brandon/Systems Press, 1970), pp. 317–25. Advertising men are sometimes shocked to discover the small role they have in the marketing orientation's view of the world. Ron Hoff, executive creative director at Foote, Cone & Belding in New York took a ten-day "renewal" course in marketing at the Harvard Business School in 1977 and learned that the marketing mix is simple: "There's the product. The price. The place it's sold. How it gets there. The promotion behind the product. The people who buy it." He sadly observed, "Advertising is notable for its absence. The Harvard folks probably throw it into something like 'promotion.' " "An Adman with Cheek at Harvard," *New York Times,* April 30, 1978, p. F–3.

23. Personal interview with a New York advertising executive who has worked on leading soft drink accounts, 1979. See also Edwin McDowell, "The Shoot-Out in Soda Pop," *New York Times,* October 19, 1980, sec. 3, p. 1.

24. Joseph M. Winski, " 'Bad' Ads Satisfying to Maker's Mark," *Advertising Age,* September 12, 1983, pp. 3, 54.

25. "A Matter of Placement," *Milwaukee Journal,* July 7, 1980. See also Ronald E. Frank and William F. Massy, "Shelf Position and Space Effects on Sales," *Journal of Marketing Research* 7 (February 1970): 59–66.

26. James O. Peckham, "The Consumer Speaks," *Journal of Marketing* 27 (October 1963): 21–26.

27. Bill Abrams, "Marketing: Packaging Often Irks Buyers, But Firms Are Slow to Change," *Wall Street Journal,* January 28, 1982, p. 25. See also Bill Abrams, "Marketing: Package Design Gains Stature as Visual Competition Grows," *Wall Street Journal,* August

6, 1981, p. 25. Shelving and display matter not only in supermarkets. Crown Books' strategy is to discount best sellers as loss leaders and make money by selling remaindered books, usually at the full remainder price. These remainders are displayed more prominently than the best sellers. See Robert Reed, "How an Industry Is Getting Crowned," *Advertising Age,* May 30, 1983, pp. M–4, M–5.

28. Margaret Loeb, "Marketing: Giving Smokers Added Value is Tobacco Firms' Latest Idea," *Wall Street Journal,* June 30, 1983, p. 27.

29. "Hershey and Advertising" (Hershey, Pa.: Hershey Foods Corporation, n.d.). U.S. Bureau of the Census, *Statistical Abstract of the United States 1981,* 102d ed. (Washington, D.C.: U.S. Government Printing Office, 1981). See also "Why They Joined the Club," *Media Decisions* 6 (March 1971); "Big Chocolate Maker, Beset by Profit Slides, Gets More Aggressive," *Wall Street Journal,* Feb. 18, 1970; and Joseph Winski, "Once-holdout Hershey Becomes Big Advertiser," *Advertising Age,* September 7, 1981, p. 3.

30. Terri Minsky, "Marketing: Beef Industry Turning to Ads to Change Meat's Reputation," *Wall Street Journal,* April 1, 1982, p. 29.

31. Neil Borden, *The Economic Effects of Advertising* (Chicago: Irwin, 1942).

32. A. Kent MacDougall, "Changing Emphasis in Ad Strategy," *Los Angeles Times,* November 26, 1981, pp. 1, 24–26. See also Kathleen A. Hughes, "Marketing: Coffee Makers Hope New Ads Will Reverse Declining Sales," *Wall Street Journal,* September 1, 1983, p. 25. For basic figures, see U.S. Bureau of the Census, *Statistical Abstract of the United States: 1982–83* (103d edition) (Washington, D.C.: U.S. Government Printing Office, 1982), p. 127. Coffee consumption continued its downward trend in 1983, down 2.6 percent from the previous year. See John L. Maxwell, Jr., "Coffee Market Still Cool," *Advertising Age,* April 30, 1984, p. 14.

33. Russell Bowman, *Couponing and Rebates: Profit on the Dotted Line* (New York: Lebhar-Friedman Books, 1980), pp. 32, 35, 42. Some 76 percent of households used coupons in 1980 with an overall redemption rate of 4 percent. William A. Robinson, *Best Sales Promotions* (Chicago: Crain Books, 1982), p. viii. See also "Sales Promotion," *Advertising Age* special section, August 22, 1983 and A. Kent MacDougall, "Coupon and Sweepstakes Game—Industry Can't Win for Losing," *Los Angeles Times,* December 6, 1981, VI–1.

34. Dik Twedt, "How Important to Marketing Strategy Is the 'Heavy User'?" *Journal of Marketing* 28 (January 1964): 71–72.

35. John R. Stuteville and Marc D. Roberts, *Marketing in a Consumer-Oriented Society* (Belmont, Calif.: Wadsworth, 1975), p. 44.

36. Michael Arlen, *Thirty Seconds* (Harmondsworth, England: Penguin Books, 1981), pp. 46, 124–25.

37. Leo Bogart, B. Stuart Tolley, and Frank Ornstein, "What One Little Ad Can Do," *Journal of Advertising Research* 10 (August 1970): 3–13.

38. U.S. Department of Commerce, Bureau of the Census, *Statistical Abstract of the United States 1981,* 102d ed. (Washington, D.C.: U.S. Government Printing Office, 1981), tables 725 and 726. Credit may also be a critical factor. Outstanding consumer credit has grown significantly in the past several decades. See *Statistical Abstract 1981,* table 865.

39. Robert D. Buzzell, Robert E. M. Nourse, John B. Matthews, Jr., and Theodore Levitt, *Marketing: A Contemporary Analysis* (New York: McGraw-Hill, 1972), p. 17.

40. Stuteville and Roberts, *Marketing,* p. 10.

41. Karen Shapiro, "The Construction of Television Commercials: Four Cases of Interorganizational Problem Solving" (Ph.D. diss., Department of Communication, Stanford University, 1981), p. 49.

42. Peter Drucker, *Management: Tasks, Responsibilities, Practices* (New York: Harper and Row, 1974), p. 61.

43. Ibid., p. 62.

44. Ibid., p. 64.

45. Buzzell, Nourse, Matthews, and Levitt use the Hollywood example, p. 20.

46. Eric Morgenthaler, "Baby-Carrier Maker Succeeds Playing It Close to the Vest," *Wall Street Journal,* April 23, 1982 p. 1.

47. "Cocaine: Middle-Class High," *Time,* July 6, 1981, pp. 56–60.

48. Leon Schiffman and Steven Schnaars, "The Consumption of Historical Romance Novels: Consumer Aesthetics and Popular Literature," in *Symbolic Consumer Behavior,* ed. Elizabeth C. Hirschman and Morris B. Holbrook (Ann Arbor: Association for Consumer Research, 1980), pp. 46–51.

49. Sandra Blakeslee, "New Contraceptive Has Brisk Sales," *San Diego Union,* August 17, 1983, p. D-3.

50. Quoted in Nancy Yoshihara, "Brandless Goods Make Their Mark," *Los Angeles Times,* November 8, 1981, p. 1. The term "satisfice" was coined by economist Herbert A. Simon. See Herbert A. Simon, *Models of Thought* (New Haven: Yale University Press, 1979).

51. John J. Wheatley, John S. Y. Chiu, and Douglas Allen, "Generics: Their Impact on National and Private Brands," *Advances in Consumer Research,* ed. Andrew A. Mitchell, vol. 9 (Ann Arbor: Association for Consumer Research, 1982), pp. 195–200.

52. See SAMI, "Interim Report on National Generic Label and Regular Private Label Performance and Trends" (New York: SAMI, a subsidiary of *Time Inc.,* July, 1983). Alan Miller, SAMI vice president for sales services, writes that the "cannibalization" by generics "has come from both name brands and regular private labels" (personal communication, July 19, 1983). For other discussion of the influence of generics, see Larry Edwards, "Also-ran brands periled," *Advertising Age,* vol. 52, May 11, 1981, pp. 3, 72; Janet Neiman, "Studies Clash on Generic Use," *Advertising Age,* January 26, 1981, p. 79; Bill Abrams, "Marketing: Reports of Generics' Success May Be Greatly Exaggerated," *Wall Street Journal,* May 7, 1981, p. 25; Robert D. Rauch, "Merchandise and Promote Your Food Bargains as Shoppers 'Trade Down' to Low-Cost Groceries," *Supermarket Business,* July 1980; and Yoshihara, "Brandless Goods."

On the origins of generics, see "French Exec Recalls Birth of Generics," *Advertising Age,* May 26, 1980, p. 34. I have also relied on an unpublished student paper by Frances Gaul, "Generics," University of California, San Diego, 1981.

53. *Popular Mechanics* quoted in Walter Henry Nelson, *Small Wonder* (Boston: Little, Brown, 1970), p. 219.

54. Data from Center for Auto Safety, *Small—On Safety: The Designed-in Dangers of the Volkswagen* (New York: Grossman Publishers, 1972), pp. 118–19.

55. The Edsel story is chronicled in John Brooks, *Business Adventures* (New York: Weybright and Talley, 1969), pp. 25–75.

56. Booz, Allen, Hamilton, *New Product Management for the 1980s* (Booz, Allen, Hamilton, 1982). The Dancer, Fitzgerald study is cited in Edgar A. Pessemier, *Product Management: Strategy and Organization,* 2d ed. (New York: John Wiley, 1982), p. 9.

57. Andrew Robertson, *The Lessons of Failure* (London: MacDonald, 1974). See also J. Hugh Davidson, "Why Most Consumer Brands Fail," *Harvard Business Review* 54 (March–April 1976) for the estimate that 70 percent of test-marketed brands in the United Kingdom do not do well enough to go national. See also C. Merle Crawford, "Marketing Research and the New Product Failure Rate," *Journal of Marketing* 41 (April 1977): 51–61 and R. G. Cooper, "The Dimensions of Industrial New Product Success and Failure," *Journal of Marketing* 43 (Summer 1979): 93–103.

58. Robert D. Buzzell and Robert E. M. Nourse, *Product Innovation in Food Processing 1954–1964* (Boston: Division of Research, Graduate School of Business Administration, Harvard University, 1967), p. 170. A good discussion of the research that goes into new

product development is in Janet Guyon, "The Public Doesn't Get a Better Potato Chip Without a Bit of Pain," *Wall Street Journal,* March 25, 1983, p. 1.

59. Buzzell and Nourse, *Product Innovation,* p. 170.

60. Janet Guyon, "Philip Morris Battles Beer and Smoke Rivals as It Enters Cola War," *Wall Street Journal,* June 30, 1982, p. 1.

61. Bill Abrams, "Marketing: Trying Again: Women's Shaving Cream," *Wall Street Journal,* November 11, 1983, p. 29. Some products survive successfully for a time before dying. Micrin mouthwash, from Johnson & Johnson, was born 1961, died 1977. See Jane Rockman, "Micrin Is Gone, Color It Blue," *New York Times,* January 15, 1978.

62. Ronald Bard of Mars Manufacturing, quoted in Helen Carlton, "The Wastebasket Dress Has Arrived," *Life,* November 25, 1966, p. 132. Oliver J. Sterling, quoted in Joseph V. Sherman, "Throwaway Bikinis," *Barron's,* August 28, 1967, p. 11. I am indebted to an unpublished student paper by Carolyn Butterfield, "The Paper Dress," University of California, San Diego, 1981.

63. There is, however, a profitable business in promoting fads that marketers know in advance will fade quickly. See Jennifer Bingham Hall, "Marketing: Fad Merchants Hustle to Sell Tomorrow's Big Craze," *Wall Street Journal,* November 17, 1983, p. 33.

64. Dean Rotbart, "In Spite of Huge Losses, Procter & Gamble Tries Once More to Revive Pringle's Chips," *Wall Street Journal,* October 7, 1981, p. 25. On failure of other chips, see Pessemier, *Product Management,* p. 37.

65. See "Kennedy Decides: It'll Be a Topper," *New York Times,* December 9, 1960, p. 24; "The Mad Hatters," *Time,* January 20, 1961, p. 81; "Kennedy Prodded Anew on Hat He Doesn't Wear," *New York Times,* July 6, 1963, p. 2; Leonard Sloane, "Swan Song for Hatmakers?" *New York Times,* February 6, 1972, p. III-2; William M. Freeman, "Cap Industry's Sales on the Rise as Season for Straw Hats Opens," *New York Times,* May 15, 1962, p. 53; "Advertising News and Notes," *New York Times,* January 8, 1949, p. 20. I am indebted to Randy Coplin for research assistance on the decline of the hat industry.

66. U.S. Bureau of the Census, *Statistical Abstract of the United States: 1982–83,* 103d ed. (Washington, D.C.: U.S. Government Printing Office, 1982), p. 785. See also William Rorabaugh, *The Alcoholic Republic* (New York: Oxford University Press, 1979), p. 232, for somewhat different figures.

67. Donna Sammons, "Bourbon and Energy: Fill 'er Up—with Old Bardstown," *New York Times,* May 25, 1980, p. F–3.

68. Frank J. Prial, "White Wine: Still America's Favorite," *New York Times,* July 24, 1983, p. 20.

69. Bill Abrams, "Marketing: Selling Wine Like Soda Pop, Riunite Uncorks Huge Market," *Wall Street Journal,* July 2, 1981, p. 25.

70. "Taking the Plunge," *Wall Street Journal,* February 18, 1971, pp. 1, 18. I am indebted to Randy Coplin for research assistance on the liquor industry.

71. Ruth Stroud, "Seagram Zeros in on Gallo," *Advertising Age,* October 3, 1983, p. 3, and Carl Cannon, "Seagram Agrees to Buy Coke's Wine Properties," *Los Angeles Times,* September 27, 1983, p. IV–1. See also "The Big Five: Top Wine Advertisers," *Advertising Age,* January 16, 1984, p. M–33. Also on liquor marketing, see "Creating a Mass Market for Wine," *Business Week,* March 15, 1982, pp. 108–18, and "Liquor's Thirst for a Younger Market," *Business Week,* April 20, 1981, pp. 114–15.

Chapter 2

1. "U.S. Advertising Agency Profiles," special issue, *Advertising Age,* March 28, 1984, pp. 1, 12.

2. See the whole development of the "production of culture" perspective in sociology,

highlighted in a special issue of *Social Research* 45 (Fall 1978) and a special issue of *Media, Culture, and Society* 4 (January 1982) and discussed in Richard Peterson, ed., *The Production of Culture* (Beverly Hills: Sage Publications, 1976) and Richard Peterson, "Revitalizing the Culture Concept," *Annual Review of Sociology* 5 (1979): 137–66.

3. With the rapid rise of the cost of television time, some advertisers have resisted paying their agencies a straight commission. A third of BBDO's clients in 1979 paid negotiated fees rather than a straight percentage. See Peter W. Bernstein, "Here Come the Super-Agencies," *Fortune* 100 (August 27, 1979): 54. See Merle Kingman, "To Fee or Not to Fee," *Advertising Age,* August 29, 1983, p. M–24; "That Fading 15%," *Advertising Age* editorial, May 2, 1983, p. 16; Philip Dougherty, "Advertising: Payment Setup Held 'Outmoded'," *New York Times,* April 21, 1983, p. D–21.

4. Bill Abrams, "Marketing: Rash of Advertisers Switch Agencies, Testing Strength of Long-Term Ties," *Wall Street Journal,* October 19, 1981, p. 25. See also Peter Dworkin, "When the Music Stops, Who Has the Account?" *Fortune* 100 (August 27, 1979): 49.

5. Nancy Milman, "Spec Presentations Alive, Well and Maligned," *Advertising Age,* February 28, 1983, pp. 3, 50.

6. David Ogilvy, *Blood, Brains, and Beer* (New York: Atheneum, 1978), p. 149.

7. Nancy Giges, "How General Foods Picked Its Fifth Agency," *Advertising Age,* July 14, 1980, pp. 45, 48.

8. Al Ries and Jack Trout, *Positioning: The Battle for Your Mind* (New York: McGraw-Hill, 1981).

9. *Advertising Age* publishes data on the one hundred leading national advertisers in a special issue every fall. See *Advertising Age,* September 8, 1983, p. 149.

10. "United Airlines Advertising," October 1982, revision no. 5, leaflet provided by United Airlines.

11. Rosser Reeves, *Reality in Advertising* (New York: Alfred A. Knopf, 1961), pp. 47–48.

12. Research to this effect goes back at least to John Watson's work for J. Walter Thompson in the 1920s. Watson discovered, to his surprise, that few smokers could identify their own brand in blind taste tests. See David Cohen, J. B. Watson, *The Founder of Behaviourism* (London: Routledge & Kegan Paul, 1979), p. 178.

13. See Philip Nelson for a discussion of "search" goods and "experience" goods, "Information and Consumer Behavior," *Journal of Political Economy* 78 (1970): 311–29.

14. This is a standard Foote, Cone & Belding model. See its use in John O'Toole, *The Trouble With Advertising ...* (New York: Chelsea House, 1981), p. 130 and also in Richard Vaughn, "The Consumer Mind: How to Tailor Ad Strategies," *Advertising Age,* June 9, 1980, p. 45.

15. This is my own unsystematic conclusion from three years of regular reading of *Advertising Age.* Marketing executives like to think that they are experts on the "consumer mind" but, in fact, it seems to me, they are authorities on the consumer mind *faced with a purchasing decision about a given array of brands for a given product category.* That's quite another matter. The popular notion of "positioning" is supposed to be a "positioning" in the mind of the consumer but is much more nearly a seeking-out of a distinct position or niche within a given product array. See Ries and Trout, *Positioning.*

16. Nancy Giges, "Coke Makes Ramblin' Move," *Advertising Age,* March 23, 1981, pp. 3, 100; John J. O'Connor, "Price Is Right for Heublein," *Advertising Age,* October 26, 1981, pp. 12, 79; "GF sends Master Blend into Battle," *Advertising Age,* January 26, 1981, pp. 1, 75; Leah Rozen, "Three Set Fast-food Ad Drives," *Advertising Age,* March 23, 1981, pp. 2, 100. See also Ries and Trout, *Positioning,* a typically overstated grand strategy for advertising that, nevertheless, has had some influence on Madison Avenue.

17. Theodore Levitt, *Marketing for Business Growth* (New York: McGraw-Hill, 1974), pp. 151–73. See also D. N. Rink, "Product Life Cycle Research: A Literature Review," *Journal of Business Research* 7 (1979): 219–42.

18. "Advertising as a Percentage of Sales," *Advertising Age,* September 8, 1983, p. 165.

19. *People Who Travel* (New York: Time, 1979) and Newspaper Advertising Bureau, "Air Travel Study" (New York: Newspaper Advertising Bureau, 1981).

20. "Air Travel Study" (New York: Newspaper Advertising Bureau, 1981).

21. Karen Shapiro, "The Construction of Television Commercials: Four Cases of Interorganizational Problem Solving" (Ph.D. diss., Communication Department, Stanford University, 1981), pp. 197–98.

22. Mary Tuck, *How Do We Choose?* (London: Methuen, 1976), p. 118. Tuck's suggestion that market research is a security blanket for advertising agencies echoes Martin Mayer's observation that advertising is a security blanket for business. He holds that the idea that advertising produces profits is more often the excuse than the reason for advertising. The most important reason for advertising is that it "satisfies that overwhelming need for security which affects business organizations in a highly developed capitalist economy." See Mayer's dated but still surprisingly valuable *Madison Avenue, U.S.A.* (New York: Harper, 1958), p. 24.

See also for Howard Rosenberg's coverage of the Christine Craft trial, "Expert Raps Research on Craft" and "Market Research Role Defended in Craft Case," *Los Angeles Times*, August 2, 1983, p. VI–1; and August 4, 1983, p. VI–1. Craft, an anchorwoman at KMBC-TV in Kansas City, was demoted and the demotion was presumably based on research that indicated that she was not popular with viewers. Some of this research was focus group research and the validity of such research became a topic of debate in the trial.

23. Lawrence E. Cole, "Entering the Age of the New Media," *Advertising Age Yearbook 1981* (Chicago: Crain Books, 1981), pp. 30, 37. An example of the kind of forecasting relevant to marketing is in *The Marketer's Complete Guide to the 1980s/A Special Report* (New York: Sales and Marketing Management, n.d.).

24. Thomas Whiteside, "Din Din," *New Yorker*, November 1, 1976.

25. Bill Ross, J. Walter Thompson, Western Division, "Market Segmentation in an Age of Change," presentation at *Advertising Age* "Advertising Week" conference, Chicago, August, 1979.

26. John Gunther, *Taken at the Flood: The Story of Albert D. Lasker* (New York: Harper, 1960) p. 96.

27. Shapiro, "Television Commercials," p. 42.

28. Bob Battenfield, "Ad Game: Forever Changing . . . And Changeless," *San Diego Daily Transcript*, April 22, 1980, p. 2A.

29. See, for instance, Herbert Gans, *Deciding What's News* (New York: Pantheon Books, 1979), pp. 229–36.

30. T. J. Jackson Lears, "Some Versions of Fantasy: Toward a Cultural History of American Advertising, 1880–1930," *Prospects*, vol. 8 (New York: Cambridge University Press, 1984). Far from the sobriety one is supposed to find in advertising at the turn of the century, Lears finds that the leading theme in national advertising was "the fun of living."

31. Richard W. Pollay, "The Identification and Distribution of Values Manifest in Print Advertising 1900–1980," History of Advertising Archives Working Paper No. 921, University of British Columbia, Faculty of Commerce, 1983. See also Jib Fowles, *Mass Advertising as Social Forecast* (Westport, Conn.: Greenwood Press, 1976) whose more modest study of *Life* magazine advertisements in 1950, 1960, and 1970 found no change in the emphasis on sexuality.

32. Merle Curti, "The Changing Concept of 'Human Nature' in the Literature of American Advertising," *Business History Review* 41 (Winter 1967): 335–57.

33. Pollay, "Values in Print Advertising," pp. 29–31.

34. Richard Pollay, "The Subsiding Sizzle: Shifting Strategies in Twentieth-Century Magazine Advertising," History of Advertising Archives, University of British Columbia, Faculty of Commerce, May, 1983. See also Richard Pollay, "The Determinants of Magazine Advertising Informativeness Throughout the Twentieth Century," Working Paper No. 917,

History of Advertising Archives, University of British Columbia, Faculty of Commerce, n.d.

35. Roland Marchand, *Advertising the American Dream: Making Way for Modernity, 1920–1940* (Berkeley: University of California Press, forthcoming). See also Donald Fleming, "Attitude: The History of a Concept," *Perspectives in American History 1* (1967): 287–365 for a marvelous discussion of how psychology's recognition of women and other non-white male groups changed its fundamental concepts.

36. "38th Annual Report of the Grocery Industry," *Progressive Grocer* 50 (April 1971): 65.

37. William Leiss, *Limits to Satisfaction* (Toronto: University of Toronto Press, 1976), pp. 27, 63, 67, 82, 84, 88–89.

38. On the cafeteria as a symbol of America, see Henry Fairlie, "Why I Love America," *The New Republic,* July 4, 1983 p. 14.

39. Shapiro, "Television Commercials," p. 39.

40. Developments in print technology helped create a more visual advertising at the turn of the century. See Neil Harris, "Iconography and Intellectual History: The Half-Tone Effect," in *New Directions in Intellectual History,* ed. John Higham and Paul K. Conkin (Baltimore: Johns Hopkins University Press, 1979), pp. 196–211. Television added movement to vision. European advertising is even more visually centered than American because advertising crosses national and linguistic barriers regularly. The visual quality of ads in Europe tends to be better than that in American advertising because advertising has had to be so much less reliant on words. See Felix Kessler, "Marketing: American TV Ads Look Bad to Some International Judges," *Wall Street Journal,* July 1, 1982, p. 21.

41. David Ogilvy, "Ogilvy on Advertising," *Advertising Age,* August 1, 1983, p. M–4.

42. On women's fashions, see *Advertising Age,* November 16, 1981 pp. 3, 92; on the "wet/dry shaver" see *Advertising Age,* February 8, 1982, p. 28; on Envoy shoes see *Advertising Age,* January 11, 1982, p. 3.

43. Morris B. Holbrook, "Introduction: The Esthetic Imperative in Consumer Research," in *Symbolic Consumer Behavior,* ed. Elizabeth C. Hirschman and Morris B. Holbrook (Ann Arbor: Association for Consumer Research, 1980), p. 36.

44. *Advertising Age,* September 8, 1983, p. 8.

45. *People Who Travel* (New York: Time, 1979).

46. *Advertising Age,* February 23, 1981, p. 5. The differences are no longer so great, although they are in the same direction. The 1983 CPM's for high income households were $4.63 for *Newsweek,* $5.09 for *Time,* and $5.57 for *U.S. News.* (Personal communication, Leslie Brody, *Time,* March 7, 1984.)

47. *Advertising Age,* July 9, 1979, p. 73.

48. *Eyes on Television 1980* (New York: Newsweek, 1980). This booklet reports on a *Newsweek*-commissioned study conducted by Audits and Surveys, Inc. The report finds that higher-income people tend to remain in the room with the television on somewhat more often than lower-income people; naturally, this is not the sort of result that *Newsweek* cared to highlight. See also the findings of Television Audience Assessment, a market research organization, that 57 percent of the audience watches all the commercials in a thirty-minute program. Bill Abrams, "Marketing: Who Watches Commercials. . . ." *Wall Street Journal,* May 20, 1982, p. 29.

49. Charles Ramond, *Advertising Research: The State of the Art* (New York: Association of National Advertisers, 1976), pp. 81–82. For a review of recent studies, see Leo Bogart and Charles Lehman, "The Case of the 30-Second Commercial," *Journal of Advertising Research* 23 (February-March 1983): 11–18.

50. John Cooney, "TV-Audience Decline, Sharper During Daytime, May Reflect Higher Number of Working Women," *Wall Street Journal,* December 14, 1977, p. 22.

51. James P. Forkan, "BBDO Report Predicts Continued Net Erosion," *Advertising Age,* December 19, 1983, p. 42.

52. Bill Abrams, "Marketing: 'Zappers' Switch Off TV Ads and Scare Some Media Buyers," *Wall Street Journal,* October 6, 1983, p. 31. Other new technologies also concern advertisers. Two-thirds of video cassette recorder owners delete commercials when they record commercial television and sixty percent of those who record the commercials skip by them when they play the program back. "Vcr Users Do Without Ads: Study," *Advertising Age,* October 31, 1983, p. 10.

53. See Mark Albion and Paul Farris, *The Advertising Controversy: Evidence on the Economic Effects of Advertising* (Boston: Auburn House, 1981) for a review of literature suggesting that television advertising is more closely related to degree of concentration in an industry than are other types of advertising, pp. 66–68.

54. Donald C. Bauder, "Radio Takes Upbeat Approach to Upscale Ad Market," *San Diego Union,* February 20, 1983 p. I–1. There are now not only specialized radio stations but specialized radio networks. There are two black radio networks and a physicians' network. See Andrew Feinberg, "Advertising Spurs Radio Revival," *San Diego Union,* May 29, 1982, and John E. Cooney, "National Black Network Builds Its Audience on the Increasing Specialization in Radio," *Wall Street Journal,* March 3, 1982, p. 25.

55. Philip H. Dougherty, "Advertising," *New York Times,* February 8, 1980.

56. Philip H. Dougherty, "Advertising: Forming Habits at Seventeen," *New York Times,* October 25, 1979, p. D–12.

57. Bernice Kanner, "Primary Audience Research Under Study Again," *Advertising Age,* July 9, 1979, p. 4.

58. John J. O'Connor and Christy Marshall, "Demographics Whip CPM in Reynolds Media Plan," *Advertising Age,* September 22, 1980, pp. 2, 110.

59. Michael J. Naples, *Effective Frequency: The Relationship Between Frequency and Advertising Effectiveness* (New York: Association of National Advertisers, 1979), p. 79.

60. Rosser Reeves, *Reality in Advertising* (New York: Alfred A. Knopf, 1961), p. 32.

61. Allan Greenberg and Charles Suttoni, "Television Commercial Wearout," *Journal of Advertising Research* 13 (October 1973): 47–54.

62. "United Airlines Advertising," United Airlines, October, 1982.

63. Michael Arlen, *30 Seconds* (Harmondsworth, England: Penguin Books, 1980).

64. John R. Stuteville and Marc D. Roberts, *Marketing in a Consumer Oriented Society* (Belmont, Calif.: Wadsworth Publishing, 1975), pp. 208–14.

65. Gail Bronson, "Why Is the Brunette in the Bentley Acting as if She's in a Huff?" *Wall Street Journal,* October 6, 1981, p. 1.

66. Ibid.

67. Jerry Della Femina, *From Those Wonderful Folks Who Gave You Pearl Harbor* (New York: Simon and Schuster, 1970), p. 26.

68. Helmut Schmitz, Volkswagen's assistant advertising manager in New York when the Doyle Dane Bernbach campaign began, cited in Walter Henry Nelson, *Small Wonder: The Amazing Story of the Volkswagen* (Boston: Little, Brown, 1970), p. 220.

69. David A. Aaker and John G. Myers, *Advertising Management* (Englewood Cliffs: Prentice-Hall, 1975), p. 416. See also Frank Rowsome, Jr., *Think Small* (New York: Ballantine Books, 1970).

70. Bill Ross, "Market Segmentation in an Age of Change," presentation at *Advertising Age* "Advertising Week," Chicago, August 1979.

71. Bernice Kanner, "Madison Avenue Is for the Cows," *New York Times,* January 27, 1980, pp. F–9, 10.

72. Nancy Yoshihara, "A Word from the Sponsor: New Zip for Tired Wheaties Image," *Los Angeles Times,* April 28, 1981, p. IV–5. See also Scott Hume, "Stars Are Lacking Luster as Ad Presenters," *Advertising Age,* November 7, 1983, p. 3 and Fred Danzig, "Ogilvy Sticks to His Guns on Celebrities," *Advertising Age,* October 24, 1983 p. 18.

73. See Bill Abrams, "Marketing: 'Ring Around the Collar' Ads Irritate Many Yet Get Results," *Wall Street Journal,* October 4, 1982.

74. Reeves, *Reality in Advertising,* pp. 47–48. See also "Ad Pioneer Reeves, 73, Dies; Proponent of Hard Sell, USP," *Advertising Age,* January 30, 1984, p. 4.

75. O'Connor, "Creative Ideas."

76. Bill Abrams, "Marketing: If Logic in Ads Doesn't Sell, Try a Tug on the Heartstrings," *Wall Street Journal,* April 8, 1982, p. 23.

77. Morris Holbrook, "Beyond Attitude Structure: Toward Informational Determinants of Attitude," *Journal of Marketing Research* 15 (November 1978): 554.

78. O'Connor, "Creative Ideas," pp. 5–6.

79. "Creatives Bemoan Current State of Advertising," *Advertising Age,* May 26, 1980, p. 10.

80. Rance Crain, "Yesterday's Rebels," *Advertising Age,* July 9, 1979, p. 18.

81. Nancy Giges, "Comparative Ads: Battles That Wrote Do's and Don'ts," *Advertising Age,* September 29, 1980, p. 59.

82. On the relaxation of comparative advertising rules, see "Advertisers Remove the Cover from Brand X," *U. S. News and World Report,* December 19, 1983, p. 75.

83. Federal Trade Commission, *Consumer Information Remedies* (Washington, D.C.: U.S. Government Printing Office, 1979), pp. 216–20.

84. Nancy Giges, "Comparative Ads: Better Than . . . ?" *Advertising Age,* September 22, 1980, p. 60 and March 11, 1982, p. 27. Bill Abrams: "Marketing: Comparative Ads Are Getting More Popular, Harder Hitting," *Wall Street Journal,* March 11, 1982, p. 27.

85. Max Gunther, "To Burke or Not to Burke?" *TV Guide,* February 7, 1981, pp. 2–8. Even if viewers remember commercials, do they understand them? One laboratory study finds that consumers, even under conditions in which they are especially attentive, misunderstand 30 percent of received information content. See Jacob Jacoby, Wayne D. Hoyer, and David A. Sheluga, "Viewer Miscomprehension of Television Communications: A Brief Report of Findings," in *Advances in Consumer Research,* vol. 8, ed. Kent Munroe (Ann Arbor: Association for Consumer Research, 1980), pp. 410–13. For an up-to-date review of the copy testing research, see John D. Leckenby and Joseph T. Plummer, "Advertising Stimulus Measurement and Assessment Research: A Review of Copy Testing Methods," March 1, 1983, manuscript.

86. Joseph T. Plummer, "Copy Research in the Coming Decade," in *Symbolic Consumer Behavior,* ed. Hirschman and Holbrook, pp. 86–89, and Jennifer Alter, "Skeptics Descend on FCB Recall Study," *Advertising Age,* May 25, 1981, p. 14.

87. Plummer, "Copy Research," p. 87.

88. Quoted in Gunther, "To Burke or Not to Burke?"

89. See John E. Cooney, "In Their Quest for Sure-Fire Ads, Marketers Use Physiological Tests to Find Out What Grabs You," *Wall Street Journal,* April 12, 1979, p. 1.

90. Plummer, "Copy Research," pp. 88–89.

91. Charlie Haas, "Charlie Haas on Advertising," *New West* 4 (November 5, 1979): 45.

92. Philip H. Dougherty, "Advertising: J. Walter's 'Bad' Year was Good," *New York Times,* March 28, 1983, p. D–11.

93. Gian M. Fulgoni and Gerald J. Eskin, "The BehaviorScan Research Facility for Studying Retail Shopping Patterns," in *Patronage Behavior and Retail Management,* ed. William R. Darden and Robert F. Lusch (New York: North-Holland, 1983), pp. 263–74. See also Fern Schumer, "The New Magicians of Market Research," *Fortune* 108 (July 25, 1983): 72–74 and Theodore J. Gage, "IRI Develops New Systems for More Exposure," *Advertising Age,* February 21, 1983, p. M–29.

94. Ramond, *Advertising Research,* pp. 49–51.

95. Ibid., p. 52.

96. Philip H. Dougherty, "Advertising: Bojangles Campaign by Rich," *New York Times,* April 15, 1983, p. D–11.

97. Philip H. Dougherty, "Advertising: Sammy Honors Winning Ad Music," *New York Times,* April 22, 1983, p. D–13.

98. Trevor Millum, *Images of Woman: Advertising in Women's Magazines* (London: Chatto and Windus, 1975), p. 51.

99. Priemer quoted in A. Kent MacDougall, "Changing Emphasis in Ad Strategy," *Los Angeles Times,* November 26, 1981, pp. 1, 24, 25.

100. Priemer quoted in Bill Abrams, "Marketing: Industry Veteran Challenges Conventional Wisdom on Ads," *Wall Street Journal,* April 9, 1981, p. 25.

101. Niko Tinbergen, *The Herring Gull's World* (New York: Basic Books, 1961), pp. 12–16.

102. These stories are drawn from *Advertising Age* for 1981. See Josh Levine and Ralph Gray, "Bidwell Tackles Hertz Dip," January 26, pp. 2, 76; Sam Harpe, "Consolidated Eyes Young Smokers," January 26, pp. 4, 79; John Revett and Pat Sloan, "New Cookery Gets Mixed Results," January 26, pp. 3, 80; Richard C. Gordon, "Pentagon Tests Recruit Education Bonuses," January 5, p. 6; Jacques Neher, "Firestone in Rebuilding Bid," March 2, pp. 1, 78; Janet Neiman, "What's Ailing Sara Lee?" March 23, pp. 4, 104; Dagmar Mussey, "German Laundry Attack by P&G," March 23, p. 20; Gay Jervey, "Polaroid Prays for Yule Developments," December 7, p. 37; Richard Kreisman, "Market Cautious for Sporting Goods," February 23, p. 32.

103. Ramond, *Advertising Research,* pp. 97–98.

Chapter 3

1. A. S. C. Ehrenberg, "Repetitive Advertising and the Consumer," *Journal of Advertising Research* 14 (April 1974): 26.

2. Ibid., p. 31.

3. Ibid., p. 32.

4. The Pulse, Inc., "A Summary of Consumer Credibility in Automobile Advertising" (March, 1953, mimeograph). See also the extensive literature on cognitive dissonance in marketing. This literature begins with Leon Festinger, *A Theory of Cognitive Dissonance* (Stanford: Stanford University Press, 1957), especially pp. 48–54. See also contributions to the literature by Sadaomi Oshikawa, "Can Cognitive Dissonance Theory Explain Consumer Behavior?" *Journal of Marketing* 33 (October 1969): 44–49; Joel B. Cohen and Michael J. Houston, "Cognitive Consequences of Brand Loyalty," *Journal of Market Research* 9 (February 1972): 97–99; and George Akerlof, "The Economic Consequences of Cognitive Dissonance," *American Economic Review* 72 (June 1982): 307–19.

5. Richard Haitch, "Gum Slander," *New York Times,* April 16, 1978, p. 45.

6. Milt Moskowitz, "General Foods Learns About Kids," *San Francisco Chronicle,* February 16, 1980, p. 31.

7. Pamela Moreland, "P&G Trying to Exorcise Devil Rumor," *Los Angeles Times,* January 22, 1982, pp. 1, 9.

8. Jennifer Alter, "P&G Sues Over Satanism," *Advertising Age,* July 5, 1982, pp. 1, 34.

9. Elihu Katz and Paul F. Lazarsfeld, *Personal Influence* (New York: The Free Press, 1955), p. 11. For a recent review of "reference group" literature, see Eleanor Singer, "Reference Groups and Social Evaluation," in *Social Psychology: Sociological Perspectives,* ed. Morris Rosenberg and Ralph H. Turner (New York: Basic Books, 1981), pp. 66–93. This review, indeed the whole volume, characteristically represents academic social psychology in ignoring studies of consumer behavior. Also see Donald F. Cox, "The

Audience as Communicators," pp. 172–87 and Johan Arndt, "Word-of-Mouth Advertising and Informal Communication," pp. 188–239, in *Risk Taking and Information Handling in Consumer Behavior*, ed. Donald F. Cox (Boston: Harvard University Graduate School of Business Administration, Division of Research, 1967).

10. Katz and Lazarsfeld, *Personal Influence*, p. 142.

11. Ibid., p. 176. See also Jacob Jacoby, "Consumer Psychology: An Octennium," *Annual Review of Psychology* 27 (1976): 341.

12. Katz and Lazarsfeld, *Personal Influence*, p. 185.

13. Ibid., p. 143.

14. A study by F. S. Bourne, "Group Influence in Marketing and Public Relations," in *Some Applications of Behavioral Research*, ed. Rensis Likert and Samuel P. Hayes (UNESCO, 1957) cited in David A. Aaker and John Myers, *Marketing Management*, pp. 365–66.

15. William O. Bearden and Michael J. Etzel, "Reference Group Influence on Product and Brand Purchase Decisions," *Journal of Consumer Research* 9 (September 1982): 183–94.

16. Michael Waldholz, "Tylenol Maker Mounting Campaign to Restore Trust of Doctors, Buyers," *Wall Street Journal*, October 29, 1982, p. 33.

17. Cox, ed., *Risk Taking*.

18. John R. Stuteville, "The Buyer as a Salesman," *Journal of Marketing* 32 (July 1968): 14–18. This is not to deny that physicians themselves are influenced by advertising. For a review of literature on drug advertising to doctors, see Mickey C. Smith, "Drug Product Advertising and Prescribing: A Review of the Evidence," *American Journal of Hospital Pharmacy* 34 (November 1977): 1208–24.

19. See the critique by Todd Gitlin, "The Dominant Paradigm," *Theory and Society* 6 (1978): 205–53.

20. Bill Abrams, "Marketing: Product Quality May Be Elusive in Ads," *Wall Street Journal*, September 8, 1983, p. 31.

21. James L. Hamilton, "The Demand for Cigarettes: Advertising, the Health Scare, and the Cigarette Advertising Ban," *Review of Economics and Statistics* 54 (November 1972): 401–11. But see also the FTC report for 1979 that argues that cigarette consumption per capita decreased steadily from 1964 through 1975 with no measurable intensification in 1968–70 or slowing in 1971, contrary to Hamilton. Richard Ippolito, R. Dennis Murphy, Donald Sant, FTC Bureau of Economics, *Staff Report on Consumer Responses to Cigarette Health Information* (Washington, D.C.: U.S. Government Printing Office, August 1979), p. 7.

22. Michael Pertschuk, *Revolt Against Regulation: The Rise and Pause of the Consumer Movement* (Berkeley: University of California Press, 1982), p. 122. Pertschuk's view gets support from Sandra J. Teel, Jesse E. Teel, and William O. Bearden, "Lessons Learned from the Broadcast Cigarette Advertising Ban," *Journal of Marketing* 43 (January 1979): 45–50. These authors find that per capita consumption of cigarettes increased slightly in the years following the ban and that the advertising cost to the manufacturer per pack of cigarettes has sharply dropped (measured in constant dollars). "In retrospect," they write, "the ban's predominant effect seems to have been reduction of antismoking communication programs' access to media while providing the cigarette industry with an opportunity for concerted action in the form of mass withdrawal from the broadcast media." Other studies confirm this conclusion. For a review of studies on the effects of the broadcasting advertising ban, see Robert H. Miles, *Coffin Nails and Corporate Strategies* (Englewood Cliffs, N.J.: Prentice-Hall, 1982), p. 264.

23. For an important general discussion of the role of brokers or gatekeepers in the "culture industry," see Paul Hirsch, "Processing Fads and Fashions: An Organization-Set Analysis of Cultural Industry Systems," *American Journal of Sociology* 77 (January 1972): 639–59. See also "Movie Advertisements and Reviews in Newspapers" (New York: Newspaper Advertising Bureau "research note no. 6," 1981). This study of American and Cana-

dian moviegoers in 1973, followed up in 1981, found that 29 percent of moviegoers read newspaper movie reviews "most of the time" in 1981 (25 percent in 1973) and 39 percent "occasionally" (33 percent in 1973). The results indicate that a positive review "is much more likely to definitely encourage seeing a movie than a negative review is to definitely discourage seeing it."

24. See Daniel Pope, "The Development of National Advertising, 1865–1920" (Ph.D. diss., Columbia University, 1973), pp. 359–61. See also Michael Schudson, *Discovering the News* (New York: Basic Books, 1978), pp. 134–41.

25. Edward Jay Epstein, *The Rise and Fall of Diamonds* (New York: Simon and Schuster, 1982), p. 124. See also Dennis Chase, "De Beers Changes Ad Tack," *Advertising Age,* July 18, 1983, pp. 42, 48. Epstein's work, among many others, attributes considerable power to advertising. Indeed, it opens with a description of an ad campaign for diamonds and notes that before the campaign began in 1968, only 5 percent of Japanese women getting married were given a diamond engagement ring—it was 27 percent by 1972 and by 1981 60 percent of married Japanese women had diamond rings. Epstein is not so quick to point out that De Beers failed utterly to pull off the same trick in Brazil, Austria, Germany, and Italy. (See Epstein, p. 256.) De Beers has worked hard in Brazil without notable success but will try soon in Taiwan, Thailand, the Philippines, Singapore, Malaysia, and Hong Kong to replicate the Japanese miracle.

26. Janet Guyon, "To Tout Merit, Philip Morris Creates News," *Wall Street Journal,* August 21, 1981, p. 25.

27. Felix Kessler, "Fresh Ideas Help World's Top Ski Maker, But Fresh Snow Might Help Even More," *Wall Street Journal,* March 3, 1981, p. 48.

28. Epstein, *Diamonds,* p. 124.

29. Joseph Winski, "Hershey Befriends Extra-Terrestrial," *Advertising Age,* July 19, 1982, pp. 1, 66.

30. See Stephen J. Sansweet, "Why Marlon Brando Passed the Milk Duds to George C. Scott," *Wall Street Journal,* May 24, 1982, pp. 1, 10 and also Janet Maslin, "Quiet on Set, 'Rocky' and Pass the Wheaties," *San Diego Union,* November 21, 1982, p. E–3.

31. Victor F. Zonana, "More Foods Today Are 'Fresh' from Factories and Quick to Prepare," *Wall Street Journal,* June 21, 1977, pp. 1, 29. Product sales may be affected by news about other matters. The Soviet invasion of Afghanistan in 1980 and its downing of Korean Airlines flight 007 in 1983 both led to a decline in sales of Russian vodka. See Gay Jervey, "Russ Vodka Sales Seen Down Drain," *Advertising Age,* September 12, 1983, p. 1 and "Vodka: It Doesn't Have to Be Russian," *New York Times,* February 24, 1980, p. III–17.

32. See Herbert J. Gans, *Deciding What's News* (New York: Pantheon, 1979), pp. 45–48, 190–97. But on this point as on other political and economic issues, journalists may be characterized more by a relative lack of strong conviction than by any particular ideological leaning. See Stephen Hess, *The Washington Reporters* (Washington, D.C.: Brookings Institution, 1981), p. 89.

33. Marc G. Weinberger, Chris T. Allen, and William R. Dillon, "Negative Information: Perspectives and Research Directions," pp. 390–404 and Carol K. Scott and Alice M. Tybout, "Theoretical Perspectives on the Impact of Negative Information: Does Valence Matter?" pp. 408–9, both in *Advances in Consumer Research,* vol. 8, ed. Kent B. Munroe (Ann Arbor: Association for Consumer Research, 1981).

34. John J. O'Connor, "Creative Ideas out of a Bottle," *Advertising Age,* July 27, 1981, p. S–6. Chervokas is a creative director at Warwick, Welsh, and Miller.

35. *San Diego Daily Transcript,* July 19, 1983, p. 2A, "Computers: Focus on Schools," *New York Times,* November 23, 1982, business p. 1, and Leonard M. Apcar and Marilyn Chase, "Apple Wants a Big Tax Break So It Can Give One of Its Computers to Every Public School," *Wall Street Journal,* March 19, 1982, p. 27. Computer manufacturers also court universities and provide them machines at large discounts, believing people will later

want to buy the computers they learned on in college. David E. Sanger, "Computer Makers Pursuing Campus Sales and Research." *New York Times,* January 20, 1984, p. 1.

36. Aimee Dorr, "Television Viewing Programs," in *International Encyclopedia of Education,* ed. T. Husen and N. Postlethwaite (Oxford: Pergamon Press, forthcoming). This includes a bibliography of recent writing on the subject of teaching critical television viewing skills. See also Aimee Dorr, Sherryl Browne Graves, and Erin Phelps, "Television Literacy for Young Children," *Journal of Communication* 30 (Summer 1980): 71–83.

37. Fred Hirsch, *Social Limits to Growth* (New York: Twentieth Century Fund, 1976), pp. 82–83.

38. Philip Nelson, "Information and Consumer Behavior," *Journal of Political Economy* 78 (1970): 321–23.

39. Bill Abrams, "Marketing: Shoppers Are Often Confused by All the Competing Brands," *Wall Street Journal,* April 22, 1982, p. 33.

40. Christy Marshall, "FCB Chief Raps TV Nets," *Advertising Age,* May 9, 1983, p. 2. See also Leo Bogart and Charles Lehman, "The Case of the 30-Second Commercial," *Journal of Advertising Research* 23 (February-March, 1983). Figures on recall differ from one method of study to another and from one date of study to another—though all seem to indicate a decline in the memory of commercials. Bogart and Lehman compare the findings of a number of studies.

41. Jack J. Honomichl, "Money Couldn't Buy Market Share," *Advertising Age,* July 19, 1982, p. M–3.

42. Ernest F. Larkin, "Consumer Perceptions of the Media and Their Advertising Content," *Journal of Advertising* 8 (Spring 1979): 5–7, 48.

43. "Credibility: The Medium and the Message." (New York: Magazine Publishers Association, n.d.). This pamphlet reports on a 1969 survey conducted by Gilbert Youth Research. Also see "The Believability of Advertising in Five Media: Results from a Recent Nationwide Survey" (New York: Newspaper Advertising Bureau, 1981).

44. *Advertising Age,* February 1, 1982, p. 37.

45. See Peter Wright, "The Harassed Decision Maker: Time Pressures, Distractions, and the Use of Evidence," *Journal of Applied Psychology* 59 (1974): 555–61.

46. Jennifer Alter, "Public Is Still Wary of Ads: Study," *Advertising Age,* June 23, 1980, pp. 3, 94.

47. "What 4As Study on Advertising Reveals," *Television-Radio Age,* August 16, 1976, pp. 28–29. See also Raymond A. Bauer and Stephen A. Greyser, *Advertising in America: The Consumer View* (Boston: Graduate School of Business Administration, Division of Research, Harvard University, 1968). A 1977 French survey found that 68 percent of the population believe that advertising makes people buy what they do not need and 66 percent say that advertising is a kind of lie. See Christiane Scrivener, Daniele Achach, and Yves Monier, *Rôle, Responsabilité et Avenir de la Publicité* (Paris: La Documentation Française, 1979).

48. Bill Abrams, "Marketing: WATS News . . . Margins Slim at Markets . . . Ernie's English," *Wall Street Journal,* September 10, 1981, p. 27.

49. See C. H. Sandage, Arnold M. Barban, and James E. Haefner, "How Farmers View Advertising," *Journalism Quarterly* 53 (Summer 1976): 303–7 for a review of some of the changes in attitudes in a variety of surveys between 1962 and 1974.

50. Donald Cox, "Clues for Advertising Strategists," in Cox, ed., *Risk Taking,* pp. 112–51.

51. *Sales and Marketing Management* 127 (November 16, 1981): 138.

52. Jacques Neher, "Firestone in Rebuilding Bid," *Advertising Age,* March 2, 1981, pp. 1, 78.

53. Peter C. Riesz, "Price versus Quality in the Marketplace, 1961–1975," *Journal of Retailing* 54 (Winter 1978): 15–28.

54. Jeffrey H. Birnbaum, "Pricing of Products Is Still an Art, Often Having Little Link to Costs," *Wall Street Journal,* November 25, 1981, p. 29. For experimental confirmation of

this inclination of consumers to be more attracted to higher-priced goods, see H. J. Leavitt, "Experimental Findings about the Meaning of Price," in Bernard Taylor and Gordon Wills, *Pricing Strategy* (Princeton: Brandon/Systems Press, 1969), pp. 37–43 and, in the same volume, D. S. Tull, R. A. Boring, and M. H. Gonsior, "The Relationship of Price and Imputed Quality," pp. 44–49. These studies find that consumers will choose higher-priced goods under some situations, especially in product areas where they believe there are large quality differences among brands.

55. For the Heublein data see Birnbaum, "Pricing of Products." The term "retrograde pricing" comes from Max Kjaer-Hansen, "The Significance of Marketing Costs," in *Pricing Strategy,* ed. Bernard Taylor and Gordon Wills (Princeton: Brandon/Systems Press, 1969), pp. 152–53. For another approach to pricing as a marketing tool, one that also assumes that cost of production should not determine price, see André Gabor, *Pricing: Principles and Practices* (London: Heinemann Books, 1977), pp. 211–30.

56. Richard L. Gordon, "Barclay lmg Claim Invalid, FTC Decides," *Advertising Age,* June 28, 1982, pp. 1, 88.

57. Surgeon General, *The Changing Cigarette* (Washington, D.C.: U.S. Department of Health and Human Services, 1981), pp. 200–206. Recent evidence indicates that low-tar cigarettes may not be any better for health than the conventional cigarette. See Neal L. Benowitz, et al. "Smokers of Low-Yield Cigarettes Do Not Consume Less Nicotine," *New England Journal of Medicine* 309 (July 21, 1983): 139–42.

58. Robert Raissman, "Mitsubishi, Hitachi Mull Ad Pullback," *Advertising Age,* July 5, 1982, p. 1.

59. The notion of "disengagement" of the elderly, hotly debated in gerontological circles, was first proposed by Elaine Cumming and William Henry, *Growing Old: The Process of Disengagement* (New York: Basic Books, 1961). William E. Oriol, staff director of the U.S. Senate's Special Committee on Aging, concluded that the main consumer problem of the elderly is the simple one that they don't have very much money. See "Federal Role in Consumer Protection," in *The Daily Needs and Interests of Older People,* ed. Adeline M. Hoffman (Springfield, Ill.: Charles C Thomas, 1970). See also H. Lee Meadow, Stephen C. Cosmas, and Andy Plotkin, "The Elderly Consumer: Past, Present, and Future," in *Advances in Consumer Research,* vol. 8, ed. Kent Munroe (Ann Arbor: Association for Consumer Research, 1981), pp. 742–47.

60. See Alan R. Andreasen, *The Disadvantaged Consumer* (New York: The Free Press, 1975) for a comprehensive review of the consumer problems of the poor. Lawrence Bowen, "Advertising and the Poor," *Journalism Monographs* 75 (February 1982) found in a study of university students from low- and middle-income families that, to the author's surprise, low-income students were *more* skeptical of television advertising content than middle-income students.

61. The quotation is from a study by Scott Ward cited in George Comstock, et al. *Television and Human Behavior* (New York: Columbia University Press, 1978), p. 199. See also Thomas S. Robertson and John R. Rossiter, "Children and Commercial Persuasion: An Attribution Theory Analysis," *Journal of Consumer Research* 1 (June 1974): 13–20. This study interviewed 289 school boys in Philadelphia Catholic schools and found that 53 percent of first-graders recognized the "persuasive intent" of commercials, 87 percent of third-graders and 99 percent of fifth-graders. Seventy-four percent of first-graders discriminated between programs and commercials, more than 90 percent of third-graders and all fifth-graders. Sixty-five percent of first-graders trusted all commercials, 30 percent of third-graders, and 7 percent of fifth-graders. These are fairly typical findings. See also T. G. Bever, et al. "Young Viewers' Troubling Responses to TV Ads," *Harvard Business Review* 53 (November-December 1975): 109–20, and Ellen Wartella, "Changing Conceptual Views of Children's Consumer Information Processing," in *Advances in Consumer Research,* vol. 9, ed. Andrew A. Mitchell (Ann Arbor: Association for Consumer Research, 1982), pp. 144–46.

62. See the comprehensive review of literature in Comstock, et al., *Television,* pp. 196–205. See also Richard P. Adler, et al., *The Effects of Television Advertising on Children* (Lexington, Mass.: Lexington Books, 1980).

63. Comstock, et al., *Television,* p. 201.

64. Michael Pertschuk, "What, Me Worry?" address to conference on "The Impact of the Mass Media on Health," University of California Extension Center, San Francisco, April 23–24, 1982.

65. Warren Hoge, "Smoking Is Flourishing in Brazil with Foes Unable to Stamp It Out," *New York Times,* January 21, 1980, p. A–2, reports on the rapid growth of cigarette consumption in Latin America and the increasing incidence of lung cancer as a cause of death among males. All but two of the ninety-five brands marketed in Brazil are high in tar and nicotine and have no health warning on the package. This includes some of the same R. J. Reynolds and Philip Morris brands which carry the warning here.

66. Milton Silverman, Philip R. Lee, and Mia Lydecker, *Prescriptions for Death: The Drugging of the Third World* (Berkeley: University of California Press, 1982). The authors note that the labeling of drugs has improved greatly in Latin America since the International Federation of Pharmaceutical Manufacturers Association passed a labeling code in 1976. Still, the center of promotional activity that would need to be examined are the detail men or "visitadores" as they are known in Latin America—the "propas" as they are called in Southeast Asia, the Japanese word for propagandists. In the United States and Europe, there is one detail man for every ten physicians. In Ecuador, the ratio is one to eight, in Colombia one to five, in Tanzania, one to four, and in Guatemala, Mexico, and Brazil, one to three. It is one to three or even one to two in Indonesia and the Philippines. (See p. 107.) See also Milton Silverman, *The Drugging of the Americas* (Berkeley: University of California Press, 1976).

67. D. B. Jelliffe, "Commerciogenic Malnutrition?" *Nutrition Reviews* 30 (1972): 199–205. The Third World phenomenon today has a counterpart in American history when infant formula first became popular here. See Rima D. Apple, " 'To Be Used Only Under the Direction of a Physician': Commercial Infant Feeding and Medical Practice, 1870–1940," *Bulletin of the History of Medicine* 54 (Fall 1980): 402–17, and Harvey Levenstein, " 'Best for Babies' or 'Preventable Infanticide'? The Controversy over Artificial Feeding of Infants in America, 1880–1920," *Journal of American History* 70 (June 1983): 75–94.

68. For a discussion of this and other marketing practices, see "Marketing and Promotion of Infant Formula in the Developing Nations, 1978," Hearing before the U.S. Senate Subcommittee on Health and Scientific Research of the Committee on Human Resources (Washington, D.C.: U.S. Government Printing Office, May 23, 1978).

69. Ibid. See, for instance, the testimony of Dr. James E. Post, especially pp. 123–24. For other evidence of the continuation of field practices in violation of codes to which the parent company had agreed, see also the testimony of Leah Margulies, director of the Interfaith Center on Corporate Responsibility, p. 37. The World Health Organization "International Code of Marketing of Breast-milk Substitutes" is printed in full in the *WHO Chronicle* 35 (1981): 112–17. The code was approved by the United Nations agency by a vote of 118 to 1, with Japan, the Republic of Korea, and Argentina abstaining and the United States alone in voting no.

As of fall, 1983, the Nestlé Infant Formula Audit Commission, established by Nestlé and headed by former Secretary of State Edmund S. Muskie, held there was still need to monitor Nestlé's activities. But in January, 1984, boycott leaders negotiated an agreement with Nestlé by which Nestlé agreed to curb its distribution of free infant formula as a promotional device, stop providing favors to physicians for their help in promotion, place warning labels on packages, and include a warning about the dangers of formula feeding in its literature. Based on these pledges from Nestlé, boycott leaders ended the boycott. "Nestle Boycott Being Suspended," *New York Times,* January 27, 1984, p. 1. For contrasting post mortems from the advertising community, see Richard Manoff, "Learning a Lesson from Nestle," *Advertising Age,* February 13, 1984, p. 16 and Rafael Pagan, "Nestle: On Going It Alone," *Advertising Age,* May 21, 1984, p. 18.

70. William Leiss, *The Limits to Satisfaction* (Toronto: University of Toronto Press, 1976), pp. 15–16.

Chapter 4

1. Quoted in Charles Sandage and Vernon Fryberger, *Advertising Theory and Practice* (Homewood, Ill.: Richard D. Irwin, 1975), p. 191. See also Andrew Tobias, *Fire and Ice: The Story of Charles Revson—the Man Who Built the Revlon Empire* (New York: William Morrow, 1976).

2. Marshall Sahlins, "The First Affluent Society," in *Stone Age Economics,* ed. Marshall Sahlins (Chicago: Aldine, 1972).

3. Adam Smith, *The Wealth of Nations* (New York: Modern Library, 1937), p. 821.

4. Ibid, p. 822.

5. From Karl Marx, *Capital,* vol. 1, quoted in Agnes Heller, *The Theory of Need in Marx* (London: Allison and Busby, 1974), p. 30.

6. Marx, *Capital,* vol. 2, quoted in Heller, p. 36.

7. *Wage, Labour and Capital* quoted in Patricia Springborg, *The Problem of Human Needs and the Critique of Civilisation* (London: George Allen and Unwin, 1981), p. 110. Marx's views on human needs have been a subject of very able scholarship recently, beginning with Agnes Heller's work. Springborg reviews the concept of human need in Rousseau, Hegel, Marx, Sartre, Reich, Fromm, Marcuse, Heller herself, Ivan Illich, and William Leiss. Leiss has written on the subject not only in his book, *The Limits to Satisfaction* (Toronto: University of Toronto Press, 1976), but in a number of essays, including, "Marx and Macpherson: Needs, Utilities, and Self-development," in *Powers, Possessions and Freedom: Essays in Honour of C. B. Macpherson,* ed. A. Kontas (Toronto: University of Toronto Press, 1979).

8. Thorstein Veblen, *The Theory of the Leisure Class* (New York: New American Library, 1953; Macmillan, 1899). For the argument that industry in advanced capitalism uses advertising to *create* the needs it then goes about satisfying, see John K. Galbraith, *The Affluent Society* (Boston: Houghton Mifflin, 1967), and John K. Galbraith, *The New Industrial State* (Boston: Houghton Mifflin, 1967). Also relevant is Herbert Marcuse, *One-Dimensional Man* (Boston: Beacon Press, 1964). Galbraith's position is frequently echoed. See, for instance, Erik Barnouw, *The Sponsor* (New York: Oxford University Press, 1978), p. 82, where Barnouw claims, "The merchandising of necessities . . . can seldom sustain the budgets applied to the unnecessary, unless the necessary is cloaked with mythical supplementary values. The focus is on the creation of emotion-charged values to make the unneeded necessary." Clearly, I find these views oversimple. For a critique of the Galbraithian position, see David Reisman, *Galbraith and Market Capitalism* (New York: New York University Press, 1980), especially pp. 72–100. I have written my own critique in "Criticizing the Critics of Advertising: Towards a Sociological View of Marketing," *Media, Culture, and Society* 3 (January 1981): 3–12.

9. On Detroit living rooms, see Edward O. Laumann and J. S. House, "Living Room Styles and Social Attributes: The Patterning of Material Artifacts in a Modern Urban Community," *Sociology and Social Research* 54 (1970): 321–42; on lifestyle in Newburyport, see W. Lloyd Warner, *Yankee City* (New Haven: Yale University Press, 1963); on yams in the Trobriands, see Bronislaw Malinowski, *Argonauts of the Western Pacific* (New York: E. P. Dutton, [1922] 1961); on curtains in East London, see Michael Young and Peter Willmott, *Family and Kinship in East London* (Harmondsworth, England: Penguin Books,

1957), pp. 159–60. See also the review article by Marcus Felson, "The Differentiation of Material Life Styles: 1925–1966," *Social Indicators Research* 3 (1976): 397–421.

10. Claude Lévi-Strauss, *The Elementary Structures of Kinship* (Boston: Beacon Press, 1969), pp. 58–59.

11. Alvin Gouldner, "The Norm of Reciprocity," *American Sociological Review* 25 (1960): 161–78. See also Russell W. Belk, "Gift-Giving Behavior," in *Research in Marketing* 2 (1979): 95–126.

12. Malinowski, *Argonauts*, pp. 81–104.

13. Carol Stack, *All Our Kin* (New York: Harper and Row, 1974), p. 41.

14. Theodore Caplow, "Christmas Gifts and Kin Networks," *American Sociological Review* 47 (June 1982): 388.

15. Eugene Rochberg-Halton, "Cultural Signs and Urban Adaptation: The Meaning of Cherished Household Possessions" (Ph.D. diss., University of Chicago, 1979). See also Mihaly Csikszentmihalyi and Eugene Rochberg-Halton, *The Meaning of Things* (Cambridge: Cambridge University Press, 1981) and Eugene Rochberg-Halton, "Remembrance of Things Present," paper presented at the 1983 meeting of Society for the Study of Symbolic Interaction, Detroit, Michigan.

16. Lévi-Strauss, *Kinship*, p. 55.

17. U.S. Department of Commerce, *Survey of Current Business* 61 (Washington, D.C.: U.S. Government Printing Office, August 1981).

18. Caplow, *Christmas Gifts*, p. 384.

19. *Advertising Age*, January 26, 1981, p. 80.

20. Susan Johnston, Florists' Transworld Delivery Association, personal communication, May 20, 1982.

21. Thomas B. Doyle, National Sporting Goods Association, personal communication, May 12, 1982.

22. *Departmental Merchandising and Operating Results of Department and Specialty Stores, 1967* (New York: National Retail Merchants Association, 1968).

23. U.S. Dept. of Commerce, *Survey of Current Business* 61 (August, 1981).

24. Gay Jervey, "Candy Makers Want No Tricks," *Advertising Age*, August 29, 1983, p. 3.

25. Advanced technology has created some means of gift giving that do not go through the market and might be taken as evidence of an extraordinarily gift-centered attitude in our society, the best case being that of donors for organ transplants. See Roberta Simmons, Susan Klein, and Richard Simmons, *Gift of Life: The Social and Psychological Impact of Organ Transplantation* (New York: John Wiley, 1977).

26. Marcus Felson and Joe L. Spaeth, "Community Structure and Collaborative Consumption," *American Behavioral Scientist* 21 (March–April 1978): 618.

27. *New York Times*, March 12, 1981, p. 39.

28. *Advertising Age*, January 26, 1981, p. 8.

29. Gay Jervey, "Polaroid Prays for Yule Developments," *Advertising Age*, December 7, 1981, p. 37.

30. U.S. Dept. of Commerce, *Survey of Current Business* 61 (August, 1981).

31. *Financial and Operating Results of Department and Specialty Stores of 1979* (New York: National Retail Merchants Association, 1980).

32. Shirley Polykoff, *Does She . . . Or Doesn't She?* (New York: Doubleday, 1975), p. 38.

33. *Chicago Tribune*, April 9, 1980, section 4, pp. 1, 9.

34. Lee Rainwater, Richard Coleman, and Gerald Handel, *Workingman's Wife* (New York: MacFadden Books, 1959), p. 184.

35. Ibid., pp. 107, 122, 225.

36. J. Davis, "Gifts and the U.K. Economy," *Man* 7 (September 1972): 424.

37. Quoted in Margaret Yao, "Gift-Giving Spirit Haunts Some People Who Can't Afford It," *Wall Street Journal,* December 24, 1981, p. 1.

38. Robert Tucker, ed., *The Marx-Engels Reader,* 2d ed. (New York: W. W. Norton, 1978), pp. 94–96.

39. Ibid., p. 76.

40. See Shlomo Avineri, *The Social and Political Thought of Karl Marx* (Cambridge: Cambridge University Press, 1968), pp. 77–81 and especially footnote 1, p. 81.

41. Leiss, *The Limits to Satisfaction,* pp. 40, 69, and elsewhere.

42. Lee Rainwater, *What Money Buys: Inequality and the Social Meanings of Income* (New York: Basic Books, 1974), p. 24.

43. Ibid., p. 35. Rainwater adopts the phrase "standard package" from David Riesman and Howard Roseborough, "Careers and Consumer Behavior," in *Abundance for What?* ed. David Riesman (Garden City, N.Y.: Doubleday, 1964).

44. Rainwater, *What Money Buys,* p. xi.

Chapter 5

1. Theodore Dreiser, *Sister Carrie* (New York: Bantam Books, 1958 [Doubleday, Page, 1900]), p. 4.

2. See Lyn Lofland, *World of Strangers* (New York: Basic Books, 1973), and Richard Sennett, *The Fall of Public Man* (New York: Alfred A. Knopf, 1976), p. 39.

3. Theodore Dreiser, *Newspaper Days* (New York: Horace Liveright, 1922), p. 139.

4. Dreiser, *Sister Carrie,* p. 17.

5. "The Department Store Question," editorial, *Chicago Tribune,* February 26, 1897, and "Big Stores Are in Scorn," *Chicago Tribune,* February 23, 1897. For a discussion of similar, and more successful efforts, in France, see Michael B. Miller, *The Bon Marché: Bourgeois Culture and the Department Store, 1869–1920* (Princeton: Princeton University Press, 1981), pp. 212–13. For a brief history of the American department store, see Daniel Boorstin, *The Americans: The Democratic Experience* (New York: Random House, 1973), pp. 101–18.

6. William Allen White, *The Autobiography of William Allen White* (New York: Macmillan, 1946), p. 400.

7. Quoted in Neil Harris, "Museums, Merchandising, and Popular Taste: The Struggle for Influence," in *Material Culture and the Study of American Life,* ed. Ian M. G. Quimby (New York: W. W. Norton, 1978), p. 152. Again, see Miller, *Bon Marché,* pp. 168–77, for a similar account of Bon Marché in Paris. As interesting and delightful as Miller's book is, his view that "it was the department store that was largely responsible for lowering prices and for creating overpowering urges to consume" (p. 184) cannot be accepted.

8. Boorstin, *Americans,* p. 107.

9. Quoted in Harris, "Museums," p. 152.

10. Joel H. Ross, M.D., *What I Saw in New York* (Auburn, N.Y.: Derby and Miller, 1851), p. 170.

11. See Michael Schudson, *Discovering the News* (New York: Basic Books, 1978), pp. 93, 206.

12. Charles Edward Russell, *These Shifting Scenes* (New York: George H. Doran, 1914), p. 309.

13. Robert Lynd and Helen Lynd, *Middletown* (New York: Harcourt, Brace and World, 1929), p. 532.

14. Joseph Appel, *Growing Up With Advertising* (New York: Business Bourse, 1940), pp. 25, 43, 92, 97. Appel was John Wanamaker's advertising manager.

15. Erik Erikson, *Childhood and Society* (New York: W. W. Norton, 1950), p. 261.

16. Peter Berger and Thomas Luckmann, "Social Mobility and Personal Identity," *Archives Européenne de Sociologies* 5 (1964): 331–43.

17. Ibid., p. 338.

18. Lynd and Lynd, *Middletown*, p. 144.

19. William Leiss, *The Limits to Satisfaction* (Toronto: University of Toronto Press, 1976), pp. 61–63 and elsewhere. Robert Lynd sensed this growing ambiguity of needs when he wrote of the proliferation of consumer goods in the 1920s, suggesting that "it is an open question whether factors making for consumer confusion in our rapidly changing culture are not actually outstripping the forces making for more effective consumption." Robert Lynd and Alice C. Hanson, "People as Consumers," in President's Research Commission on Social Trends, *Recent Social Trends in the United States* (New York: McGraw-Hill, 1933), p. 911.

20. Daniel Bell, *The Cultural Contradictions of Capitalism* (New York: Basic Books, 1976), p. 66.

21. Claude Lévi-Strauss, *Totemism* (Boston: Beacon Press, 1963), p. 89, and Mary Douglas and Baron Isherwood, *The World of Goods* (New York: Basic Books, 1979), p. 62.

22. Berger and Luckmann, *Social Mobility*, p. 339.

23. Boorstin, *Americans*, pp. 97, 99.

24. Lynd and Lynd, *Middletown*, p. 165.

25. Anne Hollander, *Seeing Through Clothes* (New York: Viking Press, 1978), p. 362.

26. There is a large literature on fashion. America's premier analyst of clothing, Thorstein Veblen, saw dress in the late nineteenth century as primarily intended for the display of economic position. See Thorstein Veblen, "The Economic Theory of Women's Dress," in *Essays in Our Changing Order*, ed. Thorstein Veblen (New York: August M. Kelley, 1964 [1934]), p. 67. The essay appeared first in *Popular Science Monthly* 46 (November 1894). See also the rich and provocative book by Hollander, *Seeing Through Clothes;* Edward Sapir, "Fashion," *Encyclopedia of the Social Sciences* (New York: Macmillan, 1933), vol. 6, pp. 139–44; Georg Simmel, "Fashion," in *Georg Simmel: On Individuality and Social Forms*, ed. Donald N. Levine (Chicago: University of Chicago Press, 1971); and Herbert Blumer, "Fashion: From Class Differentiation to Collective Selection," *Sociological Quarterly* 10 (Summer 1969): 275–91. Also valuable is Neil McKendrick, "The Commercialization of Fashion," in *The Birth of Consumer Society: The Commercialization of Eighteenth Century England*, ed. Neil McKendrick, John Brewer, and J. H. Plumb (Bloomington: Indiana University Press, 1982) on fashions in clothing and other consumer goods, from pottery to cut flowers.

27. Marcus Felson, "Invidious Distinctions among Cars, Clothes and Suburbs," *Public Opinion Quarterly* 42 (Spring 1978): 49–58 and Marcus Felson, "The Masking of Material Inequality in the Contemporary United States: Felson's Reply," *Public Opinion Quarterly* 43 (Spring 1979): 120–22.

28. George Akerlof, "The Market for 'Lemons': Quality Uncertainty and the Market Mechanism," *Quarterly Journal of Economics* 84 (August 1970): 499. For relevant comparative material on how the use of trademarks and advertising in the Soviet Union acts as a kind of quality control and consumer protection, see Marshall I. Goldman, "Product Differentiation and Advertising: Some Lessons from the Soviet Experience," *Journal of Political Economy* 68 (August 1960): 346–57 and M. Timothy O'Keefe and Kenneth G. Sheinkopf, "Advertising in the Soviet Union: Growth of a New Media Industry," *Journalism Quarterly* 53 (Spring 1976): 80–87.

29. John McPhee, *Oranges* (New York: Farrar, Straus & Giroux, 1967), p. 21.

30. Ted Roselius, "Consumer Ranking of Risk Reduction Methods," *Journal of Marketing* 35 (January 1971): 56–61.

31. Sinclair Lewis, *Babbitt* (New York: Harcourt, Brace, 1922), p. 95.

32. Mary Douglas and Baron Isherwood, *The World of Goods* (New York: Basic Books, 1979), pp. 75–76.

33. In American society, the names of products are not only culturally shared but privately owned. Brand names that become household words take from manufacturers the exclusive rights to the words. Bayer lost the right to "aspirin" and Abercrombie and Fitch lost the rights to "safari." The words cellophane, escalator, shredded wheat, ping-pong, yo-yo, thermos, and zipper all began as brand names. In recent litigation, the FTC challenged American Cyanamid's right to exclusive use of the world "formica." Xerox advertisements urge people to say "photocopy" rather than "xerox" as a verb to keep xerox in the public mind while keeping it from becoming a dictionary term. Similarly, commercials that stress "Sanka brand" decaffeinated coffee try to keep "Sanka" from being synonymous with decaffeinated coffee. The intention in these cases is to protect the name as a piece of property, to prevent its being part of a truly common culture. If culture is the sharing of names, it is also the structured absence of sharing, and this, too, requires examination. See Walter P. Margulies, "FTC vs. Formica Inc.: Trademarks Face Challenge of Their Lives," *Advertising Age*, August 13, 1979, pp. 53–54.

34. See Neil Harris, "The Drama of Consumer Desire," in *Yankee Enterprise*, ed. Otto Mayr and Robert C. Post (Washington, D.C.: Smithsonian Institution Press, 1981), pp. 196–211.

35. Lynd and Lynd, *Middletown*, p. 532.

36. Frank Presbrey, *The History and Development of Advertising* (Garden City, N.Y.: Doubleday, Doran, 1929), p. 362. See also an account of the predominance of patent medicine advertising in this period in Grace Margaret Busso, "A History of the *Des Moines Register*" (M.A. diss., University of Iowa, 1932), p. 134. For a detailed and interesting account of one key patent medicine, see Sarah Stage, *Female Complaints: Lydia Pinkham and the Business of Women's Medicine* (New York: W. W. Norton, 1979).

37. Ralph Hower, *The History of an Advertising Agency: N. W. Ayer & Son at Work, 1869–1949* (Cambridge: Harvard University Press, 1949), pp. 44, 91–92.

38. James Harvey Young, *Toadstool Millionaires* (Princeton: Princeton University Press, 1961), p. 167.

39. Ibid., p. 152.

40. Ibid., pp. 103, 169.

41. For the general analysis here, I rely on Alfred D. Chandler, *The Visible Hand: The Managerial Revolution in American Business* (Cambridge: Harvard University Press, 1977). On Royal Baking Powder, see Daniel Pope, *The Making of Modern Advertising* (New York: Basic Books, 1983), p. 148.

42. Arthur F. Marquette, *Brands, Trademarks and Good Will* (New York: McGraw-Hill, 1967), p. 33.

43. Chandler, *Visible Hand*, p. 287.

44. Marquette, *Brands*, p. 52.

45. Pope, *Modern Advertising*, p. 236.

46. Marquette, *Brands*, p. 51.

47. Chandler, *Visible Hand*, p. 299.

48. This is a much debated point. See, for instance, the account in Mark Albion and Paul Farris, *The Advertising Controversy: Evidence on the Economic Effects of Advertising* (Boston: Auburn House, 1981).

49. Vince Norris, "Advertising History—According to the Textbooks," *Journal of Advertising* 9 (1980): 3–11. Norris places too much emphasis on advertising as a weapon against retailers but he is right to call attention to the importance of this factor.

50. Hower, *Advertising Agency*, p. 16.

51. See Bertram Wyatt-Brown, "God and Dun & Bradstreet, 1841–1851," *Business History Review* 40 (Winter 1966): 432–50 and James H. Madison, "The Evolution of Commercial Credit Reporting Agencies in Nineteenth-Century America," *Business History Review* 48 (Summer 1974): 164–86.

52. Hower, *Advertising Agency,* p. 96.

53. Ibid., p. 56.

54. Ibid., p. 58.

55. See John Gunther, *Taken at the Flood: The Story of Albert D. Lasker* (New York: Harper, 1960), p. 62.

56. Daniel Pope, "The Development of National Advertising 1865–1920" (Ph.D. diss., Columbia University, 1973), p. 284.

57. Ibid., p. 309.

58. Ibid., p. 357.

59. Daniel Pope, *The Making of Modern Advertising,* pp. 239–42 and Quentin Schultze, "An Honorable Place: The Quest for Professional Advertising Education, 1900–1917," *Business History Review* 61 (Spring 1982): 16–32.

60. David Cohen, *J. B. Watson: The Founder of Behaviorism* (London: Routledge and Kegan Paul, 1979), p. 193. See also Kerry W. Buckley, "The Selling of a Psychologist: John Broadus Watson and the Application of Behavioral Techniques to Advertising," *Journal of the History of the Behavioral Sciences* 18 (July 1982): 207–21.

61. Roland Marchand, *Advertising the American Dream: Making Way for Modernity, 1920–1940* (Berkeley: University of California Press, forthcoming).

62. Quoted in Robert Wilber, "Men's Wear Stores for Women Only," *Printer's Ink,* September 15, 1917, p. 162.

63. Ibid., p. 164.

64. James Curran, Angus Douglas, and Barry Whannel, "The Political Economy of the Human-Interest Story," in *Newspapers and Democracy,* ed. Anthony Smith (Cambridge: MIT Press, 1980), pp. 288–347.

65. Walter Lippmann, *Public Opinion* (New York: Macmillan, 1922), p. 205.

66. Stuart Ewen, *Captains of Consciousness: Advertising and the Social Roots of the Consumer Culture* (New York: McGraw-Hill, 1976), p. 12.

67. Ibid., pp. 25, 33, 43, 109.

68. The one regularly cited person in Ewen's book who was not in advertising is Edward Filene, and even he was not an industrialist but a renegade department store owner. Filene supported independent unionism, helped establish the credit union movement, and, a life-long Democrat, supported Franklin Roosevelt in both 1932 and 1936, splitting openly in 1936 with the U.S. Chamber of Commerce that he had helped to found. Filene's insistence that employees at Filene's Department Store be represented in corporate decision making eventually led to his own ouster from management in 1928; he had hoped to transfer store management entirely to the employees. This is scarcely the representative voice of American capital. See Louis Filler's biographical sketch in *Dictionary of American Biography,* vol. 11, supplement 2 (New York: Charles Scribner's Sons, 1958), pp. 183–85 and also *National Cyclopedia of American Biography* 45 (1962): 17–19.

69. On the disposable income of workers in the 1920s, see Frank Stricker, "Affluence for Whom?—Another Look at Prosperity and the Working Classes in the 1920s," *Labor History* 24 (Winter 1983): 5–33. Stricker argues that ". . . the masses were not affluent enough to worry about clean-smelling breath and fancy cars." The response to Ewen's book has varied from uncritical admiration—a reviewer in *Contemporary Sociology* called it a "masterwork"—to extremely hostile criticism, especially in the history journals. Probably the most balanced review is by Daniel Horowitz, "Consumption, Capitalism, and Culture," *Reviews in American History* 6 (September 1978): 388–93, which identifies the reason for the importance of the book: "It is the first major study by a radical historian that moves from analysis of capitalist control of production to that of corporate hegemony in consumption." See also Sue Curry Jansen's review of Stuart and Elizabeth Ewen, *Channels of Desire*, in *Contemporary Sociology* 12 (July 1983): 423 and the reviews of *Captains of Consciousness* by Otis A. Pease, *American Historical Re-*

view 182 (October 1977): 1092–93 and Morton Keller, *Journal of American History* 64 (June 1977): 210. Ewen's work has had more influence in sociology than in history. See, for instance, Michael E. Sobel, *Lifestyle and Social Structure: Concepts, Definitions, Analyses* (New York: Academic Press, 1981), pp. 31–41, which closely follows Ewen's argument.

70. Ewen, *Captains of Consciousness*, p. 204.

Chapter 6

1. Daniel Boorstin, *The Americans: The Democratic Experience* (New York: Random House, 1973) emphasizes the beginning of consumer culture in the late nineteenth century; Daniel Bell, *The Cultural Contradictions of Capitalism* (New York: Basic Books, 1976) places considerable emphasis on the 1920s; and Otis Pease and Stuart Ewen, from very different viewpoints, see the roots of consumer culture in the 1920s but take the 1950s as its first real flowering. See Otis Pease, "Teaching Americans to Consume," in *Advertising and the Public*, ed. Kim B. Rotzoll (Urbana: University of Illinois, Department of Advertising, 1980), pp. 1–15 and Stuart Ewen, *Captains of Consciousness* (New York: McGraw-Hill, 1976), p. 206. The claim for England as the first consumer society is made in a set of rich, provocative essays by Neil McKendrick, John Brewer, and J. H. Plumb, *The Birth of a Consumer Society: The Commercialization of Eighteenth-Century England* (Bloomington: Indiana University Press, 1982).

2. Daniel Bell sees the expansion of consumer credit as a turning point in *Cultural Contradictions*, pp. 69–70; Christopher Lasch emphasizes a replacement of the work ethic with a new ethic of self-preservation in the 1970s in *The Culture of Narcissism* (New York: W. W. Norton, 1978), pp. 52–70; and on the revolution in economic thought beginning in the 1690s, see Neil McKendrick, "Commercialization and the Economy," in McKendrick, Brewer, and Plumb, *Consumer Society*, pp. 13–19.

3. James Truslow Adams, *The Tempo of Modern Life* (Freeport, N.Y.: Books for Libraries Press, 1970 [1931]), p. 84.

4. Neil Harris, "The Drama of Consumer Desire," in *Yankee Enterprise*, ed. Otto Mayr and Robert C. Post (Washington: Smithsonian Institution Press, 1981), p. 204.

5. Daniel Boorstin, *The Americans: The Democratic Experience* (New York: Random House, 1974), pp. 307–58.

6. On the importance of embarrassment and embarrassment-avoidance in human social life, see Michael Schudson, "Embarrassment and Erving Goffman's Concept of Human Nature," *Theory and Society* (vol. 13, 1984).

7. Robert Lynd and Helen Lynd, *Middletown* (New York: Harcourt, Brace, 1929).

8. Ibid. The "plateau" metaphor is presented on p. 83.

9. Benno Milmore and Arthur Conover, "Tobacco Consumption in the United States, 1880–1955." This is the appendix to William Haenszel, Michael B. Shimkin, and Herman P. Miller, *Tobacco Smoking Patterns in the United States*, Public Health monograph no. 45 (Washington, D.C.: U.S. Government Printing Office, 1956), p. 107.

10. *New York Times*, February 3, 1930, p. 4.

11. Erik Barnouw, *The Sponsor* (New York: Oxford University Press, 1978), p. 95. Barnouw and other observers have been influenced by Edward Bernays's recollections in *Biography of an Idea: Memoirs of Public Relations Counsel Edward L. Bernays* (New York: Simon and Schuster, 1965), pp. 383–95. Bernays takes pride in having arranged for ten women to light up cigarettes, their "torches of freedom" in the 1929 Easter Parade in New York. He smugly recalls that this created a storm of interest and front-page news stories and photos. Yet women smoking cigarettes in public had been making the front page for years without the help of Edward Bernays.

12. There is not a "field" one could call the sociology of consumption yet—despite the importance that sociologists have long placed on status and its material as well as nonmaterial symbols. "Consumer behavior" has been studied in the business schools but studied there as a kind of primitive applied psychology or sometimes applied demography. Where sociologists have themselves become market researchers without losing their interest in social theory, some good work has been produced. This was the case with Elihu Katz and Paul Lazarsfeld in the celebrated volume, *Personal Influence* (New York: The Free Press, 1955) and also the case with the work of Lee Rainwater, Richard Coleman, and Gerald Handel in *Workingman's Wife* (New York: MacFadden Books, 1962). There is still a lot to be learned from David Riesman, Nathan Glazer, and Reuel Denney, *The Lonely Crowd* (New Haven: Yale University Press, 1950). Indeed, a remark in *The Lonely Crowd* provides, in a sense, the question of this book: "Isn't it possible that advertising as a whole is a fantastic fraud, presenting an image of America taken seriously by no one?" (p. 294). Yes, indeed, it is possible—but frauds have consequences, even if they are not taken seriously. More recently, there has been a modest surge of interest in consumption, spurred by a number of unusually thoughtful works, of which I would list as being particularly important William Leiss, *The Limits to Satisfaction* (Toronto: University of Toronto Press, 1976); Fred Hirsch, *Social Limits to Growth* (Cambridge: Harvard University Press, 1976); Marshall Sahlins, *Culture and Practical Reason* (Chicago: University of Chicago Press, 1976); and Mihaly Csikszentmihalyi and Eugene Rochberg-Halton, *The Meaning of Things: Domestic Symbols and the Self* (Cambridge: Cambridge University Press, 1981).

13. Eunice Fuller Barnard, "The Cigarette Has Made Its Way Up in Society," *New York Times Magazine,* June 9, 1929, p. 18.

14. "Going Up in Smoke" editorial, *New York Times,* September 24, 1925.

15. See "Women and Cigarettes," *Printer's Ink,* February 18, 1932, pp. 25–27 and "Blow Some More My Way," *Printer's Ink,* April 14, 1932, p. 20. One later and more impressionistic estimate is much higher. Industry executives cited in *Advertising Age,* September 7, 1936, p. 19, suggested that, in big cities, women smoked more cigarettes than men. The argument was not that more women smoke than men but that women smokers smoke more cigarettes than men smokers. Why? "Men usually smoke all of every cigarette they light. Women, who cannot smoke everywhere, often throw away a cigarette after a puff or two and return to their office work, shopping, or whatever they happen to be doing. Most women devoted to the habit are young and they refuse to smoke more than half a cigarette for fear of staining fingers and nails."

16. Milmore and Conover, *Tobacco Consumption,* p. 107.

17. "The Fortune Survey," *Fortune* 12 (July 1935): 111.

18. Alfred Chandler, *The Visible Hand* (Cambridge: Harvard University Press, 1977), pp. 289–92.

19. Milmore and Conover, *Tobacco Consumption,* p. 107.

20. William Bennett, "The Nicotine Fix," *Harvard Magazine,* July-August 1980, p. 13. See also Heather Ashton and Rob Stepney, *Smoking: Psychology and Pharmacology* (London: Tavistock, 1982), pp. 29–32.

21. Richard Tennant, *The American Cigarette Industry* (New Haven: Yale University Press, 1950), pp. 76–79 and Curtis Wessel, "The First 60 Billions Are the Hardest for the Cigarette Industry," *Printer's Ink,* January 31, 1924, p. 137.

22. Wessel, "First 60 Billions," p. 137.

23. American Tobacco Company, *Sold American—The First Fifty Years* (American Tobacco Company, 1954), p. 56.

24. *New York Times,* May 23, 1918, p. 1. See also the editorial, "They've Had a Lot of Tobacco," May 24, 1918, p. 12. Controversy developed over YMCA distribution of cigarettes. See *New York Times,* May 27, 1918, p. 1 and separate article on p. 3. See also John R. Mott, *Addresses and Papers of John R. Mott,* vol. 4 (New York: Young Men's Christian Association, Association Press, 1947), pp. 808, 810.

25. Russell B. Adams, Jr., *King C. Gillette: The Man and His Wonderful Shaving Device* (Boston: Little, Brown, 1978), pp. 102–3.

26. Barnard, "Cigarette Made Its Way," p. 18.

27. For controversy over cigarette smoking in a dormitory for women war workers, see *Literary Digest* 61 (June 28, 1919): 76.

28. *New York Times,* November 25, 1928, section IV, p. 7.

29. *New York Times,* December 10, 1921, p. 10.

30. *New York Times,* January 22, 1925, p. 1; February 26, 1925, p. 13; February 27, 1925, p. 16.

31. *New York Times,* March 2, 1925, on Radcliffe and November 20, 1925, on Smith.

32. *New York Times,* October 12, 1925, p. 1.

33. *New York Times,* November 24, 1925, p. 1 and November 25, 1925, p. 20.

34. Paula Fass, *The Damned and the Beautiful: American Youth in the 1920's* (New York: Oxford University Press, 1977), p. 293.

35. Fass, *Damned and Beautiful,* pp. 295–97. But see also A. T. Allen, superintendent of schools in North Carolina who saw Bryn Mawr as the wave of the future for women's colleges. *New York Times,* November 29, 1925, section II, p. 3.

36. *New York Times,* July 5, 1929, p. 19 and July 11, 1929, p. 48.

37. *New York Times,* December 7, 1929, p. 44.

38. *New York Times,* July 15, 1921, p. 5.

39. *New York Times,* April 9, 1925, p. 18.

40. *New York Times,* July 16, 1925, p. 1 and July 17, 1925, p. 14.

41. *New York Times,* August 4, 1926, p. 21.

42. *Baltimore American,* July 15, 1925.

43. Jack Jacob Gottsegen, *Tobacco: A Study of Its Consumption in the United States* (New York: Pitman Publishing, 1940), p. 151.

44. "Woman No Longer Hides Her Cigarette," *New York Times Magazine,* August 21, 1928, p. 19.

45. Frances Perkins, "Can They Smoke Like Gentlemen?" *New Republic* 62 (May 7, 1930): 319–20. Perkins, later to be Franklin Roosevelt's Secretary of Labor, was at this time Industrial Commissioner for the State of New York. See also the complaint of an underwriter that women's ineptness at smoking causes fires, *New York Times,* June 26, 1928, p. 41. A *Reader's Digest* column complained that women "haven't yet learned how to smoke, or when, or where." See "Gelett Burgess in Your Life," *Reader's Digest* 33 (July 1938): 68.

46. *New York Times,* March 9, 1925, p. 1.

47. Wessel, "First 60 Billions," p. 6. Tennant also cites a 1926 article in *Advertising and Selling* that attests to manufacturer fear of a public backlash. See Tennant, *Cigarette Industry,* p. 139.

48. Robert Sobel, *They Satisfy: The Cigarette in American Life* (New York: Doubleday Anchor, 1978), p. 99.

49. *New Yorker,* January 9, 1926, back cover.

50. *Time,* December 5, 1927, back cover.

51. *Time,* July 11, 1927, p. 29.

52. *The Outlook,* March 23, 1927, back cover.

53. *Time,* April 1, 1929, back cover.

54. *Time,* February 4, 1929, back cover.

55. *Time,* October 14, 1929, back cover.

56. *New York Times,* February 2, 1927, p. 52 and December 2, 1927, p. 48.

57. *New York Times,* November 27, 1927, p. 30 and August 30, 1928, p. 30. See also Philip Wagner, "Cigarettes Versus Candy," *Reader's Digest* 7 (March 1929): 752–54, reprinted from *The New Republic,* February 13, 1929.

58. *Report* of the 53d Annual Convention of the Women's Christian Temperance Union, San Francisco, 1921.

59. *Report* of the 53d Annual Convention of the Women's Christian Temperance Union, Minneapolis, Minn., 1927, pp. 129–33.

60. *New York Times,* March 17, 1925.

61. *New York Times,* November 1, 1925.

62. See "Cigarets for Grown-Up Kansas," *Literary Digest* 92 (February 26, 1927): 12, on the 1927 repeal of a ban on cigarette sales in Kansas.

63. *New York Times,* July 4, 1930, p. 13.

64. *New York Times,* July 13, 1928, p. 19 and May 11, 1929, p. 21.

65. Senator Reed Smoot, *Congressional Record* (June 10, 1929): 2589.

66. See *Smoking and Health: A Report of the Surgeon General* (Washington, D.C.: U.S. Government Printing Office, 1979), especially chapter 16.

67. Sinclair Lewis, *Babbitt* (New York: Harcourt, Brace, 1922), p. 327.

68. Shirley Polykoff, *Does She . . . Or Doesn't She?* (Garden City, N. Y.: Doubleday, 1975), p. 5.

69. Harry Burke, "Women Cigarette Fiends," *Ladies Home Journal,* June, 1922, p. 19.

70. On the role of the cigarette as a symbol of new womanhood, see Peter Gabriel Filene, *Him/Her/Self: Sex Roles in Modern America* (New York: Harcourt, Brace, Jovanovich, 1975), pp. 148–49 and also his bibliography on pp. 312–13 for other newspaper and magazine coverage of the smoking controversy in the 1920s.

71. Edward Bernays, *Biography of an Idea: Memoirs of Public Relations Counsel Edward L. Bernays* (New York: Simon and Schuster, 1965), pp. 383–95. See note 11, this chapter.

72. See Lester Telser, "Advertising and Cigarettes," *Journal of Political Economy* 70 (1962): 471–99 and Richard Schmalensee, *The Economics of Advertising* (Amsterdam: North-Holland Publishing, 1972), p. 213. Schmalensee's case study of cigarette advertising found no support for an industry effect of advertising on sales or for a firm effect of advertising on sales. The same results obtain in England: "In terms of total demand for tobacco products there is no evidence that advertising has had any noticeable short- or medium-term effect on total consumption." See B. W. E. Alford, *W. D. and H. O. Willis and the Development of the U.K. Tobacco Industry, 1786–1965* (London: Methuen, 1973), p. 432. For a different assessment, see Heather Ashton and Rob Stepney, *Smoking; Psychology and Pharmacology* (London: Tavistock, 1982), pp. 148–151.

73. Lewis, *Babbitt,* p. 69.

74. Burke, "Women Cigarette Fiends."

75. "Going Up in Smoke," *New York Times,* September 24, 1925, p. 24.

76. Woodrow Wilson quoted in George Juergens, *News from the White House* (Chicago: University of Chicago Press, 1981), p. 131; *Washington Evening Star,* December 8, 1922.

77. Tennant, "Cigarette Industry," p. 140.

78. Ibid., p. 142.

79. "Going Up in Smoke."

80. Gary Becker, "A Theory of the Allocation of Time," chapter 5 in Gary Becker, *The Economic Approach to Human Behavior* (Chicago: University of Chicago Press, 1976), p. 110.

81. Staffan Burenstam Linder, *The Harried Leisure Class* (New York: Columbia University Press, 1970), pp. 17, 22.

82. Ibid., p. 71.

83. Ibid, p. 74

84. Russell Mack, *The Cigar Manufacturing Industry* (Philadelphia: University of Pennsylvania Press, 1933), p. 19.

85. U.S. Department of Commerce, Bureau of the Census, *Social Indicators III* (Washington, D.C.: U.S. Government Printing Office, 1980), p. 476, table 9/11.

86. Neil Martin, "Civic Pride," *Barron's* 54 (September 9, 1974): 11, 28.

87. Norman T. Moline, *Mobility and the Small Town 1900–1930* (Chicago: University of Chicago, Department of Geography, research paper no. 132, 1971), pp. 50–73.

88. Ibid, pp. 50–73.

89. Ibid, pp. 94–121.

Chapter 7

1. Jack Goody, *Domestication of the Savage Mind* (Cambridge: Cambridge University Press, 1977), p. 44.

2. David Potter, *People of Plenty* (Chicago: University of Chicago Press, 1954).

3. Mason Griff, "Advertising: the Central Institution of Mass Society," *Diogenes* no. 68 (Winter 1969): 120–37.

4. International Commission for the Study of Communication Problems (MacBride Commission), *Many Voices, One World* (London: Kogan Page, 1980), p. 110.

5. "A Vanishing Statue of Ulysses S. Grant," *Washington Post Magazine,* February 3, 1980, p. 4.

6. Personal interview with a Hollywood actress, 1981. Quentin Schultze argues that advertising is "acultural." He writes, "Advertising directed at distant audiences and created by professional symbol brokers shows no respect for culture that has been seasoned over time and cultivated in geographic space. Advertising is not simply false consciousness; it is acultural." This is not quite so—it is middle-class culture, homogenized, yes, with regional and ethnic wrinkles smoothed out, but middle class nonetheless. See Quentin Schultze, "Advertising, Culture, and Economic Interest," *Communication Research* 8 (July 1981): 377.

7. Gerald Miller, creative director for Young & Rubicam, told the *Los Angeles Times* that Robert Young was the choice as Sanka spokesman because "he represents deliberate, mature, seasoned advice." Nancy Yoshihara, "Advertising Success? It's in the Stars," *Los Angeles Times,* February 12, 1981, p. 12.

8. Daniel Boorstin, *The Image* (New York: Atheneum, 1962; Harper Colophon, 1964), p. 57.

9. Ainsworth Howard, "More Than Just a Passing Fancy," *Advertising Age* 50 (July 30, 1979): S–2 and Nancy Yoshihara, "Advertising Success? It's in the Stars," *Los Angeles Times,* February 12, 1981, p. 1. The abstractness of product spokespersons was challenged when Pat Boone agreed in an FTC consent decree to be held personally responsible for failure of the acne medication he endorsed, Acne-Statin, to give satisfaction. He also agreed to make reasonable efforts to verify the claims of any products he would endorse in the future. The world of celebrity endorsers was briefly shaken, but the FTC did not seek consumer refunds for Acne-Statin and the Boone case, settled in the spring of 1978, seems already ancient history. See "FTC Says Star Responsible for Endorsement," *Advertising Age,* May 15, 1978, p. 1. Martin Esslin has also observed the relative abstractness of "real people" in television commercials. See *The Age of Television* (San Francisco: W. H. Freeman, 1982), p. 50.

10. On fictional characters in commercials, see Lawrence Ingrassia, "Marketing: As Mr. Whipple Shows, Ad Stars Can Bring Long-Term Sales Gains," *Wall Street Journal,* February 12, 1981. See also Philip Revzin, "You, Too, Can Star in TV Commercials, Or Maybe You Can't," *Wall Street Journal,* March 10, 1981, pp. 1, 16.

11. F. G. Wigglesworth, "The Evolution of Guinness Advertising," *Journal of Advertising History* 3 (March 1980): 16.

12. Erving Goffman, *Gender Advertisements* (New York: Harper and Row, 1976), p. 15.

13. Ibid., pp. 15, 84.

14. Quoted in Aleksandr Fadayev, "Socialist Realism," in *Encyclopedia of World Literature in the Twentieth Century* (New York: Frederick Ungar, 1971), vol. 3, p. 299.

15. See the articles on "socialist realism" by Gero von Wilpert and Aleksandr Fadayev in *Encyclopedia of World Literature in the Twentieth Century* (New York: Frederick Ungar, 1971), vol. 3, pp. 298–301. See also Caradog v. James, *Soviet Socialist Realism: Origins of a Theory* (London: Macmillan, 1973), pp. 90–93. My own list of five features of socialist realism abstracts from these works. See also Abram Tertz, *On Socialist Realism* (New York: Vintage Books, 1960). Leo Bogart, *Strategy in Advertising* (New York: Harcourt, Brace and World, 1967), pp. 6–7, discusses advertising as propaganda and compares it to Soviet propaganda.

16. Lynn Hirschberg, "When You Absolutely, Positively Want the Best," *Esquire* 100 (August 1983): 55. For the material on the current vogue for realism in commercials, see Karen Thorsen, "Wives to celebrities: Search for au naturel," *Advertising Age*, July 21, 1980, pp. S–8, S–9, S–16. But see also T. J. Jackson Lears, "Some Versions of Fantasy: Toward a Cultural History of American Advertising, 1880–1930," *Prospects* 9 (1984) which cites ad men's concern for realism in advertising in the first decade of this century.

17. Bill Abrams, "Marketing: Anacin's New, Intense TV Ads Try to Avoid 'Sanitized' Look," *Wall Street Journal*, October 13, 1983, p. 31.

18. See especially Michael Arlen, *Thirty Seconds* (Harmondsworth, England: Penguin Books, 1981).

19. Barbara Rosenblum, *Photographers at Work* (New York: Holmes and Meier, 1978), p. 16.

20. John O'Toole, *The Trouble With Advertising . . .* (New York: Chelsea House, 1981), p. 89.

21. Raymond Williams, "The Magic System," *New Left Review*, no. 4 (July–August 1960) holds that advertising is "in a sense, the official art of modern capitalist society" (p. 27). His essay is expanded as "Advertising: The Magic System" and included in Raymond Williams, *Problems in Materialism and Culture* (London: Verso Editions, 1980), pp. 170–95.

22. See the FTC's statement of philosophy and policy, *Consumer Information Remedies* (Washington, D.C.: U.S. Government Printing Office, 1979). On court decisions regarding "commercial speech," see especially Virginia State Board of Pharmacy v. Virginia Citizens Consumer Council, 425 U.S. 746 (1976) and Bates v. State Bar of Arizona, 433 U.S. 350 (1977). These and other recent cases substantially undo Valentine v. Chrestensen, 316 U.S. 52 (1942) which established that commercial speech does not qualify for First Amendment protection. See Jerome A. Barron and C. Thomas Dienes, *Handbook of Free Speech and Free Press* (Boston: Little, Brown, 1979), pp. 155–88. While the United States itself is not a dominant buyer of advertising space, direct government advertising can be an important issue, as it is in Canada. There the government is the leading advertiser in the country, spending $58 million a year. The American government, in comparison, spent $173 million on advertising in 1981, but this made it only the twenty-fourth largest American advertiser. The Canadian ads are generally reminders of "what your government is doing for you" and have drawn public criticism. Peggy Berkowitz, "Government Is Top Advertiser in Canada, Angering Its Critics," *Wall Street Journal*, March 4, 1982, p. 29. In the American situation, government support of advertising takes place in a variety of ways, including subsidies to election campaigns that help finance political advertising, U.S. Department of Agriculture subsidies for advertising individual commodities, and very importantly preferential postal rates for magazines and newspapers—indirectly a subsidy of advertising itself. Murray L. Weidenbaum and Linda L. Rockwood discuss the ways in which the government subsidizes advertising in "Government as a Promoter and Subsidizer of Advertising," in *The Political Economy of Advertising*, ed. David G. Tuerck (Washington, D.C.: American Enterprise Institute, 1978), pp. 41–60.

Advertising has also received some support from the government during war time and has substantially improved its reputation with the public and potential critics by turning its energies to support of war efforts in both World War I and World War II. See Daniel Pope, "The Development of National Advertising, 1865–1920" (Ph.D. diss., Columbia University, 1973), pp. 331–33, on World War I and Frank Fox, *Madison Avenue Goes to War: The Strange Military Career of American Advertising 1941–45* (Provo, Utah: Brigham Young University Press, Charles E. Merrill monograph series, 1975) on World War II.

23. This is not to mention more nationalistic outbursts like the paperback book by the *New York Times* staff, *Miracle on Ice,* advertised under a banner headline, "How We Beat the Russians," *New York Times,* March 2, 1980, p. 57. On the use of the Olympics to promote private industry, see Marilyn Chase, "Firms Find Sponsoring Team for 1980 Games Is Good Way to Compete," *Wall Street Journal,* April 13, 1979, p. 1; and Roy J. Harris, Jr., "U.S. Athletes' Training Gains as Private Giving Lifts Budget for Games," *Wall Street Journal,* September 9, 1983, p. 1.

24. David Bernstein, "U.S. Advertising as Seen in the U. K.," lecture at *Advertising Age* "Advertising Week" convention, Chicago, Ill., August, 1979. See also the send-up of "American-ness" in commercials in Ellis Weiner, "Patriotic Spot (60 secs.)," *New Yorker,* June 30, 1980, p. 31.

25. See, for instance, on women, Erving Goffman, *Gender Advertisements* (New York: Harper & Row, 1976); Gaye Tuchman, Arlene Kaplan Daniels, and James Benet, *Hearth and Home: Images of Women in the Mass Media* (New York: Oxford University Press, 1978); on blacks, see the literature review in George Comstock, et. al., *Television and Human Behavior* (New York: Columbia University Press, 1978), pp. 35–39.

26. Brigitte Jordan and Kathleen Bryant, "The Advertised Couple: The Portrayal of the Couple and their Relationship in Popular Magazine Advertisements," paper presented at the Popular Culture Association and American Culture Association meetings, Pittsburgh, Penn., April 28, 1979. Forthcoming in *Journal of Popular Culture* 17 (1984).

27. Public service announcements (PSA's) produced by the Advertising Council have been criticized as thinly veiled advertisements for capitalism. See Richard Ohmann, "An Agency for All Social Ills," *Cyrano's Journal* 1 (Fall 1982): 36–37 and the companion article, by William Lutz, "The Gospel According to the Advertising Council," pp. 10–11, in the same issue. Also see Bruce Howard, "The Advertising Council: Selling Lies," *Ramparts* 13 (December 1974–January 1975): 25–26, 29–32 and David L. Paletz, Roberta E. Pearson, and Donald L. Willis, *Politics in Public Service Advertising on Television* (New York: Praeger, 1977).

28. Cowley is cited in David E. Shi, "Advertising and the Literary Imagination During the Jazz Age," *Journal of American Culture* 2 (Summer 1979): 172.

29. See John Barnicoat, *A Concise History of Posters* (New York: Oxford University Press), on the intertwining of art history and advertising history. On commercial directors moving to feature films, see Patrick Goldstein, "Leech Has Knack for Commercials," *Los Angeles Times,* September 9, 1983, p. VI–1.

30. Leo Spitzer, "American Advertising Explained as Popular Art," *Essays on English and American Literature* (Princeton: Princeton University Press, 1962), p. 265*n*22 and p. 249*n*2. Of course, advertising may be ugly as well as attractive and tasteless as well as an educator of tastes. This has been an issue especially in outdoor advertising. In the nineteenth century, when advertisers were less constrained than they are today, they covered rocks and cliffs and trees with their announcements. Niagara Falls and Yellowstone became backdrops to patent medicine advertisements painted directly on the rock formations. The *New York Tribune* in 1876 complained that scenery had become "obscenery." A wave of protest led to changes in advertising practice at the end of the nineteenth century, but outdoor signs and billboards are still often defacements of cherished landscapes. On the nineteenth century, see James Harvey Young, *Toadstool Millionaires* (Princeton: Princeton University Press, 1961), p. 123. See also Ronald Berman, "Origins of the Art of Advertising," *Journal of Aesthetic Education* (Fall 1983): 61–69.

31. Thomas Robertson and John Rossiter, "Children and Commercial Persuasion: An Attribution Theory Analysis," *Journal of Consumer Research* 1 (June 1974): 17.

32. Bill Abrams, "The 1981 TV Advertisements That People Remember Most," *Wall Street Journal,* February 25, 1982, p. 29.

33. James S. Duesenberry, *Income, Saving, and the Theory of Consumer Behavior* (Cambridge: Harvard Economic Study No. 87, 1949; New York: Oxford University Press, 1967), p. 26.

34. James Rorty, *Our Master's Voice* (New York: John Day, 1934, Arno Press, reprint, 1976), p. 16.

35. Ann Douglas, *The Feminization of American Culture* (New York: Alfred A. Knopf, 1977), p. 80.

36. Spitzer, "American Advertising," p. 273.

37. Daniel Pope, "The Development of National Advertising, 1865–1920" (Ph.D. diss., Columbia University, 1973), p. 320. See also a book just published as this volume goes to press: Stephen Fox, *The Mirror Makers: A History of American Advertising and Its Creators* (New York: William Morrow, 1984).

38. Marghanita Laski, "Advertising: Sacred and Profane," *Twentieth Century* 165 (February 1959): 118–29. On ads sponsoring "Holocaust," see Marvin Kitman, "Ads Disrupting *Holocaust,*" in *The Commercial Connection,* ed. John W. Wright (New York: Delta Books, 1979), pp. 262–64.

39. Northrop Frye, *The Modern Century* (Toronto: Oxford University Press, 1967), p. 26. See also Frye's remarks on consumer skepticism of advertising in *The Educated Imagination* (Indianapolis: Indiana University Press, 1964), p. 138, where he writes, "our reaction to advertising is really a form of literary criticism."

40. Spitzer, "American Advertising," p. 264 and p. 265*n*22.

41. Herbert E. Krugman, "The Impact of Television Advertising: Learning Without Involvement," *Public Opinion Quarterly* 29 (1965): 161. See also John C. Maloney, "Curiosity versus Disbelief in Advertising," *Journal of Advertising Research* 2 (June 1962): 2–8.

42. Budd Schulberg, *Some Faces in the Crowd* (New York: Random House, 1953).

43. Christopher Lasch, *The Culture of Narcissism* (New York: W. W. Norton, 1978), p. 74.

44. Melford Spiro, "Buddhism and Economic Action in Burma," *American Anthropologist* 68 (October 1966): 1163.

45. Roland Barthes, *Camera Lucida* (New York: Hill and Wang, 1981), p. 119.

46. Georges Duby, *The Age of the Cathedrals: Art and Society, 980–1420* (Chicago: University of Chicago Press, 1981), p. 135.

47. "Languages differ not so much as to what *can* be said in them, but rather as to what it is *relatively easy* to say in them." Charles Hockett, "Chinese vs. English: An Exploration of the Whorfian Hypothesis," in *Language in Culture,* ed. H. Hoijer (Chicago: University of Chicago Press, 1954), p. 122.

48. Clifford Geertz, "Art as a Cultural System," *MLN* 91 (1976): 1478.

49. Ibid., p. 1483.

50. "Transcript of President's Address to Country on Energy Problems," *New York Times,* July 16, 1979, p. A-10.

Chapter 8

1. Alexis de Tocqueville, *Democracy in America,* trans. J. P. Mayer (Garden City, N.Y.: Doubleday Anchor, 1969), p. 534.

2. Max Weber, *The Protestant Ethic and the Spirit of Capitalism* (New York: Charles Scribner's, 1958), p. 181.

3. Gary Gereffi, *The Pharmaceutical Industry and Dependency in the Third World* (Princeton: Princeton University Press, 1983), p. 201. Sometimes marketers direct their products not only *toward* the affluent but *away from* the poor or other "undesirable" consumers. If a product becomes too popular among a stigmatized social group, say, an ethnic minority group, this may drive away potential customers in the dominant population group. Then marketers seek methods of "demarketing." See Philip Kotler and Sidney J. Levy, "Demarketing, Yes, Demarketing," *Harvard Business Review* 49 (November-December 1971): 74–80.

4. Tom Furlong, "Adjustable-Rate Loan Marketing Triggers Concern," *Los Angeles Times*, March 25, 1984, p. V–1.

5. Bureau of Consumer Protection and Bureau of Economics, Federal Trade Commission, *Life Insurance Cost Disclosure* (Washington, D.C.: U.S. Government Printing Office, 1979).

6. See Marcus Felson, "Invidious Distinctions Among Cars, Clothes and Suburbs," *Public Opinion Quarterly* 42 (Spring 1978): 49–58 and Marcus Felson, "The Masking of Material Inequality in the Contemporary United States," *Public Opinion Quarterly* 43 (Spring 1979): 120–22.

7. See, for instance, Felix Gutierrez and Clint C. Wilson II, "The Demographic Dilemma," *Columbia Journalism Review* 17 (January-February 1979): 53–55.

8. The question of the morality of liquor advertising is at present a growing public issue, spurred in particular by a report from the Center for Science in the Public Interest: Michael Jacobson, George Hacker, and Robert Atkins, *The Booze Merchants: The Inebriating of America* (Washington, D.C.: Center for Science in the Public Interest, 1983). The controversy has an international dimension, too, with concern in activist circles about why the World Health Organization shelved its plan to study the world liquor industry. See Kathleen Selvaggio, "WHO Bottles Up Alcohol Study," *Multinational Monitor* 4 (November 1983): 9–11.

9. Richard Hoggart puts the case this way: "The overriding fact is that much of the work of this profession [advertising], as it is at present practised, consists of exploiting human weakness through language. Anyone who thinks it is better to try to understand one's weaknesses than to indulge them, anyone who thinks that language (the articulation of our thoughts and feelings in communicable form) can help in that better grasp, anyone with these two premises must regard modern advertising as, at the best, a stupid waste of good human resources and at the worst, a wicked misuse of other people." Richard Hoggart, "Where Is It All Leading Us?" in *Advertising and the Community*, ed. Alexander Wilson (Manchester, England: Manchester University Press, 1968), p. 54. On the hype behind the home computer market, see Douglas Noble, "The Underside of Computer Literacy," *Raritan* 3 (Spring, 1984): pp. 37–64.

10. A good example is the work of Richard K. Manoff on behalf of various United Nations and other international agencies. See Richard K. Manoff, "When the 'Client' Is Human Life Itself," *Advertising Age*, August 22, 1983, pp. M–4, M–5.

11. Robert Heilbroner, *Business Civilization in Decline* (New York: W. W. Norton, 1976).

INDEX

Index

Index

Index

Index

Index

Index

Index

Index